Anonymous

The Jubilee of George the Third

An account of the celebration - of the forty-ninth anniversary of his reign, 25th October, 1809

Anonymous

The Jubilee of George the Third
An account of the celebration - of the forty-ninth anniversary of his reign, 25th October, 1809

ISBN/EAN: 9783337267735

Printed in Europe, USA, Canada, Australia, Japan

Cover: Foto ©Andreas Hilbeck / pixelio.de

More available books at **www.hansebooks.com**

"Then, and Now."
1809, 1887.

"THE KING ! God bless him, and long may he reign !
"God bless our good King !" and again and again
In hall and in cottage, the toast circled cheerly,
In city, in village, the bells rang out clearly.
The poor man was feasted, the debtor set free
On the glad day of King George the **Third's Jubilee** !

Yes ! glad was the day, though the dark cloud of war
O'ershadowed the nation, and news from afar
Told of sickness in Walcheren, fighting in Spain,
Of forces outnumbered, retreating again !
Still the stout hearts of England undaunted could sing,
Through the storm as through sunshine, " God bless our good King !"

Who can tell all the brightness that happy **day brought** *
It gave hope to the hopeless, it sought the **unsought,**
It gave freedom to prisoners who'd languished **for years,**
Souls hardened by sorrow dissolved in glad tears !
With one splendid **impulse for generous** deed
King and country **both thrilled to the poor in their need.**

.   .   .   .

Nearly eighty years **now since the** King's Jubilee,
But England to-day, far more great, far more free,
Calls her sons and her daughters afar and anear,
To join her in keeping *this* Jubilee year,
To her glorious Colonies stretches her hands,
To **Indian, Australian, Canadian lands.**

"**The Queen**! **God** bless her, and long may she reign!
"**God save** our good Queen!" and again and again
In hall, and in cottage, the toast shall pass cheerly
In city, in village **the** bells ring out clearly.
The poor shall be feasted, the whole world shall see
How our hearts glow with joy at our Queen's Jubilee!

Let the flags flutter forth, the bells peal from the steeple,
She has reigned fifty years in the hearts of her people!
As Maiden, all England could worship and laud her,
As Wife, in her pure home, respected, adored her,
As Widow, has mourned with her, wept with her, grieved for her,
As Monarch, has loved her, fought for her, achieved for her—
    God bless and protect her! God grant her **long days**
    With the love of the nation her soul to **upraise**!

FRANCES ALLITSEN.

London,
  31st March, 1887.

GEORGE THE THIRD, AGED 71.

In the Fiftieth year of his reign.

OF

GEORGE THE THIRD

"*THE FATHER OF HIS PEOPLE.*"

An Account of the Celebration in the Towns and Villages throughout the United Kingdom of the Forty-ninth Anniversary of his Reign, 25th October, 1809.

With Appendix: The Celebration at Bombay.

Compiled from Authentic Sources.

WITH PORTRAIT AND INDEX OF PLACES.

"'*Twill be recorded for a precedent.*"—
Shak., *Mer. of Ven.*, iv., 1.

LONDON:
JOHN BUMPUS, 350, OXFORD STREET,
BOOKSELLER BY APPOINTMENT TO HER MAJESTY THE QUEEN.
1887.

NOTICE.—*The Old Spelling of Several Places, and Quaint Phraseology, in use at the period (1809), have been retained in the text.*

LONDON:
PRINTED BY S. & J. BRAWN, 13, GATE STREET, LINCOLN'S INN FIELDS.

CELEBRATION
OF
THE JUBILEE.

LONDON.

THE veneration and loyalty of the People of London for his Majesty, as well as their gratitude for the opportunity given them by Divine Providence, of celebrating the commencement of the Fiftieth year of our gracious Sovereign's auspicious reign, was testified by every possible demonstration of joy. The morning was ushered in by a general peal of bells from all the church steeples in the metropolis, and the display of the royal standards, in honour of the day. At ten o'clock the streets were filled in all parts of the town with well-dressed persons. The volunteers in the several districts were seen marching to their respective places of worship, as were the children of the different parishes, to return their grateful thanks to Almighty God for having graciously prolonged to this country the reign of a Monarch, who has on all occasions proved himself the benevolent father of his people, and the protector of their rights, freedom, and property. The crowd of citizens from Temple-bar to Leadenhall-street, during the whole morning, was almost impervious, and the windows, from the first floor to the attics, were filled with beautiful women.

The preparations which were made on every side announced early in the morning a general and splendid illumination. In this demonstration of joy, the unanimous and ardent feeling of the people was particularly conspicuous. It was a demonstration not only not commanded, nor invited, but even in many instances forbidden and deprecated. But the effusions of a happy and loyal people could not be restrained. Every one acted for himself, and a general illumination was the consequence. The public offices, and other public buildings; the theatres; the club-houses in St. James's-street; the coffee-houses in all parts; the residences of the principal nobility and gentry, were hung with a profusion of coloured lamps. The day opened with a splendor and mildness that seemed to recall the finest period of the summer. It was, indeed, peculiarly calculated for the purposes to which it was devoted. As such, it was hailed by the people of all ranks and classes. Sounds of joy and happiness marked the way of all; and it was impossible to listen or to look, without feeling that every Briton celebrated the Jubilee of George the Third as a festival of the heart. Private families and individuals, animated by the same zeal, thronged to every place of public worship, where extraordinary service was performed, and appropriate discourses pronounced upon texts selected for the occasion. The poor were every where made to partake of the comforts of the rich; and the generous hospitality for which Britain is famous, characterised a liberality which would be injured by the cold name of charity, or by any other name that conveys ideas of inequality, of dependence, and superiority, that belong not to an occasion upon which all feel alike.

At one o'clock a grand salute of fifty guns was fired from the Park and Tower. The regiments of Guards in town attended Divine Service at the chapel, Whitehall, formerly the Banqueting-house of Whitehall Palace, which has been repaired for their use, under the direction of his Royal Highness the Duke of York, and was opened on this occasion. The Life Guards were also out; as were also the whole of the Volunteer Corps of the Metropolis, many of which, after hearing Divine Service, had a Grand Field Day in Hyde Park, where each fired a *feu de joie* in a most capital style, in honour of the occasion.

An half past ten o'clock the Lord Mayor proceeded from the Mansion-house to Guildhall, in the City State-coach, drawn by his set of six beautiful grey horses, splendidly adorned with ribbons, and attended by the usual Officers, preceded by the trumpets sounding, and the Band of the West London Militia playing *God save the King*. At Guildhall his Lordship was joined by the Members of the Corporation, and at half past eleven o'clock the procession moved from thence in the following order:—

Four Street Men.
Constables.
City's Banners.
The River Fencibles, commanded by Commodore Lucas, in new uniforms.
Band of Music, West London Militia, commanded by Col. Newnham.
Eight City Trumpeters.
City's Banners.
Four Marshals' Men.
Six Footmen in State Liveries.
Upper City Marshal on Horseback.
Lord Mayor's State Coach.
The Aldermen past the Chair.
The Recorder.
The Alderman below the Chair.
The Sheriffs, in their elegant State Carriages.
Chamberlain, Comptroller, and City Law Officers.
Twelve Constables.
Two Marshals' Men.
Under City Marshal on horseback.
The Members of the Common Council to the number of 160, in carriages, in their violet gowns, closed the procession.

In the large space between the iron gates and great west door of the Cathedral, the West London Militia received his Lordship and the rest of the procession, with presented arms. On entering the great west door of the Cathedral, his Lordship was received by the Dean and Chapter. The centre aisle to the choir was lined on each side by the River Fencibles. An appropriate Sermon was preached by his Lordship's Chaplain, from the 8th chapter of the 2nd of Kings, verse 66. The *Coronation Anthem* was performed previous to the Sermon by the full Choir with great effect. The procession returned about three o'clock in the same order. At five o'clock the Corporation were introduced up the Grand Staircase, in front of the Mansion-house; the trumpets sounding during their entrance into the vestibule. The building had been previously decorated with a splendid illumination, consisting of elegant devices of the oak, thistle, and shamrock, in coloured lamps, in the centre a radiant display of G. R. and the crown, with "Long may he reign." The pillars were tastefully ornamented with wreaths of lamps; the whole was much admired for its general grandeur and effect. On entering the grand saloon, which was lined by the band of the West London Militia, playing *God save the King, Rule Britannia, &c.* the company were individually received by the Lord Mayor, in his robes of state, with that affability, politeness, and attention, that distinguish the worthy Chief Magistrate. The saloon was brilliantly lighted with several large Grecian lamps, beautifully painted, and displaying a scene at once novel and elegant.

At half past five o'clock the doors of the magnificent Egyptian Hall were thrown open, illuminated by the blaze of innumerable lamps, tastefully arranged round the pillars, and the elegant lustres and chandeliers suspended from the roof. The tables were laid out with the greatest taste, and covered with an elegant dinner; the whole of which was served upon plate, with a plentiful supply of Madeira, &c. The band continuing during the whole to play several delightful military and other airs. After the cloth was removed, *Non Nobis Domine,* was charmingly sung. The Lord Mayor then gave—"The King—God bless him, and long may he reign!" which was drank with three times three; and with exulting enthusiasm, amidst thunders of applause, that continued unabated for a considerable length of time.—After this effusion of loyal feeling had subsided, the national anthem of *God save the King* was performed by the professional gentlemen present, with appropriate additional verses for the occasion, the whole company standing, and joining in the chorus with the most heartfelt zeal, accompanied by the animating sounds of the military bands.

The worthy Chief Magistrate then gave—" The Queen, the Prince and Princess of Wales, and the rest of the Royal Family." After which "Rule Britannia" was sung, accompanied in full chorus by the band and company present. A great number of other loyal and constitutional toasts were drank, interspersed with many excellent songs, duets, and glees. When the health of the Representatives of the City of London was drank, thanks were respectively returned in appropriate speeches by Sir William Curtis, Mr. Alderman Combe, Sir Charles Price, and Sir James Shaw. The harmony of the evening was kept up till a late hour, with that enthusiasm and delight which the attentive politeness and splendid hospitality of the worthy Chief Magistrate must ever ensure to his guests and friends.

About Two Hundred and Fifty Gentlemen dined together, at the Merchant Tailors' Hall, to commemorate his Majesty's Accession.—Among the company were, Lords St. Vincent, Liverpool, Mulgrave, Camden, Erskine, and Leveson Gower, Mr. Perceval, Mr. Canning, Mr. Sheridan, Mr. Huskisson, Mr. Ellis, &c.—Mr. Beeston Long, the Chairman of the Committee of Merchants and Bankers, took the Chair, and dinner was served up about seven o'clock.—After the cloth had been removed, *Non nobis Domine* was sung with uncommon effect, by the first professional singers.

The Chairman then arose, and said it would not be necessary for him to preface, with many observations, the toast he was going to propose. His Majesty had, in the course of his long reign, uniformly set an example to every public and private virtue. The gratitude of his subjects was apparent from the unanimity which appeared to prevail all over the country, with respect to the public expression of their sentiments upon the present occasion. It was the ardent wish of his people that he should long continue to reign over his beloved subjects. Without any further preface he would give the health of THE KING.—This toast was drank with three times three, and the loudest applause.—Afterwards followed "The Queen and Royal Family," and "The Prince and Princess of Wales," which was drank with similar applause.—" The Wooden Walls of Old England," and "The Army of the United Empire," were also drank with three times three; as was also, "The Ships, Colonies, and Commerce" of England.—The Chairman then, after a short panegyric on the constitution, and on the virtues of the reigning family, gave as a toast, "The House of Brunswick, and may they reign over the Constitution in Church and State for ever."—Drank also with loud applause.

The Chairman then observed that last year they had met together in that hall, to welcome the deputies of our allies, the Spaniards. Our wishes for their success were now as ardent as ever, although it was evident that it must depend principally on their own exertions. He concluded by giving " Success to the exertions of the Portuguese and Spaniards, in maintaining their rights and independence."—This toast was received with loud applause. The evening was passed in great harmony and conviviality, and the company did not separate till a late hour.

The loyalty expressed by the Volunteers at the celebration, is entitled to particular notice. The Duke of Cumberland's Sharp Shooters made an excellent muster in the King's Mews, and having piled arms in the Armoury, proceeded to St. Martin's Church with the Prince of Wales's Corps. After hearing an excellent sermon, they marched to Hyde Park and fired a *Feu de joie*. The rifle regiments attached to the Surrey Volunteers, mustered at the Paragon, in the Kent-road, whence they attended Divine Service in the Chapel of the Philanthropic Society. The officers and privates of this respectable Corps made a liberal subscription for the Children of the Philanthropic Institution before they left the Chapel. They then marched to Kennington Common with the whole of the first Surrey Corps, under Colonel Gaitskil, and fired a *Feu de joie*.

The Queen's Royal Volunteers assembled on parade in Sloane-square, and marched to Battersea-Bridge, where they formed a line and fired a *Feu de joie*, and were answered from Lord Cremorne's by a discharge of fifty pieces of cannon; after which the battalion gave three cheers uncovered. The battalion then proceeded to Chelsea College Chapel, where the form of prayer for the day was read, and an excellent sermon preached on the occasion by the Rev. Dr. Butler. After service was over, the band played "God save the King," when they proceeded again to Sloane-square, and fired another *Feu de joie* at sun-set. The serjeants then received half-a-crown for every man and non-commissioned officer present.

The Old St. George's Volunteers paraded at ten o'clock, and marched to St. George's Church, preceded by their excellent band, in rich and elegant new clothing for the occasion; each man (nearly five hundred) wore a sprig of laurel in his cap, which had a pleasing effect. After a most animating discourse by the Rector, there was a collection at the doors for charitable purposes, and to which the corps liberally subscribed. The regiment, on coming out of the church, formed into companies, during which time the band formed in front of the church, and played "God save the King," at the conclusion of which, the immense number of spectators gave three hearty cheers. The regiment then marched back to their parade to receive their arms and ammunition, and repaired to their alarm post (Grosvenor Square), where they trooped their colours in a grand style of military parade; they then marched into Hyde-park, and fired a *Feu de joie* with great exactness and rapidity, giving three cheers after each repeated three rounds; the band playing, drums beating, &c., gave the whole a truly grand effect. The regiment then returned to their parade, and after lodging their arms, &c., were plentifully regaled with good old English cheer of roast beef and plum-pudding, &c., provided for them by their officers, to which the Commanding Officer (Major Harrison) added a sufficient quantity of punch to drink "Health and long life to the best of Kings."

The Shoreditch Volunteer Corps, commanded by Major Marshall, had a strong muster for the celebration of the Jubilee. After attending Divine Service at Shoreditch Church, and hearing an appropriate and excellent Sermon, preached by the Rev. Mr. Evans, one of the Curates, the Major marched the regiment to the London Field, Hackney, where it fired a *Feu de joie*, and several volleys, in excellent style, and at the close of their military movements the regiment gave three cheers uncovered. The regiment then marched to the Mermaid Tavern, at Hackney, where they were regaled with an excellent dinner. At seven o'clock the drums beat to arms, and the regiment marched back to head-quarters, in a very orderly steady manner, all pleased with the festivities that the day had afforded.

About One Hundred and Fifty Members of that valuable Corps, the Light Horse Volunteers, exclusive of visitors, sat down to a splendid entertainment at the Freemasons' Tavern, at which their Commanding Officer, Colonel Herries, presided. On the cloth being removed, many patriotic toasts were drank with enthusiastic ardour, and the utmost conviviality prevailed in the meeting until a late hour.—During the evening several songs were sung with peculiar effect; and, among others, the following **stanzas**, written for the occasion, by a member of the Corps:—

  While Tyrants, who Countries have deluged in blood,
   Have been flatter'd in song and extoll'd in oration,
  What tongue can refuse for a KING great and good,
   To join in the general acclame of the nation?
  Inspir'd ev'ry heart by the comfort possest,
   In a reign the most ardous in history known,
  This dome shall resound while the glass passes round,
   In praise of the Monarch who graces the Throne.

  If on Edward and Henry, of Albion the pride,
   Our forefathers were wont their eulogiums to pour,
  Whose high-mettled souls Gallic valour defied,
   Whose swords steep'd her vine-cover'd valleys in gore;
  If inscrib'd be each name on the tablet of fame,
   If Cressy and Agincourt glory recall,
  Britannia can boast still of warriors a host,
   The Guardians of Britain—the terror of Gaul.

  On the days of Queen Bess the Barons so bold,
   If memory dwell with peculiar delight,
  The annals of GEORGE to the world can unfold
   Men as great in the Senate, as daring in fight.
  While wreathing the crown with superior renown,
   Where'er our proud ensigns triumphantly wave,
  Art and science refin'd—to humanity join'd
   Enlighten the savage—unfetter the slave.

  While around us we view in the council and field,
   Kings and Princes to falsehood and tyranny bend
  And Nations their rights and their liberties yield;
   To Heav'n for that Sov'reign what prayers should ascend,
  Who by no passions sway'd that mortals degrade,
   'Gainst the Throne when the bolts of sedition were hurl'd,
  Ever virtuous and just, stood firm to his trust,
   And his kingdom preserv'd 'midst the wreck of the world.

  Such goodness, such valour, such truth to display,
   (The source whence our grandeur and happiness spring)
  Can Britons do less on this festival day,
   Than sing *Io pæan!* "Long life to the King?"
  Knit in amity's band, each a bumper in hand,
   Then swear while life's current shall flow thro' the veins,
  The laws to respect, and the Monarch protect,
   Whose firmness sav'd Britain from slav'ry and chains.

A general order was issued by the Lords of the Admiralty, that all our brave tars, in the ports of Great Britain, should be regaled with roast beef, plum pudding, and a pint of wine, or half a pint of rum, in addition to their usual allowance.—The Governor and Directors of the Bank of England allowed their clerks, 927 in number, one guinea each, for a dinner, to celebrate the Jubilee day.—The Directors of the Royal Exchange Insurance Fire Office gave each of their clerks ten guineas, their messengers five guineas each, and their firemen one guinea each, to celebrate the day.—The Marshal of the King's Bench, with his usual liberality, ordered a fine ox, with a butt of porter, bread, &c., to be distributed in the prison, with the very praise-worthy intention of enabling those prisoners whose circumstances would not allow them to participate in the general festivity of the Jubilee, to commemorate that auspicious day with satisfaction. The Corporation of the City of London presented the Society for the relief and discharge of debtors with the sum of £1000. And the Society of Friends, commonly called Quakers, presented the same fund with the sum of £500. By the liberality of Sir James Shaw, Bart. the president, and under the humane superintendence of R. Baldwin, Esq., the treasurer, the patients in Bartholomew's Hospital (near 500 in number) were regaled, (as far as was consistent with their respective maladies) with excellent roast beef and plum-pudding, a pint of porter to each female, and a quart to each male patient capable of enjoying it, every thing being conducted with great comfort and regularity. The Members of the Royal Academy dined together in their Council Chamber, at Somerset-house, to celebrate the Jubilee.—Mr. B. West, the President, in the chair.

The children in Christ's Hospital, after hearing Divine Service, and a sermon, by the Rev. James Crowther, were regaled, to the number of 700, in their great hall, with plenty of excellent roast beef and plum puddings (of which there were no less than 80). After dinner the youths were brought up in divisions of about 30, and received a glass of wine each, the elder boy of each class, as they advanced to the table where it was distributed, ascended a bench, and gave as a toast, "To the King; long may he reign!" which was succeeded by a universal shout from the boys at large, each being served with a glass of wine in the most perfect order. The song of "God save the King," was impressively and delightfully sung by a select party of the boys, the whole joining in the chorus, in a manner which at once charmed and affected the feelings of the auditory. The greatest credit is due to the Treasurer and Governors, who superintended and regulated this festivity, and who appeared fully rewarded for the pains they took, by the gladdened countenances and innocent joy felt by their numerous and interesting family.

The private festivities on the occasion were innumerable. That of Mr. Lawrence, of the Stable Yard, attracted considerable attention from the excellent band which attended. The festive party was select, and the fare bore the genuine character of true English hospitality. The best wines were in great profusion: and the respectable host sent on the same day a handsome donation in aid of the fund for the relief of insolvent debtors.—Messrs. Barclay, Perkins, & Co., with the liberality and loyalty which has **always** characterised that house, entertained upwards of 220 of the men employed in their Brewery with the good old English fare of plenty of beef and brown stout. In the evening the Brewery was brilliantly illuminated.—The **Worshipful** Company of Apothecaries gave each of their annual servants one guinea, and to the labourers half a guinea each. Messrs. **Hansard** and Son, Printers to **the** House **of** Commons, gave each of their **journeymen** half-a-guinea.

Mr. **Oakley,** of Bond-street, entertained all **his** artists, &c., exceeding 150 **in number,** with roast beef and plum pudding. A select party of particular **friends** likewise dined with Mr. Oakley. After the **cloth was removed, a** professional gentleman of **the** party made his appearance **on** the balcony, with his violin ; on his right stood Mr. Oakley, **and** on his left **22** gentlemen, friends of the party. In an appropriate situation the artists and artificers **took** their station.— On Mr. Shaw's striking **up** *God Save the King*, he was **joined by** the already mentioned gentlemen, and upwards of 5000 spectators assembled **in the street. Every** window in the neighbourhood displayed elegantly dressed **females.** The party afterwards sung *Rule Britannia*. During the **time the** above songs were sung the populace **remained** uncovered.

Divine Service was performed at the German **Jews' Great Synagogue,** Duke's-place ; an appropriate and most impressive Sermon **was there** delivered, by the Rev Dr. Solomon Hirschell, Chief Rabbi **of the Congregation ;** after which Masters Pike and Moss, and **a** band **of choristers, chanted** with much fervour and devotion an Ode composed for the occasion. **The** poor of the congregation were amply provided **for** by a distribution of money, exclusive of the recommendation for individuals subscribing to the general relief in their several districts, &c. The different charity schools among the Jews had likewise dinners provided **that** day. Nor were the inmates of that excellent Institution **at** Mile-end (for the purpose of inculcating the habits **of** industry in youth) forgotten on that joyful event, but all partook of the festivity **of the** day.—The following is a translation of the Hebrew **Prayer,** composed by the Rev. Solomon Hirschell, Chief Rabbi, for **the service** of the Jubilee. " O Lord ! it is thou who **art** our King from **the earliest** times, and it is thou who appointeth the Kings of the earth, **and** inclineth their hearts to all that thou dost desire. **We thank** thee, O Lord our God, for all thy wonders and all thy assistances, for **thou art** careful of thy people Israel in all places of their settlement; and with increased respect and firmness hast thou granted them shelter and protection here, under the government of **our** powerful and pious Lord, King George the Third, (may his glory be exalted !) thou hast passed the decree, and it has been confirmed, that among nations we should live under his shelter ; through thy fondness and great mercy hast thou given thy people grace in the sight of the King, his Counsellors, and Lords ; thou hast evinced a sign of goodness unto us, and we have increased in the land, that the people of the earth **may** know thou hast not rejected thy people Israel, neither hast thou despised the children of thy covenant. We beseech thee, O merciful King! be pleased to accept the prayers of thy servants this day! thou hast caused us to live and be upheld unto this time, the fiftieth year, as the Jubilee day of the reign of our Sovereign Lord King George the Third (may his glory be exalted!) For this we have consecrated an assembly in this our little sanctuary, to supplicate thee for him, for his kingdom, and for all who confide in his protection, and seek his peace and welfare. Bless, O Lord, his substance, and be graciously pleased with his actions; lengthen his days as the days of heaven, and let his throne be established as the sun at noon day; preserve him from the shafts of sorrow and trouble, and stand forth to his assistance; overthrow his foes, and make them fall before him like stubble before the wind: renovate his strength, gird him with might, and renew his youth like the eagle: may his hands be steady till the sun of his enemies go down, and their light decline, and let the sun of his righteousness shine forth to the inhabitants of all the land, and the distant isles, from one end of the earth to the other; and in peace and comfort may he reach the days of eternity which approach him; add days to his days, and his years as many generations. Amen."

The feast of the Jubilee was likewise celebrated in the first Synagogue, called the Portuguese and Spanish Synagogue. The service commenced with the usual prayers of the afternoon, including several psalms suitable to the occasion. A sensible and well arranged sermon was afterwards delivered by the Rev. Dr. R. Meldola, residing Rabbi, in the Hebrew and Spanish languages, from the following appropriate texts, Levit. chap. xxv. ver. 13. "In the year of this Jubilee ye shall return every man unto his possession;" and from Psalm xxi. ver. 1. "The King shall rejoice in thy strength, O Lord," &c. The service concluded with a prayer adapted to the religious observance of the day, composed by the above learned and respectable Rabbi. The whole of the 21st psalm was also sung in the most impressive style, to the melody of "God Save the King," by their Sub-Minister, Mr. Shalom. We must also notice that the members of this Ancient Congregation have not demonstrated their loyalty and affection by their prayers and thanksgivings only, for the prolonged felicity of our beloved Monarch's reign, but have mingled their charitable benevolence with their other fellow-subjects, in distributing alms to the poor, and by their liberal contributions for the release of the unfortunate prisoners.

Bishop Hodgson, the Roman Catholic Bishop of the London District, with a spirit of loyalty that does him and that respectable body at large the highest honour, issued the following Order to his Clergy, for the celebration of the Jubilee. "Dearly beloved brethren—The Almighty Lord and God, *by whom Kings reign*, (Prov. viii. 15) has been pleased, in mercy to us, to prolong the reign of our beloved Monarch, while in the revolutions of other empires and kingdoms many dreadful events have taken place. In these happy isles we have enjoyed **an** enviable security in our own houses, while in other countries, every thing sacred and profane, altars and thrones, have been thrown into the common mass of ruin. When we look back and contemplate all **these** blessings, and the many oppressive restraints from which Catholics **have** been released **under** the reign of his present Majesty, **we must** acknowledge that **gratitude** and thanksgiving **are** the smallest returns which **can** be **made**. For this reason, dearly beloved brethren, let us join in hymns of praise **and** jubilation to the Sovereign Disposer of all Events, and beseech **him** to prolong the days of our beloved Sovereign, **to** give wisdom **to his** councils, and vigour to **his** strength, and again to bless the land with peace. We earnestly, **therefore,** dearly beloved brethren, exhort you to assemble round your pastors, in thanksgiving and prayer, on Wednesday the 25th instant. And accordingly it is ordered that all Priests who have the care of congregations, or who officiate to such, shall after the Mass of that day say or sing, or cause to be said or sung, the Psalm ' Exaudiat,' with **the** ' V. Domine salvum fac Regem,' and the Prayer, ' Pro Rege Quæsumus Omnipotens Deus." JOSEPH HODGSON, V. G.

THE ILLUMINATIONS.

Day-light was scarcely gone, when **the full** blaze burst forth **upon the** eye, in all the skill of art, and in **all the** radiant splendour **and** varied magnificence of the general illumination of the British capital. Hands could hardly be procured to light up the innumerable lamps. All the customary demonstrations of popular satisfaction were abun**dantly** exhibited. Those who recollect similar displays after the **recovery** of the Monarch's health, and the several naval victories, require no description. Those **who** have not witnessed such a sight may find some gratification in the perusal of the details which are given.

The pillars of the portico in front of the *Mansion House* were encircled with **rows of** lamps, and the interstices decorated with golden vases and bouquets **of** oak, thistle, shamrock, **etc.**, intermixed with flowers. In the centre, **was** a large tablet, with **an** illuminated inscription, "Long may he reign," over which **was** the crown, etc.—The illumination of *Lloyd's,* **on** the north front **of** the Exchange, was appropriate and magnificent. In the centre, opposite Bartholomew-lane was the representation of the stern of a ship in full sail, 40 feet high from the keel to the main-top, with a long pendant flying. On the stern was inscribed Jubilee, 50, Lloyd's. On the right **was a** large compartment, illuminated, with the motto " Ships, Colonies, and Commerce ;" and on the left, one with the inscription, " Long live the King." At each end of the building G. R. and the crown above. In other spaces were placed anchors, cables, stars, etc. The novelty of the design of the ship, and the brilliant effect of the whole of this exhibition, created universal admiration.—The south front of the *Royal Exchange*, facing Cornhill, was also decorated in a splendid manner ; the pillars and outlines of the building were finished with variegated lamps, and under **the** archway in the centre hung a large illuminated anchor and trident, surmounted by a British Ensign. On the steeple was hoisted the Royal Standard.—The *Bank of England* was elegant and superb. The entablatures, ballustrades and arches, were all marked with lines of lamps, and the columns encircled with serpentine wreaths. In the centre was a very large brilliant star and crown, with the motto, "God save the King." All the pediments and the recesses behind the pillars in Threadneedle-street, Bartholomew lane, and Princes-street, were ornamented with stars and other devices. The new circular portico, at the corner of Princes-street and Threadneedle-street, was very tastefully decorated. The new buildings opposite exhibited, on a grand tablet, "God preserve the King." The wall of *Grocer's Hall Garden*, was adorned with the royal emblems. The *Sun* and the *Imperial Fire Offices*, and all the neighbouring buildings, lent their aid to this most dazzling and interesting scene.—The *India House* was most brilliantly decorated. In the centre of the colonnade was a display of trophies, consisting of a crown at top, beneath which was a star, and on each wing was a naval anchor, and festoons. The whole of the columns, from base to capital, were richly covered with variegated lamps, as were also the entablature and the pediment; from the centre of which an anchor was suspended, most brilliantly illuminated.—The *Trinity House*, Tower Hill, exhibited in front the royal initials, G. R. surmounted by the British crown, and supported beneath by crossed tridents, bound together by a blue wreath, and on each wing was an anchor, of appropriate colours, in variegated lamps.—The illuminations at the *Post Office* displayed very great taste and fancy. The whole of the covered passage leading to the office was decorated with arched festoons, richly hung with variegated lamps. The front was also ornamented in a brilliant and appropriate manner.—The illuminations of *Mercer's Hall*, in Cheapside, were well designed, and beautifully adorned by a splendid display of lamps. A transparency containing a full-length portrait of his Majesty in his state robes, under which was, "Long live the King."—*St. Paul's Free School*. Of all the public buildings inferior to the Bank, none exceeded this establishment in point of brilliancy and chaste design. At the top was a crown of variegated lamps, on each side of which were two vases of combustible light. Beneath the cornices at the top of the building, lamps were thickly studded, then followed two rich double lines of dazzling lustre, within which were the words, "Vivat Rex," in bold characters, to which a festoon of lamps gave an elegant finish. On the bottom stories the four arched windows were surrounded by a double row of lamps, and between them were two oblong transparencies, each containing a branch of olive and oak entwined, and bound by crimson fillets. In a garter at the top of the first was the inscription, "*Quo semel est imbuta Recens*," and at the bottom, "*Servabit odorem testa diu;*" at the top of the other was, "*Prospera lux oritur*," and at the bottom, "*Linguis avimusque favete.*" The *tout ensemble* had a most happy and elegant effect, and was universally admired by all who witnessed it.—The fronts of the *Albion, Hope, Eagle, Atlas, Globe*, and other *Insurance Offices*, were illuminated with considerable taste and effect.—The front of *Bridewell Hospital* was splendidly illuminated. The arched entrance and the windows were ornamented with lamps. Above these was a large inscription, VIVAT REX, with festoons depending. At each end were transparencies representing the arms of Bridewell and Bethlehem (these two Hospitals being united under the same Governors). The centre window over the arch was enriched by twisted pilasters of lamps, and filled with a star, and on each side were the letters G.R. The whole was surmounted by a large crown, which occupied the centre window of the second floor.—The *Ordnance Office*, Pall-mall, afforded a most magnificent display of lamps in pyramidical columns. The centre of the front of the pile of building was occupied by a magnificent transparency, executed by Mr. Pocock. The centre represented the Guardian Angel of Britain, with her wings extended, in the act of supporting the busts of the King and Queen. Underneath were placed the Order of the Garter, and an inscription in large characters, "God save the King." —*Somerset Place* presented a beautiful *coup d'œil*, from the advantages afforded by the uniformity of the buildings ; among which the Navy, the Navy Pay, the Stamp Offices, etc., were principally distinguished by the royal insignia, anchors, etc., etc.—The *Admiralty* was particularly splendid ; the grand colonnade at the entrance of the hall being ornamented with spiral rows of different colours, from the ground to the top, amounting, it is said, to 3000 for each pillar, and the minor colonnade in front being also decorated in a splendid manner.—The illuminations at the *British Museum* were not inferior to that of any other in point of simplicity and elegance. The front of the gateway forming a triumphal arch, had a row of lamps on every architectural line. In the pediment were the letters G. R., and on the angle at the top of the pediment was a brilliant crown, within the arch, on a transparency, were the words *Vota publica quinquaguagies suscepta.*— *Covent Garden Theatre* was lighted up by rows of lamps round the window frames, etc,—The *Horse Guards*, towards Whitehall, had a motto in the centre, "God save the King," with G. R., crown, etc., etc. On each wing, the crown, etc., etc., were repeated with superb festoons. The *Treasury* and *Office for the Home Department* were tastefully decorated.—The *War Office* had its share of illumination, ornamented with the crown, regal insignia, etc.—The *Opera House* illumination did not extend along the whole front, but was confined to the space over the entrance doors. There was a suitable transparency, with the crown and G. R.—The Hon. Corporation of the *Royal Exchange Assurance*, the [*Gresham Committee*, and the *River Dee*, illuminated jointly, and displayed the royal standard.—*Mr. Abraham Goldsmid* had a very grand display of lamps affixed to the veranda in front of his magnificent town residence, with a transparency, and the words "God bless our King."—The Hon. *Hudson's Bay Company*. The words " God save the King," crown, and G. R. and a tasteful display of festoonery.—The *West India Dock House.* The words " Long live the King," and a very elegant display of festoonery, together with G. R. and crown.—The *East India Dock House*. The crown and G. R.—

The *Subscription Houses* and *Insurance Offices*, in Pall Mall and St. James's-street, were lighted up with taste and splendour.—In Piccadilly, opposite St. James's-street, an excellent effect was produced by transparencies, at a window blind painter's, where, in the centre of some beautiful landscapes, there was a large representation of his Majesty in his coronation robes, with an angel, symbolical of Providence, hovering over him.—The whole front of the *Warehouse for the Yellow Fever Remedy*, exhibited one brilliant blaze. Besides the star and anchor, the letters G. R. displayed by an immense number of variegated lamps, and a very beautiful and appropriate transparency in the centre of which was a portrait of his Majesty, and in other parts of the transparency was written, in letters of gold, " The fiftieth year of the reign of George the Third, a real Patriot, the best of Kings and the only virtuous Sovereign in Europe ; every heart is filled with joy for thy long reign, O King !"—The *New Public Library*, in Cornhill, was particularly distinguished for its splendour and appropriateness. A transparency, containing a correct portrait of his Majesty, supported by a figure of Prudence on one side, and Minerva on the other, had a good effect, over whose head was suspended, " Magna Charta," and a group of boys sustaining the emblems of Literature, the Arts, and Sciences.—The *Hay-market Theatre* was neatly illuminated —*Astley's Olympic Pavilion*, in Wych-street, and his *Amphitheatre* over Westminster Bridge, were both very handsomely lighted up ; as was also *Elliston's Royal Circus.—Lyceum Theatre.* Festoons of laurel to which was suspended the word " Lyceum," with the motto " Laus Deo."—*City of London Tavern.* A transparency, 12 feet by 9, painted by Howard, R.A., above appears a figure of Time, unrolling a scroll, on which is written " Jubilee ;" immediately under Britannia is placing a wreath of honour on a colossal bust of his Majesty ; on the right, the city of London, accompanied by a figure of Commerce, is represented returning thanks to Providence for the many blessings of his reign ; on the left, Science and the Arts are looking up to him as their Patron and Protector, and one of the group is tracing on the pedestal, " Inscribed by a grateful people to their King and Father, on entering the 50th year of his reign, Oct. 25, 1809."—The whole front of *Vauxhall Gardens* was so mechanically arranged as to represent a brilliant temple of loyalty, upwards of 70 feet in height, closely studded with variegated lamps, each compartment displaying different splendid and appropriate devices, in number exactly fifty, and terminating with an imperial crown, and other regal insignia. This had a very grand and striking effect, as the crown alone contained upwards of 1000 lamps.—The most general decorations were the Crown and G. R., and the mottos were mostly the same as those given. It is impossible to enter into further particulars of these numerous exhibitions of loyalty and splendour.

———0———

CITY ADDRESS TO THE KING.

TO THE KING'S MOST EXCELLENT MAJESTY.

The humble and dutiful Address of the Lord Mayor, Aldermen, and Commons of the City of London, in Common Council assembled;

"MOST GRACIOUS SOVEREIGN.—We, the Lord Mayor, Aldermen, and Commons of the City of London, in Common Council assembled, approach your Majesty's sacred person with our most lively and unfeigned congratulations on the recent Anniversary of your Majesty's Accession to the Throne of these realms; with joy and gladness we hailed the day on which your Majesty entered into the fiftieth year of your Majesty's reign, not only over the persons, but in the hearts of your Majesty's subjects.—When it pleased the Almighty Ruler of Princes to place the sceptre in your Majesty's hands, the brave, free, and loyal people, whom your Majesty was ordained to govern, received with pleasure your Majesty's first declaration to the great Council of the nation, that 'born and educated a Briton, the peculiar happiness of your Majesty's life would ever consist in promoting the welfare of your people, and your Majesty's resolution to maintain our most excellent Constitution both in Church and State, with an assurance that the civil and religious rights of the subject were equally dear to your Majesty with the most valuable prerogatives of the crown.'—We experience and acknowledge the blessings of this security to our religion and laws, and that great charter of liberties which in virtue of the glorious revolution your Majesty's illustrious house was chosen to defend. Through the lapse of nearly half a century your Majesty has proved yourself on every occasion, unwearied in the maintenance and practice of all the principles so graciously pledged.—It is a proud subject for your Majesty's faithful citizens of London to record, that in the midst of all our unexampled struggles, your Majesty is enabled to say, now, as at the commencement of your Majesty's reign, that your Majesty can see with joy of heart, the commerce of these kingdoms, that great source of our riches, and fixed object of your Majesty's never failing care and protection, flourishing to an extent unknown in any former war.—Deeply impressed with gratitude to Almighty God for the innumerable blessings he has been pleased to pour down upon this highly favoured nation, and more particularly for his wonderful and great goodness, in having continued his divine protection to your Majesty until this joyful period, we, your Majesty's faithful citizens of London, have implored heaven to accept our fervent prayers of praise and thanksgiving, and to continue that same providential care and protection to your Majesty for many years yet to come.—Believe, Sire, that it is the warmest wish and most fervent prayer of your Majesty's Citizens of London, that Providence may long continue to this nation so distinguishing a mark of divine favour, and that in the fulness of time, when your Majesty shall be called from your earthly to a celestial crown, the memory and example of so beloved a Sovereign may secure to a grateful people the imitation of your Majesty's virtues, in the successors of your Royal House, till time shall be no more.

"Signed by order of Court,

HENRY WOODTHORPE."

To which Address his Majesty was pleased to return the following most gracious Answer:—

"I thank you for this testimony of zeal and affection for me and my Government. It has ever been my anxious care to maintain the rights and privileges of every class of my subjects; and it is a great satisfaction to me, to reflect, that, in the midst of all our unexampled struggles, and notwithstanding the duration of the wars in which, for the safety of my people, I have been engaged, the Commerce and Manufactures of my City of London have been carried to an extent unknown at any former period."

They were all received very graciously, and had the honour to kiss his Majesty's hand. After which his Majesty was pleased to create the Lord Mayor a Baronet, and conferred the honour of Knighthood on William Plomer, Esq. Alderman.

The following was sung at the dinner given by the Merchants and Bankers at Merchant Tailors' Hall.

TO THE ANACREONTIC TUNE.

The day our lov'd monarch ascended his throne,
   In mirth each true Briton should ever employ,
But now, forty-nine anniversaries gone,
   The fiftieth solemnity hallows our joy !
'Tis a Jubilee year, 'tis a festival dear,
To all who their King and their Country revere.
Our voices we'll raise, 'till the firmament ring,
With a loud loyal chorus of "GOD SAVE THE KING !"

And well, at devotional gratitude's call,
   Our bosoms, exulting, with bliss may expand,
When the blessings by Providence destin'd for all
   Yet linger on earth but to gladden our land.
While Europe's fair soil is of robbers the spoil,
And force reaps the harvest of industry's toil,
Our sea-guarded isle unmolested may sing,
Heaven prospers my sons, and may "GOD SAVE THE KING."

Religion, to guide and enlighten mankind,
   Here finds her asylum and fixes her sway,
Where no superstition debases the mind,
   Nor black infidelity skulks from the day.
The sympathies here drop for mis'ry a tear,
And charity hastens its anguish to cheer;
Extracting from penury's wound the sharp sting,
She bids all her vot'ries pray "GOD SAVE THE KING."

Here Justice, immaculate, sits on her bench,
   While at even pois'd balance determines her choice ;
No tyrannous edict her sentence to wrench,
   No bribe to corrupt her deliberate voice.
No twelve good men and true ever fast'ning her view,
To her suppliants alike she dispenses their due ;
And, when ask'd what on Britain these blessings should bring,
She points to the throne, and shouts "GOD SAVE THE KING."

What leads Britain's sons, from the pole to the pole,
   To trace o'er the globe their infallible way ;
That, where'er the winds whistle, where'er the waves roll,
   Both the waves and the winds their intentions obey ?
'Tis freedom divine wafts them over the line,
And to them bids the earth all her treasures resign ;
Secur'd by her arm, and upborn by her wing,
They make the world echo with "GOD SAVE THE KING?

Dear liberty's tree, such as Englishmen show,
    All sappy its stem and mature all its fruit,
Once France would have planted ; but how could it grow,
    With no leaves on its branches, nor life at its root?
'Tis to Britain alone this rare plant can be known,
    Its growth and its product exclusive her own ;
Her manners **its** autumn, **her** virtues its **spring**.
Her Monarch **its** sunshine : O "GOD SAVE THE KING !"

Its seed by **our** ancestors early was **sown**,
    And the ground to upraise it **manur'd** with **their** blood ;
'Tis our birth-right **to** watch **now** the tree is full grown,
    Lest a blight crop **its** bloom, or a blast nip its bud.
Corruption's the blight that its blossoms would smite,
    And faction the blast that would strip it outright,
Yet, while thus from concord our energies spring,
The crown of **our** wishes is "GOD SAVE THE KING !"

Let all, then, who Britain's free Monarch obey,
    Their religion and liberties join to maintain,
Their country invites them to hallow this day,
    When GEORGE opes the fiftieth year of his reign.
'Tis a Jubilee year, 'tis a festival dear,
    To all who their king and their Country revere ;
Our voices we'll raise till the firmament ring
With a loud loyal chorus of "GOD SAVE THE KING !"

ACTS OF ROYAL FAVOUR.

His Majesty **was most** graciously pleased on the day he entered the 50th anniversary of his reign, to grant a free pardon to all **deserters** in his fleets **and** armies, without the distressing condition usually annexed of serving upon the most odious stations ; and all persons confined for military offences, were released.—His Majesty likewise took the same opportunity of gratifying the officers of both services, by a general brevet promotion ; that of the Navy consisted of five Admirals, ten Vice-Admirals, ten Rear-Admirals, twenty Post Captains, and twenty Commanders ; all taken in regular succession from the top of their respective lists, neither one being passed over, **nor** one selected out of his turn.—All persons confined for debts due **to the Crown were** released by his Majesty's command ; the only **exceptions** being those which were distinguished by peculiar circumstances of fraud or violence, and in all instances of official delinquency ; the latter exception being dictated by his Majesty's determination never to **screen** those from punishment who have abused the powers derived **from him** to the injury of his people.—His Majesty **was pleased** graciously **to permit** all prisoners of war heretofore on **parole, to return** to their own countries. The prisoners of the French **nation were** rendered a necessary exception to this extreme indulgence, **by the** unparalleled severity of their ruler, in detaining all **British subjects** in France.—To these instances of his Majesty's favour must be added, his royal bounty in appropriating the sum of 2000*l*. out of his own privy purse, for the release of poor debtors in England

and Wales; the distribution of which sum was graciously intrusted by his Majesty to the Society for the Relief of Persons confined for small Debts, as being qualified to judge most correctly of the cases worthy of the royal favour.—1000$l.$ were likewise appointed to the like purpose in Scotland, and 1000$l.$ in Ireland, out of funds remaining at his Majesty's disposal.

---o---

WINDSOR.

The commencement of the festive sports was announced at six o'clock in the morning by the sound of trumpets; after which, the drums beat to arms, the Royal Horse Guards (blue), the Staffordshire Militia, and the Volunteers, paraded, and the bells rung a merry peal.—Between eight and nine o'clock their Majesties, Princess Elizabeth, and the Dukes of York and Sussex, attended divine service at the private chapel in the Castle. At half past ten o'clock her Majesty, Princess Elizabeth, and Lady Ilchester, went in the carriage from the Castle towards the Town-hall, and passed under the triumphal arch; the Royal Horse Guards (blue) lined the street from the Town-hall towards Frogmore, where her Majesty went for the purpose of inspecting the preparations going forward for the entertainment. At one o'clock, the Queen, Princess Elizabeth, the Dukes of York, Kent, Cumberland, and Sussex, attended by Lady Ilchester, Lord St. Helen's, the Mayor and Corporation of Windsor, with white wands, and others, walked to the Bachelor's Acre, for the purpose of seeing the ox roasted whole, her Majesty leaning on the Duke of York's arm. Her Majesty having graciously announced her intention of accepting an offer made by Mr. and Mrs. C. Buckeridge, of all the accommodation, which their house and garden could afford, to view the scene commodiously, Mr. Buckeridge had a stand erected adjoining his garden, which was carpeted, for the accommodation of the royal visitors.—A little after one the royal party arrived at Mr. Buckeridge's house. Fifty Bachelors were ready, at the outside of the gate, which opens to the Acre; and, when the royal party descended from the stand, guarded them to the fire-place, where the ox was roasting; they then proceeded to view the construction of the grates and walls for roasting the ox, which were so well contrived as to roast two whole sheep at the same time, and then returned to the booth. The butchers employed in managing the cooking of the whole animals, were dressed, upon the occasion, in blue frocks and silk stockings; they cut the first prime pieces from the ox and sheep, and put them upon silver plates, and the bachelors and butchers waited upon the royal party with them. They all tasted and appeared highly pleased with the novelty. The royal party then returned to Mr. Buckeridge's, and partook of an elegant collation, prepared on the occasion, and were attended by the Master and Mistress of the house; and also by the Colonel and Mrs. Buckeridge, and their sons.—At two o'clock, they departed for the Castle, and the populace gave them repeated huzzas. A party of the Royal Horse Guards, dismounted, attended to keep off the populace. At one o'clock fifty pieces of cannon were discharged from the Grove in Windsor Park. The grand arch by the Town-hall was adorned with figures emblematical of the four seasons, likenesses of their Majesties, and other devices, the whole surmounted by the King's Arms, beneath which was inscribed on the one side, "God save the King," and on the other, "King and Constitution."

At St. George's Chapel, after the prayers of the day and the performance of the Coronation Anthem, one of the Canons, rising in his stall, delivered an oration upon the occasion, which might have been called a sermon, if it had been preceded by a text, and read in a pulpit. It expatiated but little upon the character of the Sovereign, the Reverend Orator justly observing, that to an audience, great part of whom were witnesses of his virtues, this was unnecessary. They knew with what equity he exercised his authority, with what moderation he enjoyed the advantages of his station, with what patience, and, he would add, with what humility, he bore its difficulties and cares. The chief purpose of the address was to impress upon the minds of his hearers a religious sense of the mercies of Providence, in granting to this country, in the midst of the desolation of Europe, that permanence and due balance of the different parts of our happy constitution, under which all ranks enjoyed the highest degree of liberty compatible with order, and every one was secure in his person, in his property, and every just mode of increasing it.— The Archbishop of Canterbury was one of the audience, amongst whom were several other persons of rank.—The most brilliant thing of the day was the *Feu de joie* in the long walk of the Great Park, fired by the Oxford Blues, the Staffordshire Militia, and the Artillery, the latter of whom fired fifty rounds. The spectacle of these fine corps, formed in so superb an avenue, the noblest, perhaps, in the world, was indeed a grand union of the dignity of natural objects with the splendour of military ceremonies. The King, the Duke of Cumberland, and the Princess Augusta, rode through the lines, at the conclusion of their ride, immediately before the *Feu de joie*.—Immediately afterwards, the Princess Augusta accompanied the Queen to Bachelor's Acre, already described. Here the Duke of Clarence, the Duke of Sussex, and the Duke of Kent, also attended their Royal Mother. The Duke of Sussex, with his hat off, held the tray, from which the Queen took two or three pieces of beef and bread. The Duke of Clarence distributed the plum pudding. The Queen was in high spirits, spoke to several of the Committee of Bachelors, who brought up the dishes, said frequently they were good, and waved her hand, on going away, in a manner which drew loud acclamations from a crowd, consisting of persons of all ranks.— His Royal Highness the Prince of Wales and the Princess Charlotte arrived at Windsor about twelve o'clock.

The town was brilliantly illuminated. The triumphal arch (designed by Mr. Wyatt), with allegorical paintings, executed in a most masterly style by Mr. Wyatt, had a grand and imposing effect. It extended from the Town-hall to the Castle Inn, and contained some thousands of lamps, medallions of the King and Queen, military trophies, &c. The Town-hall was brilliant, and each end contained transparencies, the subjects of which were, Prudence, Fortitude, Temperance, and Justice. All houses were lighted, and the King's tradesmen vied with each other in their testimonials of loyalty by illumination, &c., but it would be invidious to point out the most approved, as each was beautiful, some grand, and all of the superior order.

His Royal Highness the Prince of Wales subscribed 50*l.* towards regaling the poor of Windsor on the joyous day of the Jubilee, to which laudable purpose, each of his Royal Brothers added 20*l.*, and each of the Princesses 10*l.*

————o————

FROGMORE.

The splendid fete given by her Majesty at Frogmore surpassed the expectation of every one. In the midst of an immense sheet of water, on an island, appeared a magnificent temple, dedicated to Britannia, within which an appropiate device met the eye. A beautiful star ascended from the summit of it, in which Mr. Turnerelli's bust of his Majesty was exhibited. In the front of the temple, and close to the margin of the water, appeared a transparency, with these words :—" *Britannia celebrates the fiftieth year of a reign sacred to virtue and piety.*"—On the left of the temple a temporary bridge was erected over the lake, brilliantly illuminated, and inscribed "Rule Britannia, Britannia rules the waves," which had a beautiful and magnificent effect. Behind this the fire-works were exhibited, and a more striking spectacle was never witnessed, as may be conceived from the following enumeration of them, and the order in which they were fired :—*First Division.* A salute battery of fifty maroons. —Two pyramids, Bengal fire.—Twenty-four half-pound rockets, two at a time.—Two double triangle wheels, illuminated with diamond pieces.—Two planks saucissons.—Two air balloons.—Two large mines.—Two regulated pieces of three mutations.—Two planks pots de brins. *Second Division.*—Twenty-four half-pound rockets.—Two air balloons.—Two regulated pieces, of three mutations.—Two large mines.—Two figure pieces, with spiral and scroll wheels.—Two planks pots de brins. *Third Division.*—Twenty-four half-pound rockets.—One grand figure piece, of three mutations.—Two air balloons.—Two balloon wheels, with Roman candles, rockets, &c.— Two flights of rockets.—Two grand regulated pieces, with globe wheels.—Two planks pots de brins.—*Fourth Division.*—Twenty-eight one-pound rockets.—Two figure pieces, with spiral wheels and rayonet fire.—Two flights of rockets.—Two Pyramids, Bengal fire.— A grand illuminated temple, with decorations, fixed sun, diamond pieces, and pots d'aigrets, &c.—One plank pots de brins—Two planks saucissons. Three flights of rockets.—One large air balloon.—One battery of maroons. The rockets, balloons, &c. ascending when fired, were again reflected by the lake in a thousand directions, and heightened inconceivably the splendour of the scene. Two cars or chariots, drawn by sea horses, in one of which was a figure representing Britannia, in the other a representative of Neptune, appeared majestically moving on the bosom of the lake, followed by four boats filled with persons dressed to represent tritons, &c. These last were to have been composed of choristers, who were to have sung "God save the King" on the water, but unfortunately the crowd assembled was so immense, that those who were to have sung could not gain entrance. The high treat this could not but have afforded was in consequence lost to the company.—The cars had a very superb appearance. On coming to the temporary bridge erected over the canal opposite the garden front, transparencies were displayed in an equally sudden and unexpected manner on the battlement, with the words, "Rule Britannia, Britannia rules the waves," inscribed on them. At the same moment the band struck up the tune. Opposite the bridge, an elegant Grecian Temple was erected on a mount surrounded by eight beautiful marble pillars.—The interior of the temple was lined with purple, and in the centre was a large transparency of the Eye of Providence, fixed, as it were, upon a portrait of his Majesty, surmounted by stars of lamps. From the temple a double staircase descended to the water's edge. On the windings of the staircase were erected nine altars with burning incense.—On the lawn 12 marquees were erected, where the company partook of tea and coffee during the fire-works. Covers were laid in the principal dining rooms, and at 12 o'clock the company sat down to an elegant supper, consisting of all the delicacies of the season. The frames were beautifully done in emblematic figures, part of which represented Britannia kneeling by the lion, the Eye of Providence above, and underneath was written by her Royal Highness the Princess Elizabeth, "Britannia, grateful to Providence, celebrates the 50th year of a reign sacred to piety and virtue."

The Queen was attended by the Dukes of York, Clarence, and Sussex, and the Princesses Augusta, Elizabeth, and Sophia.—The Princesses and nobility wore blue ribbons, inscribed—"The 50th year; may God bless him who blesseth us."

In Frogmore, the company was mixed in a manner suitable to an occasion, on which all classes have shown such affectionate respect to the King, and on which, therefore, the Queen resolved to dispense, in a great measure, with distinctions for the day. All ranks, she said, were united in thankfulness, and therefore all should share in what entertainment she could give them. Tickets were accordingly sent to every family in Windsor, who had subscribed any thing to be distributed amongst the poor on that day. There was a great number of tradesmen's wives and daughters present, mixed with the first nobility, and the accommodation for their reception was excellent; the whole way from the entrance of the grounds to the house and the temporary buildings erected about it, being covered with an awning, and matted. The refreshments were tea and all kinds of sweetmeats and wines before the fireworks; an excellent supper afterwards. The Queen withdrew between twelve and one: but the Royal Dukes remained till three, and it was four before the whole company retired. Several bands of music attended.

BEDFORDSHIRE.

BEDFORD.—The Jubilee was celebrated with the utmost loyalty and attachment to our illustrious sovereign. The morning was ushered in with merry peals from the bells of several churches, divine service commenced at the usual hour, and appropriate discourses were delivered. Upwards of £300 was subscribed, and distributed in bread and money, whereby the poor were enabled to join in the festivities of the day. Nearly 3000 persons were relieved, including the military in the town. Five fine fat sheep were roasted whole, and disposed of with a good supply of bread and strong ale to the populace. Dinners were provided at the Swan and other inns, where mirth, good humour, and festivity prevailed. In the evening some beautiful transparencies were exhibited, but no illumination; and on Thursday evening there was a ball on the occasion. An address to his Majesty was also unanimously agreed to.

BIGGLESWADE.—The widows, and aged and decayed tradesmen, were provided with a handsome dinner, money was also distributed to them.—At Moggershanger House, the seat of Stephen Thornton, Esq., an ox was roasted, on which, with a profusion of pudding and ale, the whole of the lower tenantry were regaled, on returning from divine service. A most brilliant display of fire-works was exhibited in the Park in the evening, after which the higher order of tenants, and a party of the neighbouring gentry, adjourned to the mansion, where a dance and supper concluded the festivities of the day.

DUNSTABLE.—A subscription had been opened by a few gentlemen of the town, and a considerable sum was raised, to provide a dinner for inhabitants of the town; 950 persons sat down to old English fare, roast beef and plum-pudding, with plenty of ale. Afterwards about 40 gentlemen sat down to an excellent dinner, provided at the Crown Inn, when a band of music performed the song of "O! the Roast Beef of Old England," and the charity boys sung the anthem of "God save the King;" and many loyal toasts were afterwards drank. Perhaps there never before was an instance where the whole population of a town, so fully inhabited as Dunstable, have been so well entertained, and made so completely happy in one day.

LEIGHTON BUZZARD paid every mark of loyalty and respect to its beloved sovereign; the poor were regaled by the liberality of a voluntary subscription from the Lord of the Manor, seconded by the neighbouring gentry. Upwards of 50 gentlemen dined together at the Swan Inn; and in the evening there was a ball at the Eagle and Child, attended by upwards of 200 of the inhabitants of the town and vicinity.

RENHOLT.—The poor were liberally supplied with bread, beef, and beer, and the tenants regaled with a good dinner, and plenty of punch, by order of J. Polhill, Esq., whose loyalty and attachment to his Sovereign is surpassed only by his liberality to the poor and indigent. In the evening, there were a bonfire, fire-works, and other demonstrations of joy.

SOUTHILL HOUSE.—Samuel Whitbread, Esq., M.P., gave to each of the poor tenants on his extensive estates in Bedfordshire, whose rent was under £5 per annum, one quarter's rent of their respective dwellings; and to every workman employed upon his premises, one day's additional pay.

———o———

BERKSHIRE.

READING.—The loyalty of the inhabitants of this borough manifested itself in the most conspicuous manner, by the spirit with which they celebrated the Jubilee. At six o'clock in the morning three volleys were fired by the Royal Berks Regiment of Local Militia, in the Market-place, which, accompanied by the ringing of bells, the display of flags from the different towers, and the acclamations of the populace, announced the commencement of the festivities of the day. At nine o'clock all the Danish prisoners of war, nearly 200 in number, on parole in the town, assembled in the Market-place, and the happy news of their being set at liberty, in consequence of this joyful event, was announced to them by Mr. Lewis, the agent; the joy manifested by them was expressed by the most hearty and reiterated shouts. As a tribute of gratitude for the hospitality manifested towards them by the inhabitants, they presented the Mayor and Corporation with a complete model of a ship of war, constructed by one of them, named Sivert Rübert.—At eleven o'clock, the Corporation, the Royal Berks Regiment, the Woodley Cavalry, three troops of the Royal Horse Guards (blue), the different Benefit Societies, and the Children belonging to the different Sunday and Charity Schools, went in procession to St. Lawrence's Church where the Coronation Anthem was performed.—The Rev. Mr. Marsh delivered a Discourse, from 1 Sam. ch. x. verse 24. The Royal Horse Guards marched into the Forbury, and fired three volleys; and a very fine fat ox, and three barrels of strong beer, the gift of the Master Butchers, together with a proportionate quantity of bread, the gift of the Master Bakers, were distributed to the surrounding populace, who greeted this act of liberality with loud cheers of acclamation.—About three o'clock the Royal Berks Regiment, under the command of Major Wilmshurst, arrived in the Market-place, and again fired three excellent volleys in honour of the day; the men were afterwards marched by companies to the different public houses, where they partook of a plentiful dinner, provided by order of their Colonel, the Most Noble the Marquis of Blandford, and the Officers. The Mayor and Corporation, and a numerous company, dined at the Town-Hall; a party of Gentlemen, the Officers of the Royal Berks Regiment, the Woodley Cavalry, and the Officers of the Royal Horse Guards (blue), at the Bear; indeed, every Inn was crowded with visitors.—J. Jesse, Esq., of Castle-hill House, entertained his poor tenants, their wives and children, at his residence, with roast, baked, and boiled meat, plum-puddings, strong beer, and punch; he afterwards distributed some money among them, and ordered the women to attend next morning, and bear away the fragments of the table.—The House of Finch and Co. in the Market-place, on this festive occasion, exhibited a scene truly gratifying.—At six o'clock upwards of 260 of their Work People sat down to a most excellent dinner of roast beef and plum-pudding, with plenty of strong beer; the whole evening was spent with the greatest harmony and conviviality, and the company departed highly pleased with the liberality of their benefactors.—Relief was afforded by the Town Subscription to 480 poor persons in the three parishes, distributed in half-crown tickets, for bread and meat, and measures were taken for the release of the whole of the debtors confined in the county gaol, by means of the same liberal benefactions.

ABINGDON.—The morning was ushered in by the ringing of bells at both churches, and a display of flags in various parts of the town. At nine o'clock the cavalry and infantry assembled, and went through their manœuvres. After which they attended divine service, as did the Mayor and Corporation of this ancient town, preceded by upwards of two hundred of the Sunday school children, and nearly one hundred charity children, all arrayed in a new suit of clothes, made expressly for the occasion. As soon as the congregation (upwards of four thousand being present) were seated in the church, the organ and choir struck up "God save the King;" it had a most impressive effect. The Coronation Anthem was also sung. After a most excellent sermon from the Rev. W. Price, "God save the King" was again sung by the congregation. From Church, the regiments proceeded to the Market-place, where they fired a *Feu de joie*. The respectable part of the inhabitants of the town dined with the Mayor at the Town Hall; nearly 2000 poor men and women receiving 3s. a piece, and 9d. for every child, and were also regaled in the evening by a number of barrels of beer being placed in the Market-place, and a great quantity of cakes were thrown from the top of the Market-house amongst them, the same ceremony as was performed when his Majesty ascended to the throne fifty years ago. One of these cakes was exhibited by Mr.

John Waite, a member of the Corporation, he having kept it in his possession ever since; it has been since shown to his Majesty. The evening concluded with a display of fire-works, and a ball.

ALDERMASTON.—The cavalry attended divine service, after which they paraded in front of Aldermaston House, where they fired three *Feux de joie* in honour of the day; they afterwards marched to the Hind's Head Inn, where they partook of a sumptuous entertainment given by their Commander, W. Congreve, Esq., to which his tenants were invited. Near forty score of beef, a donation of Mr. Congreve's, and a due proportion of bread and beer, purchased by the inhabitants, were distributedt among the poor families residing in the parish.

BEACH HILL.—Nearly 200 persons were plentifully regaled with roast and boiled beef, plum-pudding, potatoes, and good ale, by C. Musgrave and R. Halhed, Esqrs.

EAST HAMPSTEAD.—Mrs. Nesbitt regaled upwards of 200 of the inhabitants with the best fare; after dinner, the health of the King was drank with three cheers, and the singers, with the band of music, sang "God save the King," in full chorus. After several loyal toasts, between five and six o'clock, the whole company paraded before the house of their hospitable Patroness, singing and playing "God save the King," and then went to the house of Mr. and Mrs. Vidal, who had entertained 50 children of the parish, with beef, pudding, &c., and saluted them with the loyal song, when the children greeted their fathers, mothers, and relations, with the same, accompanied by a piano forte and harp.

FARLEY HILL.—The Jubilee was celebrated with great joy and festivity, under a tree that was planted in commemoration of his Majesty's accession to the throne. The cottager who planted the tree, now 80 years of age, was chaired by the neighbouring tenantry with great pomp, and made president of the feast. A fat sheep was roasted whole upon the occasion, was and given among the poor cottagers.

FARINGDON.—The morning was ushered in by the ringing of bells and the firing of six pieces of cannon. The Volunteers after attending divine service proceeded to parade, and went through different evolutions. The privates were afterwards regaled with roast beef, plum-pudding, and two quarts each of ale to drink the health of their King. At twelve o'clock the company sat down to a most sumptuous supper: they afterwards resumed the merry dance till six in the morning.

GROVE-HOUSE, BINFIELD.—At an early hour the whole of the poor of the extensive parish of Binfield were assembled in front of the house of Askew Hillcoat, Esq., from whence, preceded by a band of music, attended by that gentleman and most of the respecfable farmers and tradesmen, they proceeded to the church. On entering the church-yard, "God save the King" was sung in chorus by the whole company, consisting of upwards of 500 people, with a very happy effect. After an excellent sermon by the Rev. Mr. Ashley, nearly 400 persons were presented by their benefactor with a quartern loaf, a pound of meat, and a quantity of strong beer each, to drink his Majesty's health.—Sixty of the principal farmers and others sat down to a substantial dinner of beef and plum-pudding, in the old English style of hospitality; many loyal and constitutional toasts were drank, with appropriate songs; and in the evening the mansion and gardens were brilliantly illuminated, accompanied with a large bonfire and a display of fire-works.

HINTON.—The Rev. Mr. Symonds gave a dinner to the poor inhabitants of his parish, nearly 300 persons, men, women, and children. After dinner, they were amused by a lottery of all prizes, consisting of shirts, shoes, coals, and other articles, which were given by Mr. and Mrs. Symonds.

HUNGERFORD.—The poor were supplied from a public subscription with beef, upwards of 2800 pounds having been divided amongst the poor families, in proportion to their numbers. The Corporation, and the Hungerford Volunteer Cavalry and Infantry, attended divine service, where a sermon was preached by the Rev. Mr. Bradford, after which a *Feu de joie* was fired by a detachment of the King's Own Stafford Militia, and also by the Volunteer Infantry. The Cavalry performed their sword exercise, and the day was spent with the greatest festivity, by public dinners at the Town-hall and Inns, and the evening concluded with a grand display of fireworks.

MAIDENHEAD.—The Mayor and Corporation attended divine service with their gowns, insignia of office, and band of music, when anthems were sung, and an appropriate sermon preached. Large quantities of provisions were distributed amongst all the poor families of the town. In addition to which, a fat ox was roasted whole, and given amongst the populace. The Corporation, with a great number of the respectable inhabitants of the town and neighbourhood, dined at the Town-hall, where many loyal and constitutional toasts were given.

NEWBURY.—By the handsome donations of Colonel Stead, Mr. Montague, and C. Dundas, Esq., in conjunction with the liberal town subscription, 3000 people were enabled to share the enjoyments of the day. In the evening, the ball was honoured by the presence of a large assemblage of beauty, elegance and fashion.

NORTHSTOKE.—The day was ushered in with the ringing of bells, and flags were flying on the tower, while the Local Militia of the parish, with a few of the Earl of Macclesfield's Troop of Yeomanry Cavalry, fired three excellent volleys and a *Feu de joie* in honour of the day. At ten o'clock the troops, attended by the inhabitants, marched to church, where a sermon was preached by the Rev. Mr. Wright, who came forward with his accustomed spirit and liberality, in aid of the poor, who were most amply furnished with roast beef, plum-pudding and strong beer, to celebrate the day; his Majesty's health was drank with enthusiasm, and the Jubilee was concluded with a ball, which was attended by a brilliant assemblage of beauty and fashion.—A resolution was also entered into by the gentlemen of Northstoke to commemorate the Jubilee annually, during **the remainder of his present Majesty's reign.**

SWALLOWFIELD.—The Right Hon. Lord Rivers presented five guineas, which, with the joint subscriptions of the gentlemen, yeomanry, and others, resident in the parish, furnished to 557 people an ample portion **of** beef, with money sufficient for beer, to keep up this happy event.

WALLINGFORD.—The Corporation, accompanied by the inhabitants, and preceded by a capital band of music, went in procession from the Mayor's house to St. Peter's Church, where an excellent sermon was preached by the Rev. Wm. Mairis, D.D. A dinner was provided at the expense of the Corporation, for about 200 repectable persons of the borough, and greater regularity, harmony and conviviality, never inspired a public meeting. When the King's health was given, it produced a burst of grateful and patriotic feelings from every heart, and **was** afterwards repeated with 49 successive cheers. The band then struck up "God save the King," and was joined by the whole assembly in full chorus, with an enthusiasm not to be described. The poor (nearly 800) were liberally supplied with meat, bread, and strong beer. A further subscription of 23 guineas was received from W. L. **Hughes,** Esq., one of the Members for the borough, making the whole amount of the subscription for the poor upwards of 160 guineas.

WOKINGHAM.—The Jubilee **commenced** with **a ball in** the Town-hall, **on** the evening of the 24th. **The entrance of the** auspicious day was greeted by the bells from the tower, and three excellent volleys of musketry from **the** Market-place. The company in the ball room, accompanied by the band, sang "God save the King," with most impressive fervour and animation; the dancing then recommenced and continued with much vivacity till a late hour in the morning. **The Corporation went in** procession to church; an excellent sermon was preached **by** the Rev. Wm. Bremner. After divine **service a** liberal subscription from the inhabitants was distributed **to all the** poor families in the town and parish, to enable them to participate in the general festivity. The inhabitants afterwards dined together **at the** Town-hall, and spent the remaining part of the 24 hours in **most perfect** concord.

WOODLEY.—J. Wheble, Esq., gave bread, meat, money, and beer to upwards of 300 persons; a quantity of blankets were also given away by the farmers in the same liberal spirit.

YATELY.—J. Halhed and ———— Caswell, **Esqs.,** gave a shilling to every poor man, woman and child.

BUCKINGHAMSHIRE.

BUCKINGHAM.—A handsome subscription was raised by the inhabitants to regale the poor with bread, meat, and beer, and upwards of 1900 partook of this bounty. After attending divine service, a large party, consisting of the principal inhabitants of the town and neighbourhood, dined at the Cobham Arms Inn, where many loyal and constitutional toasts were drank, and the day passed with the greatest conviviality.

AMERSHAM.—A subscription was set on foot for providing the labouring classes (upwards of 1700) with a comfortable dinner at their own houses on the day of the anniversary. The worthy representatives of this ancient borough subscribed £50 each; and a fund was raised in the course of a few hours of nearly £300, which proved fully adequate to the purpose intended, so that on this festive occasion every countenance seemed to express "God save the King."

ASTON CLINTON.—An ox was roasted whole, and distributed, with plenty of beer, to the poor. Lord Viscount Lake likewise gave a most liberal entertainment to his tenants and neighbouring farmers.

FARNHAM.—On Tuesday was delivered, to upwards of 400 persons, two pounds of prime beef, exclusive of bone, and a quartern loaf to each. On the following day a quart of strong beer was given to each man and woman, and half a pint to each child. The parish bells began to ring at six o'clock, and continued till ten at night. The village was illuminated, the church likewise, and the tower, with patent lamps. A bonfire, on an eminence commanding Windsor Castle and the surrounding country, concluded the festivity of the day.

HARTWELL.—The handsome donation of the unfortunate Prince Louis XVIII., the rightful monarch of the throne of France, ranks high in the list of generous actions performed on the joyous day of the Jubilee. To the poor inhabitants of Hartwell, in which he resides, and in the neighbouring parishes of Aylesbury and Stowe, he gave £100 to be distributed.

LILLINGSTONE DAYRELL.—The day was celebrated with every demonstration of happiness and joy; upwards of 80 of the poor inhabitants were regaled upon the lawn of Richard Dayrell, Esq., with a plentiful supply of roast beef, plum pudding, and beer.

MARLOW.—The Jubilee was celebrated with every demonstration of joy; the morning was ushered in by the ringing of bells and a display of colours. Col. Sir W. Clayton, with the Desborough squadron of Bucks Yeomanry, attended divine service, when an excellent sermon was preached by the Rev. Mr. Hicks. After divine service the Yeomanry fired a *Feu de joie.* The inhabitants subscribed upwards of £150, which enabled the Committee appointed to regale 2135 poor persons with a pound of good meat, a half-quartern loaf and plenty of good strong beer each; the poor in the workhouse, on the same joyful occasion, were supplied with a good meat dinner, plum-pudding, and plenty of strong beer. A large porty of the town, and neighbouring gentlemen, dined at the Town-hall, where a number of loyal songs were sung, and appropriate toasts drank.

MEDMENHAM.— The whole of the poor of the parish of Medmenham were regaled by Mrs. Scott, of Danesfield, and on the following Saturday, they were all again treated by the parishioners.

OLNEY.—A public subscription enabled a committee to distribute to every man, woman and child, who would accept it, one pound of beef or mutton and a half quartern loaf, which were most gratefully received by upwards of 1350 persons. A cow and ten sheep were also given away on the occasion.

STONY STRATFORD.—A collection was made throughout the town, and likewise at the church door after divine service, which enabled the parishioners to distribute one shilling to every man, woman and child in the town, who thought proper to accept the same; and the surplus of the collection was reserved till a future time, to be applied in the most beneficial manner. An excellent dinner was provided at the Cock Inn, where harmony and conviviality prevailed; and the day was spent with every demonstration of joy.

UNTON-CUM-CHALVEY.—The inhabitants of this parish subscribed a sum amply sufficient to provide upwards of 500 of the poor with a quartern loaf and a pound of meat each, and plenty of strong beer, as additional means of rejoicing on the 25th.

———o———

CAMBRIDGESHIRE.

CAMBRIDGE.—In the morning divine service was read, and discourses appropriate to the occasion preached in the different churches: very numerous congregations assembled to return solemn thanks for the blessings continued to the King and the people during a reign unexampled in the history of nations for the dangers with which the country has been threatened, but which have been averted by the wisdom bestowed upon its councils, and the courage with which its troops have been inspired. Many of the principal persons of the county (among whom was his Excellency the Earl of Hardwicke) had an elegant entertainment at the Rose Tavern; the members of the University celebrated the day in their respective college halls; and the Mayor and Corporation dined together upon the occasion. The Master and Fellows of Emanuel College entertained 200 inhabitants of the parish of St. Andrew, with a plentiful dinner of good beef and plum-pudding, the college ale being delivered out without limitation. The whole went off with much spirit, and this large party, after drinking the King's health with three times three, and singing "God save the King" in full chorus, retired in the greatest good humour highly gratified by the hospitality with which they had been received. The other colleges gave entertainments to the poor of the different parishes; and the subscriptions on the occasion amounted to such a large sum, that a great number of poor families had money distributed amongst them also. The servants of the colleges were liberally entertained by the Masters and Fellows of the respective societies. Nearly 200 boys of the Lancastrian School were regaled with beef and plum pudding in their school-room. Some of the governors, amongst whom was the Vice-Chancellor of the University, attended on the occasion; and the little fellows drank the King's health with loud and repeated huzzas. There was not a poor family in the place who did not participate of the liberality of the higher order of persons on this happy occasion. The North Lincoln Militia attended divine service in the morning at St. Mary's Church, and in the afternoon fired three volleys in the great court of Trinity College, the band playing "God save the King" between each volley, and all joining in three cheers as a mark of their loyalty. The men were then regaled with plenty of ale, and the officers afterwards dined with the members of the college. In the evening the band of the regiment paraded the streets, playing many loyal tunes, and the populace attended singing "God save the King," "Rule Britannia," etc., and testifying their joy by frequent cheers. The Masters and Seniors of Trinity College unanimously voted and transmitted a donation of 50 guineas to the British and Foreign Bible Society for the purpose of diffusing the glad tidings of redemption.

BLUNTISHAM—.In the parish of Bluntisham with Earith, upwards of forty guineas were gathered and distributed to 150 poor families in coals, meat, and flour.

CHEVELEY PARK was a scene of joy and festivity in honour of the day. The morning was ushered in by the ringing of bells, and at twelve o'clock, upwards of 900 of the surrounding poor assembled on the lawn fronting the dining parlour, where the Duchess and Dowager Duchess of Rutland, and several persons of distinction, were collected to witness the distribution of the donations which the liberality of her Grace had provided. Shortly afterwards the ladies Charlotte and Elizabeth Manners came out of the grand entrance-door, followed by servants loaded with clothing of every description, and bed linen, which was distributed to every one, by order of her Grace. The happy multitude sat down to old English fare, to the number of 900. At four o'clock, 80 persons of rank and fashion sat down to a most sumptuous dinner. In the evening the house was most splendidly illuminated.

ELY.—The officers of the Ely battalion of Local Militia met in celebration of the Jubilee, and attended the cathedral, with the staff on permanent pay. The non-commissioned officers fired three volleys in the Market-place, after which they (together with the band, in all about 70) were provided with an excellent dinner at the Lamb and Red Lion Inns, by Lieut.-Col. Brackenbury. The officers and the gentlemen of the place dined together at the Red Lion, and spent the day in the utmost conviviality. There was a concert in the evening. It was a most gratifying sight to observe in several respectable families 20, 30, 50, and upwards, of their poor neighbours, with their children, sit down to a comfortable dinner, and afterwards regaled with good home-brewed ale, to drink the health of their excellent sovereign.

NEWMARKET.—Mrs. Panton gave a dinner to nearly 100 of the poor in the town and vicinity, together with the tenants attached to her estate.

WIMPOLE.—The Earl of Hardwicke gave a very handsome entertainment to the labourers and other inhabitants of Wimpole and the adjoining parishes. A bullock and six sheep, with a proportionate quantity of bread and **ale**, were distributed at Wimpole House; the number of those who partook of his Lordship's liberality amounted to about 600.

WISBECH.—The day was celebrated with loyalty and beneficence. The officers of the Wisbech battalion of Local Militia, attended by their band, and staff on permanent pay, formed part of a numerous congregation at church,—where an appropriate discourse was delivered by the vicar, from Psalm 78. v. 72.—Immediately after which a collection was made at the church doors for the purpose of enabling the widows, orphans, and afflicted poor of the parish, to participate in the general joy.—Three excellent volleys were fired by the non-commissioned officers of the Local Militia. In the afternoon Col. Watson, with his brother officers and the gentlemen of the town, assembled at the White Hart Inn, to drink the long continuance of life and glory to our beloved sovereign; when several loyal and patriotic toasts were given. The evening concluded with a ball, which was graced by all the beauty and respectability of the town and neighbourhood. All the boys and girls of the charity schools, were regaled by the Colonel with cake and wine; and, being united with the choir belonging to the church, joined in an anthem of praise to Divine Providence for vouchsafing to continue to us a life so justly dear as that of our revered monarch, concluding with "God save the King." Nor were the poor men, women, and children in the workhouse forgotten, for their hearts were cheered on this happy occasion, by the liberality of the same benevolent individual.

---o---

CHESHIRE.

CHESTER.—The Jubilee was celebrated with a degree of magnificence of show, and cordiality of character, never before witnessed. The morning was ushered in with peals of bells from all the churches. An ox, the gift of John Egerton, Esq., of Oulton Park, (one of the members for the city) which had been slaughtered for the purpose of being roasted whole, was paraded on the preceding evening ready spitted, with horns and tail gilt, decorated with ribbons, and attended by a band of music, and the colours of the several clubs of the city. Behind the ox, on the same carriage, rode the butcher, with knife drawn; thus the procession proceeded to the Power Field, near the walls of the city, where a building was erected for the purpose of roasting. The fire was lighted at two, and the ox put down at eight on the Tuesday evening; by twelve o'clock the next day it was as well and as regularly roasted as any joint of meat could have been done by the most experienced cook. It was then taken down and the body carved up in great style, and divided in smoking portions, to the multitude, at the same time that four hogsheads of excellent old beer were also distributed among them. But the liberality of Mr. Egerton did not stop here; he ordered a sum of money to be given to all the poor prisoners in the city and county gaol, that they might regale themselves with a good dinner, and a quart of ale each on the joyful occasion. He likewise caused bread, meat, and ale to be plentifully distributed throughout the neighbourhood of his seat at Oulton.—Mr. Harrison, the architect, proposed to erect, by subscription, a column, in one block of stone, 40 feet high, and the whole height, including the basement and termination, to be 56 feet, in some proper situation within the walls of the city. A stone of this magnitude, it is conjectured, has not been taken from the quarry, and raised upon its pedestal, since the dissolution of the Roman Empire; such a memorial will no doubt be the pride of their descendants, so long as time shall leave it an ornament to the capital of the county.

BEBINGTON.—A numerous congregation attended divine service, and heard a most excellent sermon preached by the Rev. R. Jackson, whose hospitality to his parishioners was unbounded; 50 of whom, and upwards of 50 children, sat down to an elegant dinner with their worthy rector.

EASTHAM.—Lady Smith Burgess gave an ox, coals, and ale, to her tenants, at Eastham, and Havering Bower.

KNUTSFORD.—The celebration of the accession of our good and virtuous King on the 50th year of his prosperous and happy reign, commenced with a joyous peal on the bells. The flag presented to the town by their patriotic townswoman, Lady Jane Stanley, to be used upon all occasions of rejoicing, was placed upon the top of the steeple, and the streets were all cleaned and sanded into various appropriate mottoes, a custom peculiar to Knutsford: at nine o'clock, the cavalry and infantry began to assemble, and marched to church, preceded by the Sunday School scholars; an excellent sermon was preached by their new vicar, the Rev. Harry Grey; with the anthem of "God save the King," sung by Captain Leech.—After divine service, the military were reviewed upon the race ground by Lieut.-Col. Sir John F. Leicester, Bart. At the George and Angel Inns large parties of the officers and gentlemen dined; many patriotic songs were sung, and toasts drank. At seven o'clock a grand display of fire-works was let off by Charles Cholmondeley, Esq. the band of the Volunteer corps playing "God save the King" the whole time; after which a a very large bonfire was lighted on the race ground, and around were to be seen, in all directions, scenes of happy groups dancing hands round. At nine o'clock, the Volunteers at the door of Major Wright, sung "God save the King," and cheered that worthy officer with loud and hearty huzzas. Afterwards there was an elegant and well attended ball at the George Inn. A liberal subscription was made for the poorer inhabitants, who enjoyed and partook of the festivities of the day; to each man, woman, and child 2lbs. of prime beef were given, besides a quart of good ale to every man, and a pint to every woman.

MACCLESFIELD.—The morning was ushered in by the ringing of bells; and the inhabitants assembled in large congregations at both churches, where loyal and appropriate sermons were preached by the respective Ministers. At twelve o'clock a troop of the 7th Dragoon Guards, and a party of the Royal Cheshire Local Militia, fired three volleys; who as well as all those on the recruiting service were furnished with money to enable them to drink his Majesty's health.—At one o'clock upwards of 1000 poor persons assembled to dine at different inns, where they were plentifully regaled (by subscription) with roast beef, plum pudding, and ale. A surplus of nearly 50*l*. remaining after the expenses of the day were defrayed, it was appropriated to the purpose of buying blankets for poor indigent families. After dinner all parted in good order and good humour, blessing the King and the donors.—200 poor orphan children dined in the Sunday School. The following address (printed at the expense of a very active and intelligent Magistrate, Charles Wood, Esq., to whose zeal and public services the town of Macclesfield is under indelible obligation) was read aloud at the respective tables, and upwards of 1000 copies of it distributed among the people:—

An Address to those Persons who partake of the Jubilee Dinner, in Macclesfield; October 25, 1809.

FRIENDS AND NEIGHBOURS,

I most cordially congratulate you on the pleasing event which has brought you together, and on the benevolence and patriotism of the gentlemen of the town, who contrived, and have now so liberally patronised, the design of enabling you to partake with them in the general joy. What country in Europe, besides our own, can boast of such an interesting scene as this, where the people of every rank and degree are celebrating the longevity and virtues of one of the best Kings that ever swayed a sceptre! A King, who is the father of his people, and whose highest pleasure and gratification consist in seeing his subjects and happy; but whose lot, in common with our own, it has been to live at a period, and in a day, pregnant with events of uncommon interest and magnitude. Perhaps some of you will understand me better when I say, it has been his fortune and ours to live in very troublesome times, though the evils we have known have been but trifling and partial, when compared with those of other nations. We have heard of the horrors and devastation that war has made; we have heard the sound of the trumpet calling our brave sons to the defence of their country; but our eyes have not seen their swords bathed in blood; we have lived in comparative peace and security. In almost every other country, we have seen Kings hurled from their thrones, and constituted authorities (venerated and admired for ages) trodden under foot, despised, and obliterated. And what have been the consequences of all this? Has a greater share of human happiness fallen to the lot of those countries? by no **means.** Misery, distress, anarchy, confusion and blood have rapidly followed. **And** most of us remember the period, when the same dreadful evils awaited and threatened us. Thanks to Divine Providence, and the wise counsels **of that** day, the efforts that **were** then made by wicked and designing **men, at** home and abroad, **to** introduce them into England, were happily **frustrated and confounded. And** your meeting, this day, is a lively evidence, **that our country** is still preserved amid the mighty wreck. May it continue **to prosper, the** envy **and the** admiration of surrounding nations, **to** the end **of** time! Should any ask, **what are** the advantages of this country above those of **others?** I answer, **they** are many and various. To enumerate them all is incompatible with my design. Suffice it to say, that our religion is Christianity, the **last** best gift of God to man. We have a national church, apostolic, orthodox, and evangelical in her doctrines; mild, pacific, and tolerant towards those who conscientiously dissent from her. We have all the advantages of civil and religious liberty which a *good* man can possibly wish for or desire. **And** here, too, there is more real goodness, more beneficence, more liberality, more philanthropy, and charity, flowing from the benign principles of Christianity, than in any other country upon the face of the globe. **I** rejoice that I was *born* in such a country, and that is **has been** my lot to *live* in such a country. O happy, happy England! May **heaven** continue to thee, "the blessings of peace and security, and restore concord and independence to the contending and bleeding nations!"—Would you show gratitude to the Almighty, by whom Kings reign, for national mercies, and in what high estimation you hold **the** privileges of Britons? Evidence **both by** your love of order, and obedience to the laws; by fearing **God, and** honouring the King. And, in this way, testify your affection and **loyalty to your** sovereign, and your love and attachment to your native land.

AN ENGLISHMAN OF **THE OLD STAMP.**

POYNTON.—The seat of Lord and Lady Bulkeley, large bonfires **were made** in the Park, which were seen at an immense distance, at which sheep were roasted whole, **and** distributed, with bread and cheese, and two quarts of ale, to each of the colliers, **labourers, and** workmen, consisting of upwards of 200, and during the festivity, two brass mortar-pieces were fired fifty rounds, and some fire-works displayed on a boat, in Poynton water.

SANDBACH.—The morning was **ushered** in by the ringing of bells; at ten o'clock the club and friendly society, and the Sunday school children walked in procession to church, where an excellent sermon was preached by the Rev. R. L. Salmon, from the 42nd chapter Isaiah, and the beginning of 10th verse. A subscription was **raised** by the ladies of Sandbach **and its** vicinity, to supply beef, **bread,** potatoes, and ale to the **poor, which** was distributed to 400 people, **at** the Free School, **at twelve** o'clock. At three o'clock 119 people dined **together** at the George Inn, appropriate songs and toasts were given.—In the evening a sheep was roasted, and three barrels of ale given **by the** gentlemen to the populace.—Fire-works closed the **scene of festivity.** On Thursday morning sixty gallons of broth were

D

sent to 100 poor families, and in the evening a ball was numerously attended, at the George.

STOCKPORT.—The day commenced by the firing of a royal salute, and the ringing of bells; after which the Jubilee was proclaimed by the sound of trumpet. At nine o'clock a considerable number of inhabitants of the town partook of an elegant public breakfast, at the Warren Bulkeley Arms Inn, from whence they walked in procession, accompanied by several associated bodies, to St. Mary's Church, where a sermon was preached, and a collection made in aid of a subscription for the relief of debtors confined in the county gaol. At St. Peter's there was religious service, and a collection made for the same purpose. From St. Mary's the procession moved to the Market Place, where a large bonfire had been previously lighted. The Non-Commissioned Officers of the Local Militia then fired a *Feu de joie*, and a discharge of fifty pieces of cannon commemorated this Anniversary of his Majesty's long reign. Here also "Long life to the King" was drank with enthusiasm, and the populace were regaled with a plentiful supply of roasted mutton, bread and cheese, in addition to a copious libation of two-year-old October. At two o'clock the sports for the amusement of the public commenced. In the evening there was a grand display of fire-works. Many gentlemen feasted their numerous companies of workmen with the substantial dinner of old English times.

———o———

CORNWALL.

LAUNCESTON.—Immediately after midnight, a merry peal on the musical bells and the bells of the adjoining parishes, announced the approaching Jubilee. About nine o'clock, the inhabitants were given to understand that the Mayor, Deputy Recorder, and others belonging to the Corporate Body, intended to meet at the town-hall, and proceed from thence in their robes to church. The procession was admirably arranged by Major Rowe, of the late Launceston Volunteers.—The inhabitants walked two and two, amounting in the whole to upwards of one thousand.—All was order and regularity. Both the *Te Deum* and *Jubilate Deo* were sung by the choir, with the Anthem of *Zadok the Priest*, and grand chorus of "God save the King." An excellent discourse was delivered by the Rev. Mr. Rowe, from ii. chap. 1st Epistle to Timothy, v. 1, 2, 3; the whole concluded with "God save the King." The same order was preserved in returning from Church to the Guildhall, the band playing "God save the King;" and three times three finished the business of the morning. The Corporation, with about forty respectable inhabitants, partook of an excellent dinner at the White Hart Inn, and about forty respectable inhabitants at the King's Arms Inn. Eleven public-houses were opened for the other part of the inhabitants, and they were entertained with a good dinner, etc., which was provided for by a subscription of near one hundred pounds, for that and other charitable purposes. The evening was spent in the ringing of bells, bonfires and fire-works. The loyalty and good order of the public were truly praiseworthy. The ladies of Launceston and its vicinity gave a supper and ball, on Thursday, at the White Hart and King's Arms Inn. The greatest harmony, decorum, and good order, reigned throughout the day among all ranks of people.

BODMIN.—A handsome subscription was made for the poor, to which Lord de Dunstanville contributed £20. A numerous company supped at the King's Arms, and another at the Fountain, where an elegant transparency was exhibited, with a suitable motto.

CAMBORNE.—The morning was ushered in by the ringing of bells, and the 'dulcet peal' served also as a signal for the assembling of the poor, for the relief of whom a very liberal subscription had been entered into. Above 1400 lbs. of beef and 2500 lbs. of flour, were then distributed. The aged and those who were confined to the bed of sickness, were particularly attended to. The number thus relieved amounted to at least 700. Six guineas were then given to a few poor women and children who had not partaken of the former distribution. Morning service was performed at the church, where an excellent sermon from Timothy xi. 1, 2, was delivered to a large congregation. An Anthem, composed for the occasion, by Mr. Gribble, of Camborne, was sung to the tune of "God save the King." Public worship was fully attended at the respective Methodist chapels in the town and neighbourhood. The hills which surround the parish were illuminated with tar barrels elevated on poles, which produced a very pleasing appearance.

CAMELFORD.—The Mayor, Corporation and inhabitants of Camelford, united to celebrate the Jubilee with harmony and loyalty no where exceeded. The subscription, which was very liberal, was not confined to the Recorder, Mayor and Aldermen; the capital burgesses subscribed handsomely; a fine fat ox, with a quantity of bread, &c., was distributed to the poor: a loyal address to the King was unanimously voted and signed by the inhabitants; an excellent sermon from the text, *Fear God and honour the King*, was preached on the occasion by the Rev. Mr. Hockin: a party of the North Cornwall Local Militia, under Capt. Rosevear, fired three excellent volleys: the principal inhabitants dined together, and bumpered the King and his friends with heart-felt loyalty and patriotism: and bonfires and fire-works illuminated the night.

CARYTHANICK.—At Carythanick, the seat of Peter Hill, Esq., the neighbouring poor and their families were entertained. H. C. Brewett. Esq., presented the Crowan miners with a fat ox, seven barrels of beer, and three sacks of flour, with raisins, &c., for making them figgy puddings. The same gentleman presented a considerable quantity of beef, with beer, &c., to the poor in the neighbourhood of Hayle foundry.

CUBY.—Sir Thomas Dyke Ackland, in a very handsome manner (in a letter to his tenants in the parish of Cuby), expressed himself so convinced of the attachment and loyalty of all Cornishmen to their Sovereign, that he requested that his name might be added to the list of subscribers, for the purpose of celebrating the day, at the same time mentioning his donation, which was immediately followed up by the farmers of Cuby, with such spirit and liberality, as will ever entitle them to rank amongst the most true and loyal of his Majesty's subjects. The hearts of the poor of the parish were enlivened with a plentiful supply of mutton, bread, &c., &c., and a reserve made for them until winter. The farmers met at the Queen's Head Inn, in Tregony, and after spending the evening in perfect harmony, drinking and cheering the most loyal toasts and songs, parted with reluctance from the scene of mirth and jollity. Tea and coffee were prepared at the King's Arms Inn, in Tregony, for the ladies. Dancing commenced early, and continued until a late hour in the morning.— Thus closed a scene of loyalty and attachment to our good old King, that will ever be remembered with heartfelt pleasure by the inhabitants of Cuby.

FALMOUTH.—The splendour of the Jubilee at Falmouth, was truly worthy of the loyalty and spirit which characterise the place. From a liberal subscription, about 1,700 poor persons received at the Town-hall, on Tuesday, a supply of beef, bread and beer. The officers of the Pendennis Artillery Local Militia breakfasted together at Commin's Hotel, and with their non-commissioned officers and drummers, amounting to about 80, headed the procession to the Church—next followed the Free Masons' lodge and their numerous visiting brethren —the Mayor, Corporation, and principal inhabitants—the Charity children, &c., &c. The procession extended nearly a mile. On its approach to the Church, the military bands played "God save the King." The Church would not contain all who pressed for admittance. The Rev. Mr. Hichens preached a most excellent sermon on the occasion from Psalm 147th. Several public dinners followed ; while a good dinner was provided at the regimental store-room for tht non-commissioned officers and drummers. S. H. Pellew, Esq., gave a good dinner to the numerous inferior officers of the establishment, at the Custom-house, which was brilliantly illuminated in the evening. A plentiful dinner was provided for the Charity children, &c., innumerable parties, or rather one great party, filled the town with festive loyalty. About eight o'clock the numerous cannon on the batteries of Pendennis and St. Mawes Castle, illuminated the night and thundered out the climax of public joy—these were answered by the cannon of several men of war and packets—while innumerable bonfires studded the surrounding hills, and sky-rockets, blue lights, &c., from the ships and from the shore, spangled the atmosphere. One of the packets (the Mary, Capt. Cock) was beautifully illuminated throughout. The Royal Glamorganshire Militia, drawn up on the elevated horn-work of Pendennis, answered the roar of cannon with repeated volleys of musketry: and when the firing ceased, they, the garrisons, the crews of the several ships, &c., cheered each other, and their good old King, with shouts of enthusiasm, that will never be forgotten. It was a most glorious finish of a glorious day.

GRAMPOUND.—After attending at the Church, where a suitable sermon on the occasion was delivered by the Rev. Mr. Gregor, the Mayor and principal inhabitants distributed several fat sheep, and a large quantity of bread, among the poor, whose countenances expressed the warmest gratitude to their benefactors. In the evening most of the respectable inhabitants assembled at the inn, where they drank, in a cheerful glass, the health of the King and Royal Family.

HELSTON.—The Church Bells rung a merry peal in the morning —and a sermon was preached at the Methodist Chapel. At eleven o'clock the Corporation assembled, and with the staff of the Loyal Meneage Local Militia, Capt. Scott's troop of Cavalry, and the members of the Helston Lodge of Free Masons, formed a procession to the Church, where an excellent sermon was preached by the Rev. T. Stabback, from Psalm 21. ver. 7. After divine service a collection was made for the poor, which, added to the subscriptions collected by John Rogers, Esq., the worthy Mayor of the borough, amounted to about 120*l*. At one o'clock, a capital dinner was given to 60 poor families at the Seven Stars, by the Society of Free Masons, at which Brother Pearse Rogers presided. The evening concluded by balls, at the Angel and Red Lion Inns.

ILLOGAN.—Lord De Dunstanville distributed food to all the poor of the parish and sent 20*l*. to each of the subscriptions in the three towns of Redruth, Penryn, and Camborne. At night there was a grand display of well-selected fire-works, while the surrounding hills, with the venerable mountains of Carn-Brae and Carn-Kie, were illuminated by innumerable bonfires.

LANSALLOS.—In the morning a sermon was preached in Lansallos church, by Rev. J. C. Millett, from the 29th chap. of the Proverbs of Solomon, and 2nd verse. The parochial poor and daily labourers received a liberal supply of good fat mutton, purchased for them by the inhabitants.

LISKEARD.—The celebration of the Jubilee at Liskeard should be deemed to have commenced on Tuesday the 14th. On which day a numerous party of gentlemen dined together. The Right Hon. Lord Elliot, presided at dinner, the sumptuousness and abundance of which were commensurate with the noble host's design of a distribution of the fragments that remained, on the following day, to the neighbouring poor. The choice old wines produced on this occasion received an additional zest from the many patriotic toasts that were given. The charity committee dealt out beef and bread, in liberal portions, to the poor inhabitants, who were regaled also with two hogsheads of good ale. The morning service of the church was well attended, and a discourse was delivered there by the Rev. **A. T. Greene.** At one o'clock the old cannon (a piece of curious antiquity) commenced firing its fifty rounds in honour of the anniversary. Large parties dined at the several Inns, and numerous loyal and appropriate toasts and sentiments were given with reiterated and unbounded applause. Tea parties were formed in the principal streets by the ladies, in booths, elegantly ornamented for the occasion. The juvenile ball commenced at six o'clock in the Guildhall, which was brilliantly illuminated and decorated with exquisite taste, with a grand display of transparencies, lustres, ever-greens, and wreaths of artificial flowers, interspersed with suitable devices. The evening's amusements concluded by a grand display of fire-works.—The ball was very fully attended, and exhibited much beauty and fashion.

LOSTWITHIEL.—The day was ushered in by the ringing of bells, while a band of music played "God save the King," "Fame let thy trumpet sound," etc., through the streets. Three bullocks and six bushels of wheat made into bread, were distributed to the poor inhabitants. An excellent sermon was delivered on the occasion by the Rev. John Barron. After service the streets again resounded with music. A ball at the Talbot Inn was kept up till a late hour. The evening closed with a bonfire and fire-works, and the inhabitants vied with each other in tokens of loyalty.

MADDERN.—The morning was ushered in by the ringing of bells, the British Ensign proudly waving from the lofty tower. At an early hour the curling smoke from the different cottages bespoke the preparations carrying on below for the comfortable meal provided for the poor inhabitants by the munificence of their more opulent neighbours, who on the preceding evening had distributed fresh beef to nearly 600 persons. The paupers were regaled at the poor's house with the solid surloin, to which was added a pint of beer to each person to drink his Majesty's health. Satisfaction shone in every countenance throughout the parish on this memorable and joyful occasion.

MYLOR.—From the hospitable mansion of Carclew, the seat of Sir William Lemon, Bart., a liberal supply of beef, bread, and strong beer, was distributed to the numerous poor of Mylor. Capt. James, R.N., gave a liberal treat to the poor inhabitants of the neighbourhood of Woodlands, and their children, at which he presided in person. An enormous sea-pie, of nearly 200 lbs. flanked by the good old surloin, &c., &c., were followed by ample cans of strong beer, till the hearts of the poor people sung with joy.

NEWLYN.—Sir Thomas Dyke Acland, Bart. presented the parish with 15 guineas, which, added to a subscription opened in the parish, amounted to about 42l. The happy day was ushered in by the ringing of bells. An excellent sermon was preached by the Rev. Mr.

Williams. The officers and principal inhabitants of the parish distributed a quantity of good beef, bread, and beer, to every poor family in the parish.

NEWPORT.—A liberal subscription was raised by the inhabitants for the benefit of the poor.

PADSTOW.—The inhabitants of this town entered into a liberal subscription for providing bread, beef, and coals for the poor inhabitants. The day was concluded with a splendid ball at the Golden Lion Tavern.

PENRYN.—The morning was ushered in by successive peals, rung on six newly-set-up bells. Flags were displayed at the top of St. Gluvias tower, and the royal standard, hoisted at the Golden Lion. Mr. Williams (the deputy Recorder) regaled his workmen at Parken-Gew, with beef, plum-pudding and porter. All the inhabitants of Penryn seemed to vie with each other, who should be foremost in showing their unfeigned attachment to the best of Kings, and so perfectly orderly and decorous was the conduct of every class, as to call forth the public thanks of the first magistrate. Mr. Elliot, of the canvass manufactory, near Penryn entertained the people employed by him, to the amount of more than 150 men, women, and children, with good beef, mutton, and brown stout.

PENZANCE.—The morning was ushered in by firing a gun at sun-rise, and hoisting the flag on the rock battery. At ten o'clock the Mayor and the Corporation proceeded to church. A numerous assembly of the sons of Crispin joined in the procession, with their flags and emblems. More than 200 persons each received three shillings, with bread, cheese, and strong beer. The paupers in the poor-house, and the singers of the churches in the neighbourhood, were feasted with beef and plum-pudding. At three o'clock a numerous party partook of a splendid dinner at the Hotel. At eight o'clock the ball commenced. The Ladies and Gentlemen wore ribbons with mottos, and one old Lady wore the same favour, which she had worn on the day of the King's Coronation. At twelve o'clock the company retired to the supper-rooms, where an elegant collation was prepared. More than ninety sat down, while several, who were not able, or rather did not wish, to procure seats, attended upon the ladies.

PROBUS.—After divine service at the church (where an excellent sermon was preached by the Rev. Mr. Ferris, from Tim. ii. ver. 1, 2) a liberal supply of bread and a fat bullock were distributed to the poor. Mr. Ferris also gave a good dinner to several poor widows. The bells rung throughout the evening, which closed with perfect good order.

REDRUTH.—A subscription by the respectable inhabitants, provided a comfortable repast of bread and beef for upwards of 1,200 individuals, which were distributed on the afternoon of Tuesday.

The Jubilee morning was ushered in by the ringing of bells, and the parade of a thousand inhabitants, accompanied by vocal and instrumental music, through the town, and from thence to the residence of their minister and magistrate, Mr. Rogers. A sermon was preached to a very large congregation. A dinner at Gray's Hotel, attended by the principal inhabitants, produced much conviviality; loyalty to our King and attachment to our glorious Constitution, were evinced by characteristic toasts received with rapturous enthusiasm; and the illumination of Carn-Brae-hill, with a considerable quantity of tar barrels, produced a very grand effect.

ST. AUSTELL.—The Charity-school children were entertained, and the collections made on the preceding day, given in bread to the poor. An excellent supper was given at the White Hart Tavern, which displayed a beautiful transparent likeness of his Majesty. The usual toasts were drank, with " John Bull, and confusion to his bastard calves." The dissenters also entertained the poor of their society, and several masters treated their workmen.

ST. COLUMB.—A handsome sum of money was collected for the poor, and distributed to them after divine service. The Ladies and Gentlemen of the town and neighbourhood concluded the day with a ball and supper at the Red Lion Inn.

ST. GERMANS.—The anniversary was ushered in by the ringing of bells. Lord Elliot, Francis Glanville, Esq., and the Rev. Thomas Penwarne, joined also by subscriptions from the parishioners at large, distributed three capital oxen, part of a fat heifer, and bread, to 313 poor families, consisting of about 1,100 persons. The St. Germain's troop of Yeomanry Cavalry met in honour of the day; and after the usual evolutions, and firing ten rounds, adjourned to the Elliot Arms, and spent the evening with the greatest conviviality. Strong beer was also given by his Lordship to the populace on the occasion.

ST. IVES.—The Mayor and Corporation, with the Friendly Societies, went to church in procession. After the service a royal salute was fired from the batteries. The clubs dined together, as did the Corporation and other gentlemen, by whom (assisted by a donation of ten guineas from Sir Christopher Hawkins, the recorder) a subscription was raised, which supplied the poor with beef and beer. Between thirty and forty pounds were also distributed to the poor of St. Ives, by Samuel Stephens, Esq., M.P., and his friends, after which an elegant dinner was given at Tregenna Castle, in a style truly characteristic of old English hospitality. Colonel Sandys laid the foundation of a Sunday School House, on the Jubilee day, at his seath of Lanarth, in St. Keverne; which is to be conducted on Lancaster's plan, and supported by the bounty of the worthy Colonel. Subscriptions for the poor were also made in the parishes of St. Kew, St. Tudy, Eglushayle, and St. Mabyn.

TREGONY.—The Mayor, Corporation and principal inhabitants of this ancient and loyal Borough (after attending divine service, where an impressive discourse was delivered by the Rev. R. Gurney) met at the Queen's Head, and partook of a handsome entertainment; when the health of the good old king, and many other loyal toasts were drank, after which the gentlemen joined the ladies at a dance, which was kept up to a late hour. A liberal subscription was also raised for the poor; so as to enable all persons in this ancient Borough to partake of the general Jubilee.

TREGOTHNAN.—The Tenantry of Lord Falmouth, to the number of 130, were entertained at Tregothnan, in the absence of his Lordship, who partook of the festivities of Mount Edgcumbe. The health of our gracious Sovereign was drank with three cheers, with other appropriate toasts. Dancing commenced at seven, and continued with great spirit till supper; another round of loyal toasts and songs followed. Dancing was recommenced, and was kept up till four o'clock. The poor and aged of the adjoining parishes of Merther and Lamorran were supplied with clothing, and about 50 pairs of shoes were given to the children of the Free School. The poor of his Lordship's own parish (St. Michael-Penkivell) had a fat ox distributed among them in proportion to their families. And thus the three parishes held jubilee on the munificent bounty of the Noble Viscount.

TRELLISSICK.—Ralph Allen Daniell, Esq., entertained a select party of friends at his seat—while a fat bullock, three sheep, and several barrels of strong beer, fed and rejoiced the spirits of the labouring poor of the neighbourhood and their families; of whom the younger part, at intervals, danced upon the lawn, while the aged rekindled their loyalty and gratitude by liberal potations, loyal songs, and generous toasts to the long life of the King and their beneficent patron.

TREVENNEN.—William Slade Gully, Esq., plentifully regaled his labourers with a substantial dinner and good old strong beer at his seat.

TREWARTHENICK.—Francis Gregor, Esq., entertained his friends, tenants, and poor of his neighbourhood, at his seat of Trewarthenick, and, with his amiable consort, joined the grand chorus of "God save the King," which was sung by the whole company with a fervour of loyalty and devotion, worthy of the "age of chivalry."

TRURO.—The inhabitants of Truro and its neighbourhood having previously contributed very liberally to the fund for the entertainment of the poor, about sixty pounds were disposed of to nearly 900 men, women, and children; reserving the remainder as a fund for their relief during the ensuing winter. The morning was ushered in with the ringing of bells—the shops were shut—and flags displayed at General M'Carmick's, the Cornwall Gazette Office, Pearce's Hotel, and in several other quarters. At eleven the Corporation and other principal Inhabitants assembled at the Town-hall, where they were soon joined by the St. Mary's Benevolent Institution, with their flags and other insignia; and proceeded to the church, which was extremely crowded. A most excellent sermon, from the text—*Fear God; honour the King*—was delivered by the Rev. Mr. Carlyon. The procession returned to the Town-hall, where an Address to the King was signed by a great number of the inhabitants. A truly splendid dinner was prepared at Pearce's Hotel. The Royal Standard waved over the roast beef of Old England, while the British Union and other flags, with apposite inscriptions, intermingled with the solid dishes, and pyramids of lighter articles, produced a *coup d'œil* truly picturesque and beautiful. Fifty-six persons sat down to dinner. "The King" was drank with three times three, and followed by "Duke of Cornwall," and innumerable others, intermingled with excellent songs, kept up the spirit of festivity to a late hour. The Ball in the evening was also well attended. The St. Mary's Institution dined at the Bear Inn. Their first toast from the chair, which was drunk with enthusiasm, was—"The King."—A collection made round the table, produced a handsome sum for the relief of the poor. The Methodist Society of Truro also made a collection for the same benevolent purpose. Several other parties were formed, and one spirit pervaded the whole.

CUMBERLAND.

CARLISLE.—The fiftieth anniversary of his Majesty's Accession to the throne was observed by the inhabitants of this city in a manner which fully evinced the loyalty of its inhabitants. By desire of the Mayor, the shops were shut; and in the morning the Chief Magistrate and Corporation, the Lodges of Harmony and Union, Carlisle, and Wigton's St. John (preceded by the band of the Cumberland Rangers), and all the military stationed in that city, proceeded to the two churches of St. Mary and St. Cuthbert, where excellent and appropriate discourses were delivered; at the former place by the Rev. Browne Grisdale, D.D., from Samuel x. verse 24th; and at the latter place by the Rev. John Fawcet, M.A., from Levit. xxv. verse 8th, 9th, 10th, and part of the 11th. An anthem was most admirably performed by the choir of St. Mary's, accompanied on the organ. In the afternoon, 131 gentlemen met in the Assembly Room, where an excellent dinner was served up by Mrs. Irving. Loyalty, good humour, and harmony, gave a double zest to the entertainment; many loyal and patriotic toasts were given: that of his Majesty was received with unbounded enthusiasm. Thomas Blamire, Esq., Mayor, presided on the occasion. At two o'clock, the Loyal Cumberland Rangers, and the detachment of the 2nd West Suffolk (the ground being kept by the Cumberland Light Horse, and the recruiting parties) fired a *Feu de joie*, which was succeeded by three cheers. The men afterwards drank his Majesty's health—the Corporation having very generously treated them with two whole barrels of ale. Private parties met at the Bush, King's Arms, Duke's Head, Old Queen's Head Inns, and at Mr. Sheffield's, Caldewgate, to celebrate the auspicious event—in fact, joy, gratitude, and harmony, were the order of the day. A handsome sum was subscribed for the enlargement of poor debtors; and four unfortunate persons confined in the city gaol, were liberated accordingly. A Ball, at the Assembly Room, was extremely well attended. At Morresby, Egremont, and Cockermouth, the day was appropriately observed: at the latter place £200 were subscribed for the relief of the poor.

MUNCASTER CASTLE.—The day was kept by the noble owner of Muncaster Castle, in the true old English style; after Divine Service at Muncaster Church, his Lordship's tenants assembled at the Castle, and about two o'clock, after the firing cannon, between 200 and 300 dined in the Hall; it consisted of roast beef and plum pudding, and a variety of other good things, &c., and as soon as the dinner was over, the cannon were again fired, after which his Lordship, attended by his family, entered, and addressing his tenantry, said, " He was glad to see them upon that happy occasion, when their beloved Sovereign entered upon the 50th year of his reign, and during whose mild government he had shown them every example of goodness, and was truly religious, and an affectionate Father of his People; under him, thro' the blessing of God, this country had been protected, while all other nations were laid waste by fire and sword, and were groaning under oppression and arbitrary government. Our commerce, our trade, and our manufactures, were happily carried on and flourished; our agriculture greatly improved, and the people the happiest under Heaven." He then said, that at all times the county of Cumberland had been noted for its love of freedom and loyalty. His Lordship then produced the well-known cup, called *The Luck of Muncaster*, which is curiously cut in glass, and of great antiquity, having been given to the family by Henry VI. 400 years ago, as a pledge of his regard, and in gratitude for the protection they had afforded him in the civil wars, with this blessing, " that so long as they kept it whole, they should have plenty, and should prosper;" and tradition has carried down the account from father to son for ages back. His Lordship said, he did produce this from any superstitious idea, but to urge his tenants to bring up their sons to be loyal and honest, and their daughters virtuous and good; to fear God and to honour the King; and he hoped the future owners of the Castle would be as zealous for their welfare as he had ever been, and that he heartily wished *The Luck of Muncaster* might attend them all through life. He then sang " God save the King," in which the family and the whole company joined in chorus. His Majesty's health was drank with three times three, and that he might long live a blessing to his people. The merry dance was kept up in the Hall till 10 o'clock, when a plentiful supper was served up, after which the company separated, all truly grateful for the noble manner in which they had been entertained by his Lordship.

PENRITH.—The day was kept here with the greatest solemnity. An excellent sermon was preached on the occasion by the Rev. Mr. Bewsher. After divine service, the officers and non-commissioned officers, &c., belonging to the Loyal Local Penrith Militia, assembled in Sandgate, when 21 rounds were fired from four brass field-pieces, and three excellent volleys by the non-commissioned officers. The officers belonging to the above corps adjourned to the New Crown Inn, where they partook of a most excellent dinner,—and the non-commissioned officers. The whole of the business was conducted with the greatest propriety.

WHITEHAVEN, &c.—The anniversary was celebrated at Whitehaven, with every mark of respect and gratitude. The flags were hoisted at all the usual places; and a royal salute was fired by the Whitehaven Local Militia Artillery, amid loud huzzas. There were several dinner parties in the town: the paupers in the poor-house where also plentifully regaled, and treated with money.

WORKINGTON—At Workington a most impressive and excellent sermon was preached by the Rev. Peter How, A.M., from the first Epistle General of Peter, ii. chap. 17th v. After divine service, 240 poor persons received proportionate relief from the alms of the congregation, and also from a very liberal subscription raised by the inhabitants of the place.

———o———

DERBYSHIRE.

DERBY.—On the Tuesday evening there was a Ball at the Old Assembly Room, very respectably attended by the commercial part of the town, who ushered in the day with dancing and other festivity. The 37th Regiment, commanded by Lieut.-Colonel Spread, the non-commissioned officers of the Local Militia, commanded by Major Sir Robert Wilmot, (in the absence of their Colonel Sir Henry Crewe,) assembled in the Market-place, and proceeded with the Mayor, Aldermen, and other Members of the Corporation, to All Saints Church, where an excellent and appropriate discourse from 1st Samuel, chap. x. verse 24, was delivered by the Rev. Charles Stead Hope, who in a very able and impressive manner pointed out the many invaluable blessings we have so long enjoyed under our beloved Monarch. After service the above regiments were drawn up, and each fired three excellent volleys. The Corporative body and a large party of Military and other Gentlemen of the town and neighbourhood, sat down to dinner at the George Inn. There were various other public dinners in the town, very respectably attended, and a ball in the evening for the benefit of the poor debtors, under the direction of Major Sir Robert Wilmot, and D. P. Coke, Esq., closed this glorious event so as to leave a lasting impression of the loyalty and affection of this town and neighbourhood to our most gracious Sovereign. The prisoners in the county gaol were obliged to Charles Upton, Esq., the

High Sheriff, for a very plentiful supply of roast beef, plum-pudding, and strong beer, which he kindly afforded them to celebrate the Jubilee day.

ALFRETON.—The morning was ushered in by the ringing of bells; and from a subscription, eighty stone of beef, and thirty stone of plum-pudding, were distributed to the poorer classes of the people, to enable them in comfort, with their families at home, to join in the national festivity of the day; and in the course of the afternoon the populace were regaled with ale in the market-place, "Health and long life to his Majesty," was drank by them with repeated huzzas.

ASHBORNE.—The Jubilee was observed at Ashborne in a manner very appropriate to the occasion. A subscription was raised, by which upwards of 900 persons were relieved. Divine service was well attended, and an excellent sermon was preached by the Rev. Samuel Shipley, M.A., the Vicar, in which he expatiated on the virtues of our beloved sovereign, the blessings of toleration, and the glory of our constitution. The afternoon was spent with the greatest hilarity, public and private dinner parties abounded, at which many loyal toasts were drank, and all was joy. The evening concluded with balls at the Black's Head and Green Man Inns, which were numerously attended. Thus the day was marked with festivity, sobriety, and order.

BAKEWELL.—The morning was ushered in with the ringing of bells, and the South High Peak Volunteers, under the command of Major Carleill, fired ten rounds. The non-commissioned officers and privates of the corps, were regaled with ale. The officers and several other gentlemen of the neighbourhood dined together at the Rutland Arms Inn, where a number of loyal and constitutional toasts were drank, and the day was spent with the greatest hilarity. On the following evening there was a ball which was numerously attended. Afterwards "God save the King," was sung in full chorus, and the company separated.

CHESTERFIELD.—The day was ushered in at Chesterfield by the ringing of bells, bonfires, display of flags, and the other usual demonstrations of joy, and was throughout observed with a peculiar degree of loyalty and benevolence. A very liberal subscription for the poor was entered into by the inhabitants, (aided by a contribution of 20 guineas from Sir Sitwell Sitwell, Bart.) by which nearly 2500 poor persons were supplied with a handsome allowance of meat, bread, and ale, and were thereby enabled to participate in the general rejoicing, manifested upon this happy occasion. Not a single poor person within the town, went without a good dinner, and a suitable proportion of ale, with his family at his own house. The Mayor and Corporation went in procession to Church, where an admirable sermon was preached by the Rev. Edward Goodwin, M.A., from Tim. chap. 2. v. 1, 2, and 2. About one o'clock, ten volleys, and a *feu de joie*, were fired by the non-commissioned officers of the Scarsdale regiment of Local Militia. An excellent dinner was provided at the Angel Inn, and numerously attended by the Gentlemen of the town and neighbourhood; many loyal toasts were drank and patriotic songs sung, and "God save the King," in particular, was admirably sung in full chorus. In the evening, there was a very grand exhibition of fire works, to a large concourse of spectators. The pleasures of the day concluded by a ball in the evening, at the new Assembly Room, which was both numerously and fashionably attended.

DRONFIELD.—The young Gentlemen of Mr. Taylor's Academy generously selected from the town and quarter of Dronfield all the poor men of equal age with the King, and furnished them with a new hat, a good dinner, and a shilling to drink his Majesty's health in their own way. These venerable characters preceded the boys to church, graced like themselves with an elegant appropriate Medal, pendent at the left breast, and on their return joined in a rapturous paraphrase of "God save the King," with three loyal cheers. All spent the day in the utmost hilarity, and closed the evening in innocent mirth and recreation.

ECKINGTON.—Sumptuous dinners were provided at the different Inns, where many loyal and appropriate toasts were given by large parties who spent the day with the greatest conviviality and decorum. Bonfires blazed in every street, and the welkin resounded with the ringing of bells, firing of guns, and loud reiterated shouts of "Long live the King." About 400 persons (consisting of the children of the Sunday schools, and the aged poor of both sexes,) partook of a Fete Champetre, given by Sir Sitwell Sitwell, Bart., where roast beef, plum-pudding, and beer, were served up in the old style of English hospitality, by Lady Sitwell, Master and Miss Sitwell, and the Clergymen and Gentlemen of the neighbourhood.

HASSOP.—The seat of Francis Eyre, Esq.—The day of the Jubilee was one of great festivity; all the tenants and labourers, to the number of between 400 and 500, sat down at his expense, to a plentiful dinner of roast beef, plum-pudding, &c., with a liberal proportion of ale; to his labourers he gave a holiday, and the evening concluded with a dance in the Coach-house. "God save the King," was played and sung in full chorus, and all departed delighted with the hospitality of their loyal benefactor.

THE OAKES,—The seat of Sir W. C. Bagshaw.—The Jubilee was celebrated with peculiar hospitality. In the morning the Church bells were rung, a band of music played "God save the King," and other loyal tunes, and the Royal Standard was hoisted from the house. At eleven o'clock Sir William and Lady Bagshaw, followed by a numerous tenantry, accompanied also by the children of the Free School, walked in procession to Church, where an excellent sermon was preached by the Rev. R. Robinson. At the return of the procession to the Oakes a Royal Salute was given from the terrace, by cannon;

other volleys were fired by a company of Royal Marines, and there were further discharges from two brass swivels on board a ship on the water in the park. Two hundred children were afterwards supplied with frumenty. At two o'clock Sir W. C. Bagshaw and 400 persons sat down to dinner. Many loyal and patriotic toasts were drank. At night an immense bonfire was lighted, consisting of a pile of wood eight yards in height, and thirty-six yards in circumference. In the front of the Oakes House there were five splendid transparencies exhibited, consisting of a bust of his Majesty, with the crown above and G.R. on the right and left, in the centre, surrounded by suitable national emblems. Fire-works were exhibited on the lawn, and the whole concluded with a dance of the tenantry.

OSMASTON.—After divine service was over, William Bates, Esq., entertained about 100 persons, the whole of the poor belonging to the parish, and a few tradesmen and their wives, with roast beef, plum-pudding, and strong ale. After regaling themselves till midnight, they all assembled in front of the house, formed a circle, and sang "God save the King," with three huzzas, and then retired in peaceable order to their separate homes.

RADBORNE.—Mr. Pole gave a liberal entertainment to his tenantry and the labouring families at Radborne, in celebration of the day.

SUDBURY.—The Jubilee was celebrated by Lord Vernon at Sudbury, with his accustomed hospitality. After attending divine service at the church, where a most excellent sermon was preached by the Rev. Frederic Anson, from the appropriate words, "Fear God, honour the King," to a very numerous congregation, all the poor men, women and children of the parish, to the amount of more than 200, sat down to dinner in the court yard of the Hall, to a good old English dinner of roast beef, plum-pudding, and ale. In the evening the tenants of his lordship were also regaled with punch, etc. Loyalty and conviviality closed the joyous day. The Rev. F. Anson, the tenants, etc., entered into a very liberal subscription to provide clothes, coals, etc., for the poor during the following winter.

TICKNALL.—At Calke Abbey an abundant repast was provided by Sir Henry Crewe, Bart., consisting of roast beef, mutton, plum-pudding, and plenty of good ale, for the work people employed by him, with their wives and children, amounting to upwards of 200. Sir Henry also contributed ten guineas towards a subscription entered into by his tenantry for the purpose of celebrating the event in the parish of Ticknall. The sum of £70 was collected, with which all were well regaled with roast beef, mutton, and ale; and the day was spent with the greatest loyalty.

TIDESWELL.—Three sheep were roasted, with which, and a proportionate quantity of bread and ale, the poor were plentifully regaled.

WILN.—The principal inhabitants of Wiln and Draycott commemorated the event by distributing to 110 poor families half a ton of coals each, with a quantity of bread and ale.

WIRKSWORTH.—The day was ushered in with ringing of bells, and other demonstrations of joy. At an early hour the principal inhabitants assembled to assist in the distribution of bread and meat to the lower classes, when upwards of 400 families were supplied with a proportion of each, according to the number of their respective families. The officers and non-commissioned officers of the Wirksworth regiment of Local Militia, commanded by Lieut.-Colonel Hurt, attended divine service, and an appropriate sermon was preached by the Rev. N. Hubbersty. The non-commissioned officers afterwards fired three most excellent volleys, and a hogshead of ale was given to the populace. At four o'clock the gentlemen and respectable inhabitants of the town and neighbourhood, together with the officers of the Wirksworth regiment, amounting to nearly 100 persons, dined at the Red Lion Inn, where many loyal and constitutional toasts were drank, and the utmost conviviality and harmony prevailed till a late hour.

―――――o―――――

DEVONSHIRE.

EXETER.—The day was announced by discharges of artillery and musketry, the ringing of bells, etc. Soon after the streets resounded with vocal and instrumental music, playing "God save the King." The town was decorated with laurel, ensigns, festoons, and triumphal arches. About ten the processions began to move from the Guildhall to attend divine service at the Cathedral. The brethren, constituting the different lodges of Free and Accepted Masons in the city, etc., met in the Free Grammar School, where, being arranged in due form, they proceeded to the Cathedral, and after divine service repaired to their different Lodge-rooms, and spent the remainder of the day with the greatest conviviality. The Hon. and Right Rev. the Lord Bishop of Exeter preached an excellent and suitable discourse on the occasion, to a very crowded audience, from the 1st of Samuel, 10th chapter, 24th verse. The 9th regiment of Light Dragoons, and the North Hants Militia, with the Royal Train Artillery, after attending divine service, marched to the barracks near the city, and fired a *feu de joie*. Distribution of money and provisions to the poor, and feasts, were abundant in every part of the city; conviviality and good humour prevailed throughout the evening, and towards night the public were amused with bonfires and a brilliant exhibition of fireworks. The prisoners in the gaols were liberally treated by the High Sheriff, Sir Thomas Dyke Ackland, Bart. Those confined in the new house of correction, 60 in number, sat down to a plentiful dinner provided for them at the expense of S. F. Milford, Esq., one of the Magistrates of the county. The arcades of that extensive building were ornamented with laurel, interspersed in the evening with lights.

ASHBURTON—The inhabitants vied with each other in liberality and rejoicings ; **upwards** of £150 were subscribed, and more than 1700 poor persons received donations of beef, bread, and beer, which were distributed from a marquee pitched on the lawn of the vicarage. The Volunteers fired a *feu de joie*, and rural sports commenced for the amusement of the multitude ; not less than 5000 persons were assembled in the grounds of the hospitable vicar. The gentlemen dined in the old English style, on roast beef and plum-pudding ; at night fireworks were displayed, and a splendid ball took place at the Golden Lion, first opened on the occasion, which was crowded with beauty and fashion.

AXMINSTER.—A band of martial music, with a numerous choir, assembled on the church tower at break of day, and a full chorus of voices and instruments performed part of Handel's Coronation Anthem, "God save the King, long live the King, may the King live for ever." The party then descended, and paraded through the principal streets, repeating the chorus, in which the inhabitants joined, and on its termination the bells rung out a merry peal. Divine service at the several places of worship was fully attended, after which Major Bawden's two troops of Royal East Devon Yeomanry Cavalry fired a *feu de joie*. The populace then retired to their homes to enjoy their dinner, two pounds of the finest beef having the preceding evening been distributed for every individual, to upwards of 1000 of the poor inhabitants, with an adequate quantity of cider. Dinners were provided at the several inns, and numerously attended. At the George Inn about 60 gentlemen of the town and neighbourhood sat down to a most sumptuous entertainment; a fine turtle, presented by Sir William Pole, Bart., of Shute, and two haunches, etc., of excellent venison, the gift of William Tucker, Esq., of Coryton, graced the table. The latter filled the chair; a number of most appropriate and loyal toasts were drunk with enthusiastic pleasure, and some excellent songs suitable to the day were sung by several of the gentlemen. Soon after eight o'clock the party retired, to accompany the ladies to see a brilliant display of fireworks, afterwards to the ball, where the merry dance was kept up by a numerous assembly till five in the morning.

BEAFORD.—The Church was fully attended. The Rev. Mr. Knight delivered a very appropriate discourse ; after which he, with several of the principal inhabitants, assisted in the distribution of several sheep (boiled and roasted) and a quart of strong beer to each person, to drink his Majesty's health. A subscription had been entered into by the parishioners, but before the celebration took place, a handsome donation from the Right Hon. Lord Rolle was sent in aid of the fund, and another from Sir Thomas Dyke Acland, a young baronet, who has proved himself worthy of the stock from which he sprung. In a field adjoining the village a large pile of wood had been collected, and with the aid of tar barrels and other combustible matter, our inveterate enemy was burnt in effigy, to the no small amusement of the populace; after which the Yeomanry retired to the inn, where they drank of the cup of cheerfulness till a late hour. The utmost harmony prevailed, and each guest departed with regret that a new born day had put an end to their conviviality. It must not be omitted that the truly charitable Lady Rolle was not unmindful of the approaching winter, and ordered a large quantity of blankets, and other bedding, to be distributed amongst the poor, in this and several neighbouring parishes.

CASTLE HILL,—The seat of Earl Fortescue, Lord Lieutenant of the county. After divine service a plentiful dinner was given to all his lordship's labourers and their families, with the poor of the parish and its vicinity, on the terrace before the house; and in the evening the Earl and Countess Fortescue, with their family, and a party of their friends, drank tea in the Castle, where a bonfire and fireworks were exhibited, and a large concourse of people entertained with strong beer.

DARTMOUTH.—The day was ushered in by every demonstration of joy. The Mayor, Corporation, and principal inhabitants walked in procession to church, where an admirable sermon was preached on the occasion by the Rev. Caleb Rocket, to an immense congregation. From divine service the Corporation, &c., proceeded to the coffee-house, where a loyal address to his Majesty was signed by the most respectable characters in the neighbourhood. At three o'clock about 70 gentlemen set down to dinner at the Castle Inn. In the course of the afternoon some excellent constitutional toasts and sentiments were drank. The dinner party having spent the day with the greatest conviviality till about eight o'clock, adjourned to the ball-room, where the spirit of the day was kept up to a late hour next morning. Three royal salutes were fired from the fort and the vessels in the harbour. At noon the Volunteers fired three volleys, and at night there was a display of fireworks on the New Ground. A general subscription was raised for the poor, to be laid out for their use in the approaching winter. The Corporation supplied every poor person with a dinner, and about 100 persons were regaled in the Rope Walk in the old English style, with roast beef, plum-pudding, and strong beer, by Messrs. A. Hunt and Co.

DAWLISH.—A handsome subscription was collected for the poor, and at Crewkerne, Chard, and Honiton the festivals were kept with great liberality and spirit.

ILFRACOMB.—The morning was ushered in by the ringing of bells. At four o'clock an elegant dinner was served up at the Britannia; Mr. Locke presided; the King's health was drank with three times three, and mirth and loyalty prevailed in an eminent degree. A vast number of poor people were relieved by a liberal subscription.

KILLERTON.—The seat of Sir Thomas Dyke Ackland, the High Sheriff of Devon, was marked with peculiar festivity. A subscription having been entered into by the gentlemen and farmers for the poor, Sir Thomas, with his accustomed liberality, gave in addition a handsome sum of money and a donation of twenty sheep.

MOUNT-EDGCUMBE.—The revered and enchanting seat of Mount-Edgcumbe was a scene of festivity. Early in the morning the noble owner distributed a large sum of money and two oxen to the poor of Maker, Milbrook, Kingsand and Cawsand. At half past five a grand dinner was served up in the first style of elegance to a numerous party from Devon and Cornwall.

OAKHAMPTON.—The Jubilee was celebrated here under the auspices of Mr. A. Savile, the Recorder, in a manner worthy of the occasion. The morning was ushered in by the ringing of bells. The Corporation met, and voted an address to His Majesty, and afterwards walked in procession to Church, with their Member at their head, to hear an excellent sermon preached by the Rev. Mr. Hole.

OTTERY ST. MARY.—The day was ushered in by the ringing of bells and every demonstration of joy. A fund having been raised by the inhabitants, the poor—to the amount of upwards of 1,300—were supplied with beef, bread, and cider, with which they regaled themselves at their respective homes; besides which, sheep were roasted and distributed indiscriminately to the people. There was a grand dinner at the King's Arms for the principal inhabitants. At the barracks, the South Devon Militia, after firing a *feu de joie*, were—with their wives and children—entertained by their Colonel, Lord Rolle, with a good dinner, consisting of the substantial fare of English roast beef and plum pudding, with a plentiful supply of cider, in the barrack-yard. The health of His Majesty was given with three times three, after which the band struck up "God save the King," which was sung with enthusiasm by the whole regiment, joined by a concourse of spectators. In the evening there was a splendid exhibition of fire-works; and the officers of the South Devon Militia gave a grand ball and supper at the barracks, which displayed an extraordinary assemblage of beauty and elegance.

OTTERTON.—Lord Rolle gave to fifty parishes, wherein he has property, ten guineas each, besides cider; at Littleham and Exmouth, the gentlemen-farmers and other inhabitants added so large a sum, that upwards of 600 poor persons were amply fed on a most excellent dinner. The gentlemen and tradesmen dined at the Globe; and the most perfect order, good humour, and loyalty were conspicuous throughout the day, which concluded with a ball.

PLYMOUTH.—The day was observed here with every mark of loyalty and affection. The morning was ushered in by the ringing of bells and the firing of fifty cannon. The royal standard was hoisted at Government House, on board the flagships, and the union flag at all the Public Offices, on St. Andrew's Tower, and the Guildhall. At nine o'clock the Mayor, Recorder, Town Clerk, Aldermen, and the Common Council, in their robes, attended by the freemen and inhabitants, marched in procession to the first turnpike-gate on the New Road, where they met the Members of the Embankment Company, and formed in one line of march, on their way through the town, to St. Andrew's Church, where the procession were received with the Coronation Anthem; 600 charity children, formed in rows round the altar, was a most gratifying sight. A very excellent sermon was preached by the Rev. J. Gandy, M.A. The procession then returned to the Guildhall, to sign a loyal and affectionate address of congratulation to His Majesty; a roasted ox was distributed to the populace; and at four o'clock 120 gentlemen sat down to a sumptuous dinner in the Guildhall, where loyal and appropriate toasts were given, and many excellent and well-selected songs and glees sung. At eight o'clock fire-works were exhibited. The procession was the grandest and best conducted ever seen in the West of England. It is supposed there were nearly 50,000 people assembled on the glorious occasion. A subscription of £200 had been collected, and was distributed among 2,000 poor people. Fifty pounds were collected and given to the poor by the people of the Jewish persuasion. The different regiments of infantry assembled at three o'clock before Government House and fired three volleys. The square of the First West York barracks was covered with tables, and a good dinner laid out for the wives and children of the men. The East Devon Militia also feasted their soldiers' families. The poor at the Workhouse, and the charity children at Plymouth Dock, were feasted. The officers of the Royal Marines gave an entertainment to upwards of 500 women and children, the majority of whose husbands and fathers were at sea, fighting the battles of their country in almost every part of the world. At half-past one o'clock this numerous company sat down to a most excellent dinner of roast beef, plum-pudding, &c., in the spacious drill room of the corps, at Stonehouse Barracks, after which each individual was regaled with a quart of eight-penny beer, and all departed highly gratified with the attention shown them by the officers. The women had finished the afternoon with a dance. The surplus of the roast beef and plum-pudding (which was immense) was distributed among the children to enjoy themselves with at home. At the same time, in honour of the day, Mrs. Strike, the sutler, gave to each marine at head-quarters one quart of eight-penny beer, to drink His Majesty's health, which was distributed on the square in front of the barracks, Major-General Bright taking the first glass, and drinking "health and long life to our most gracious sovereign;" the band during the whole time playing the national airs of "God save the King" and "Rule Britannia."

PLYMOUTH DOCK.—Upwards of £50 worth of bread were distributed to the poor. At Stoke Church an excellent and impressive sermon was preached by the Rev. John Hawker.

SALTRAM.—Lord Boringdon commemorated the joyful day by

distributing money among the poor of his parish of Saltram, in proportion to their several wants, and by regaling all his labourers with an excellent dinner, and strong beer, at Saltram House.

STONEHOUSE.—The principal inhabitants of the parish subscribed nearly £80 (to which Lord Mount Edgcumbe added £10) for the relief of their necessitous parishioners, which was distributed in bread, &c., to upwards of 500 poor people. In the evening a large bonfire and a display of fire works took place.

WOODBURY.—The merry bells ushered in the morning: at eleven about 500 persons attended divine service at the parish church, where an excellent sermon was preached by the Rev. John Edsall, and at the conclusion the whole congregation joined in the song of "God save the King." The charity children, and children from three Sunday schools, were provided with suitable entertainment. A liberal subscription, at the head of which stood the names of Lord Rolle, Lord Heathfield, Marchioness of Headfort, &c., &c., afforded an opportunity to distribute a quantity of beef, bread, cider, &c., to the poor of the parish.

The following lines are inserted by particular request :—

Most humbly addressed to the Queen's most excellent Majesty, upon our most gracious Sovereign's entering into the Fiftieth Year of his Reign.

The prayer was heard,* Britons attentive hear,
Thy Monarch pray'd that he the Fiftieth Year
Might happy reign o'er this high-favour'd Isle;
The prayer was heard, and Heaven in mercy smil'd.
    The year of Jubilee is come,
    Loud acclamations speak the Nation's joy.

Thus rich in gooodness, King of kings,
    Thy gracious favours how divine;
The blessings Britain this day sings,
    With brightest, noblest lustre shine.
    The year of Jubilee fulfil,
    Let Britain hail her Sov'reign still.

Join all to bless this happy morn,
    Let plaudits sound from shore to shore :
Swell, swell the trump and martial song,
    And bid the mighty cannon roar.
    The year of Jubilee we sing,
    And Britain hails her much-lov'd King.

Exult with patriotic breast;
    Let every free-born Briton pray
That Britain's throne may long be blest,
    And George the sceptre sway.
    The year of Jubilee is come,
    Old Time records the Fiftieth Year.

Near Fifty Years his scepter'd hand
   Has held the equal scales of power,
And shower'd blessings round the land,
  Tho' war and devastation lower.
    The year of Jubilee fulfil,
     Let Britain hail her Sovereign still.

Our leader God, our songs proclaim ;
   Each heart with throbbing valour glows ;
We lift our banners in his name,
  And march against our madd'ning foes,
    The year of Jubilee fulfil,
     Let Britain hail her Sov'reign still.

A people's joy, a pious King,
   What hostile realm can proudly boast ?
Then let each Briton loudly sing
  The triumphs of our sea-girt coast.
    The year of Jubilee fulfil,
     Hail ! Britons, hail ! your much-lov'd King.

JANE WEBB.

Plymouth, 25th October, 1809.

* Mr. Mawman, at the Court held at the Guildhall by the Lord Mayor, said that it was the prayer of our most gracious King, that he might be permitted to enter the 50th Year of his Reign.

DORSETSHIRE.

DORCHESTER.—The auspicious event was celebrated here in the general manner, by ringing of bells, attending divine service, and in contributions for the poor.

IBBETSON. — Among the various acts of benevolence which marked the Jubilee, stands eminently conspicuous that of Joseph Daubeny, Esq. of Ibbetson. The whole of the poor of Ibbetson were made partakers of this Gentleman's liberality.

BROAD WINDSOR.—The propitious morning was ushered in by the ringing of bells, and flying colours. At eleven, the congregation —the largest that had been known for many years—assembled at the Church, where their behaviour was strikingly serious and devout. Divine service was performed, and an appropriate sermon preached by their exemplary Vicar, the Rev. Dr. Nott ; who, anxious to diffuse and excite that spirit of loyalty which cannot be kept too much alive, relieved the poor, the aged, and infirm, entirely at his own expense. He invited the farmers, and respectable inhabitants, to a plentiful and hospitable dinner at the George Inn, where upwards of 70 persons sat down to table ; and that all might have an additional motive to bless the King, as the cause of their comforts and enjoyments, he concluded the evening by giving a ball to the younger people. The festivity of the day was unclouded ; every one present was animated with sentiments of loyalty, love, and veneration, towards their Sovereign, and gratitude to the Supreme Giver of all good, for having so long continued to them the blessings of his reign.

HINTON ST. GEORGE.—Earl Poulett gave a fat ox and eight sheep, with 150 loaves. Every poor person in the village of Hinton St. George received about 6lb. of meat, a loaf, 60lb. of potatoes, and a gallon of cider. All the persons in his Lordship's employ were regaled with an excellent dinner. A triumphal arch, decorated with laurel, and inscribed with "Long live the King," was erected over a butt of the best stout, and four hogsheads of cider, with which the company enjoyed themselves in many loyal songs and toasts until a late hour.

LULWORTH CASTLE—The seat of Thomas Weld, Esq. was very gay; the great guns at one o'clock in the morning announced the approaching day by a discharge of twenty-one, and the like number at ten; the colours were up by six, and the bells sounded their merry peals; two fat beasts were distributed amongst the poor of the neighbouring villages, and they were plentifully regaled with ale, and in the evening treated with a dance.

LYME.—The joyful event was ushered in about half-past five in the morning, by a band playing "God save the King," &c. At one o'clock the ships in the harbour fired a royal salute of 21 guns, with colours flying; the inhabitants paraded the streets with muskets and fowling pieces, saluting those who had been employed in distributing two large bullocks and mutton. In the evening two hogsheads of old strong beer were given away in the market-place, and on the new wall leading to the harbour. A subscription was gathered, so as to enable the committee appointed to defray every expence, and to purchase five hundred bushels of coals, (equal to one thousand Winchester measure) for the poor during the approaching winter.

MELBURY HOUSE.—The Earl of Ilchester gave a plentiful dinner at Melbury House, to all his workmen and to the poor; and at the same time three fat bullocks, and three hogsheads of strong beer, were distributed to the poor of his Lordship's parishes of Evershot, Melbury, Osmond, and Abbotsbury.

MILTON.—Lady Caroline Damer gave a plentiful dinner to 200 of the poor of Milton, and ten guineas to the poor of the parish of Ham.

NETHERBURY.—The poor were assembled, at ten o'clock, and five bullocks and four sheep were distributed amongst them. After divine service the gentlemen of the parish dined together, and two hogsheads of cider were given in the village, to drink the health of our beloved Sovereign. The day concluded by a subscription ball.

POOL.—A subscription having been made, seven bullocks, six sheep, and 2000 loaves, were distributed to 647 poor families, including 2000 persons and **upwards, each** of whom received the price of a pint of strong beer.

SHAFTSBURY.—At Shaftsbury **the** Jubilee was **celebrated** in **the most loyal** and respectful manner.

SHERBORNE.—The Jubilee was celebrated by the inhabitants of the town in a sober and becoming manner. Four fat bullocks, and a quantity of strong beer, were distributed amongst the poor, so as to enable about 400 families to dine at their respective homes in quietness and comfort. The Volunteers were regaled with a dinner by **Captain** Helyar. In the evening there was a display of fire-works.

STOCK HOUSE.—The **Rev. F.** H. Yeatman liberally treated the neighbouring poor. Here **the** day of rational festivity was concluded by an immense bonfire.

WEYMOUTH.—Weymouth was on this day a scene of the most general festivity, **and** besides exhibiting the same tokens **of** joy, as those noticed at other places, was distinguished by the laying the foundation of a pedestal for erecting a statue of his Majesty, which was done in due Masonic order. At eleven her Royal Highness the Princess **Mary**, and the Duke of Cambridge, attended by Sir Harry Burrard **Neale.** Gen. Garth, Lady G. Murray, and the Misses Murray, attended divine service, preceded by the Mayor and Corporation, and **the** different Public Bodies, and Masonic Lodge, assembled together **to form** the procession to lay the foundation stone of **a** Pedestal for erecting a Statue of his Majesty on, as a memento to future ages of **our** august Monarch. On the procession arriving at the spot fixed **on for** laying the stone, at the entrance of the town, the military **formed a** square, in the centre of which the carriages of the Nobility were drawn up. A carpeted platform was fitted up in the most convenient situation for the accommodation of his Royal Highness the **Duke** of Cambridge, the Princess Mary, and their attendants. The ceremony of laying the stone in due form commenced about two o'clock, and notwithstanding the immense concourse of people that assembled together in all parts of the country, it was conducted with a degree of solemnity and silence highly becoming. After the usual forms had been gone through, the three Sojourners of the Royal Arch Procession moved forwards with the silver vessels, containing corn, wine, and oil, each strewing the contents on the surface of it, the Master Mason repeating the following ejaculations:—" May the bountiful hand **of** Heaven supply with abundance of wine, and oil, and **all other** necessaries of life, this my native town." The inscription was then handed over by 'the Master to the Royal Party for inspection, on which was engraving:—" This foundation stone of a Pedestal, **on** which **a** Statue of his Majesty is to be erected, was laid Oct. 25, 1809, (being the day on which his Majesty entered the 50th year of his reign), by J. H. Browne, Esq., Master Mason of All Souls' Lodge, No. 226, in Masonic order, the Brethren attending in due from, in the presence of their Royal Highnesses the Duke of Cambridge and

Princess Mary." After the stone was laid, and the inscription fixed, the Master finished his work by delivering a speech to the following effect, in a very impressive manner:—"As we have now laid this Foundation Stone, may the Grand Architect of the Universe, of his kind Providence, enable us to carry on and finish the work we have now begun. May He still be the protector of our most gracious Sovereign, whose Statue we are about to erect, and may he preserve it from decay and ruin to the latest posterity." The ceremony being finished, three times three cheers were vociferated by the multitude in a strain of loyalty and exaltation that re-echoed from all parts of the Esplanade, and very visibly affected the feelings of the Royal Party.—The procession then returned to the Guildhall with the same regularity, when the different societies separated. Lord Eardley joined the All Souls' Lodge, and with his usual liberality made a voluntary gift of 100 guineas, for the relief of his suffering countrymen in France. The different Lodges returned to the King's Head and Red Lion, and dined together in their usual perfect harmony, enjoying the pleasing reflection of having previously contributed with their fellow townsmen to the comfort of 1500 men, women, and children, by providing them a dinner at their own houses, in the following proportions: heads of families, 2lb. of beef, half a quartern loaf, and a quart of ale each; children seven years old and upwards, half a quartern loaf, 1 lb. of beef, and a pint of ale each; younger children, half a quartern loaf, and a half a pound of beef each; and the poor in the Alms-Houses regaled with a quart of ale each. On the approach of night, the Royal Sovereign yacht was most brilliantly illuminated with an immense number of lamps, forming a triangular blaze, and the Royal Barge was anchored opposite the Palace, bearing a well executed transparency, with the inscription, "May the King live for ever," in a wreath of the rose, shamrock, and thistle, suspended by an angel. The evening concluded with a town ball at Harvey's Rooms, (at which upwards of 100 persons were present), and a most brilliant display of fire-works on the water, opposite the Palace, presented on the occasion by Sir John Johnstone, Bart. as well as a most liberal subscription to the poor.

DURHAM.

The Jubilee was celebrated throughout the county of Durham with that pure loyalty and liberality of sentiment, which reflect lasting honour on its inhabitants; the affluent contributing towards the the relief and comforts of the poor, who partook largely in the general festivity. In the city of Durham divine service was performed in all the Churches and Chapels. The Mayor, Corporation, Volunteers, and Blue Coat Scholars, attended the Cathedral, where a sermon was preached by the Rev. Dr. Price, from Psalm 21, v. 7. The fraternity of Free Masons walked in procession to St. Giles's Church, where an excellent discourse was delivered by the Rev. Mr. Blacket. At ten o'clock the Volunteers fired three volleys in the Market-place, followed by three times three, the band playing "God save the King." The Dean and Chapter voted 100*l.* towards the relief of insolvent debtors. Above 100*l.* subscribed by the inhabitants, was distributed to the poor. The Rev. Mr. Bouyer gave an excellent dinner to the Boys of the School founded on the plan of Dr. Bell, and a proper portion of stout ale to drink his Majesty's health. An additional quantity of beef and bread was allowed to the Paupers in the Workhouses. T. Wilkinson, Esq., of Oswald House, gave half-a-crown each to 77 poor parishoners of St. Oswald. The Mayor and a large party dined at the City Tavern, where the conviviality of the day was enlivened by many loyal and patriotic toasts and songs. The Free Masons dined at the Hat and Feathers Inn, their worthy master, A. Logan, Esq., in the chair, and the day was spent in good humour and festivity. The Free Gardeners dined together, and intended to have given a dinner to the poor in the Workhouse, but they had been anticipated by the generosity of the Overseers; they however, sent each person a pint of porter, and a glass of spirits, to drink his Majesty's health, and ordered them a dinner on Friday. There were several other dinner parties equally loyal and festive. In the evening a ball and supper were numerously and fashionably attended. There was a large bonfire in the Market-place, and the day closed with the greatest harmony and tranquillity.

BERNARD CASTLE.—Lord Strathmore gave to the poor inhabitants 460 threepenny loaves, two fat beasts, and 460 pints of ale. Stenton, Gibside, and Glams Castle, partook likewise of his Lordship's bounty.

CHESTER-LE-STREET.—The Volunteers attended divine service, and heard an appropriate and eloquent discourse by the Rev. W. Nesfield, from Prov. 22, v. 2. After divine service the Volunteers fired nine volleys, and then received three and a half barrels of ale, to drink his Majesty's health. A large party of Gentlemen dined at the White Hart Inn, where many appropriate toasts were given, and the day concluded in social festivity.

DARLINGTON.—The inhabitants resolved to build a Dispensary, as the best and most permanent testimony of their loyalty and affection. At the head of the subscribers, towards building this lasting monument of compassion and benevolence, is George Allan, Esq., 50*l.*

HARTLEPOOL.—A good substantial dinner was given by the principal inhabitants to their poor neighbours, and half-a-crown each to 37 persons whose ages exceeded the King's.

HAUGHTON.—At Haughton, a small village near Darlington, the inhabitants gave to the poor a Pic Nic Supper, each subscriber to this plan providing a large joint of meat, with vegetables, a loaf of bread, and a pudding or pie, all ready dressed. The bells were ringing the whole day, and the cottagers, when they returned from their daily labour, dressed themselves in their holiday clothes, and attended the singers, with musical instruments, belonging to the Church, to the top of the tower, and there, with the true spirit of loyalty, joined in one chorus in the patriotic song of "God save the King." At the conclusion of which they retired to partake of the feast provided by their more affluent neighbours. The evening, being very fine, the happy group, exceeding 100 in number, were joined by the ladies and gentlemen of the place, and after having given three cheers at the door of each of their benefactors, they retired to their respective homes with grateful hearts. The young men and maidens were provided with music, and enjoyed the cheerful dance to a late hour. A Sunday School was likewise established for the children on Dr. Bell's plan, which leaves no doubt of the benefit they will derive from the institution.

HELMINGTON HALL.—The Rev. R. Spencer gave a plentiful dinner, in the true Old English style, to nearly 100 persons of his township; in the evening the inhabitants of Hunwick and Helmington joined in the merry dance, which was kept up with great spirit to a late hour, concluding the festivity with "God save the King."

RAVENSWORTH.—Sir T. Liddel, Bart., gave a plentiful dinner to his tenants, and a number of poor inhabitants; he distributed to each of the men a new jacket, and to the females a flannel petticoat.

SHOTTON.—The Rev. R. H. Brandling distributed a fat ox to the poor,—his tenants and neighbours were regaled with good cheer, at the Black Bull Inn.

SOUTH SHIELDS.—The Loyal Independent Armed Association, under the command of Lieut.-Col. Bulmer, and the 1st South Shields Volunteers, commanded by Sir Cuthbert Heron, Bart., attended divine service. An excellent discourse was delivered by the Rev. W. Maugham, from 1st Peter, chap. 2, v. 17, "Fear God, honour the King." The Officers of the Association, the bench of Magistrates, and several other Gentlemen of the town and vicinity, dined with Lieut.-Col. Bulmer. The officers of the Volunteers, and a large party of Gentlemen, dined at the Hop-Pole Inn, where the day was spent in social harmony. Several charitable subscriptions were raised in honour of the day.

STOCKTON.—The day was ushered in by ringing of bells. The Loyal Stockton Volunteers, the Brethren of the Lodge of Philanthropy, in Masonic order, and the Mayor and Corporation, attended divine service. An appropriate sermon was delivered by the Rev. T. Baker, Vicar of Stockton. Afterwards the Volunteers fired a *feu de joie*.—The officers of the Corps, with the Mayor, and several other Gentlemen, dined together at the Town Hall,—the day was spent in harmony and conviviality. A subscription was raised to give the poor a substantial dinner. In the evening there was a **very** respectable ball, which concluded the festivities of the day.

SUNDERLAND and BISHOP WEARMOUTH.—Early on Wednesday morning, the happy event was announced by the ringing of bells, and other demonstrations of joy, which continued during the whole day. The Sunderland Volunteer Infantry, under the command of Sir R. Milbanke, Bart., attended divine service at Bishop Wearmouth Church, where an appropriate discourse was delivered by the learned and worthy Rector. The impression it excited will not readily be effaced from the recollection of those who heard it. At four o'clock, above 70 Gentlemen dined together at the Bridge Inn : George Robinson, Esq., presided. The King's health was drank with that enthusiasm of loyalty which springs from the noblest feelings of Englishmen, and is the spontaneous emotion of love and affection towards their Sovereign, combined with an ardent love of the country. Sir R. Milbanke and Col. Robinson spoke with great propriety. The Vice President, Cuthbert Sharp, Esq. spoke nearly to the following effect : " Mr. President, I beg leave to propose 'The House of Brunswick, and the principles which placed the House of Brunswick on the Throne of Great Britain.' It will not be necessary for me to search the pages of history, to prove that the House of Brunswick has always been the steady supporter of the cause of liberty. In the few remarks which I shall have the honour of offering to your notice, I shall confine my observations entirely to recent events. The present state of civilized Europe becomes naturally a subject of consideration, at a moment like this ; but I will not wander through the disgusting annals of duplicity and blood, which have exalted to the throne of France a man, as singularly marked by fortune as by his crimes. My remarks will be devoted to the Brunswicks of modern days, and our attention is naturally directed to the gallant veteran, who at the head of the Prussian Army, was determined to stand or fall with his country,—he fell on the plains of Jena ! and with him fell the Prussian Monarchy !—as his life was honourable, so was his death glorious,—he did not survive his country. It will hardly be credited by posterity, that the tyrant who adds insult to conquest, refused to his disconsolate family, the last sad consolation of placing the remains of this great man in the tomb of his ancestors! But let us hope that Eternal Justice does not sleep,—that the day of retribution will come, and that the man who, in the plentitude of ephemeral power, tramples on every law, human and divine,—who has deluged suffering humanity in blood, will receive the reward due to his unparalleled crimes and atrocity. During the present campaign, we have seen with admiration another Brunswick, animated with the same noble spirit of patriotism,—determined to live or die with the liberties of his country,—his efforts have proved unavailing,—but his example will live in the grateful recollection of posterity. Had all Germany been animated by the same principles which fired the soul of the Duke of Brunswick Oels, her citizens would no longer groan under the oppression of a military despot. The battle of Wagram, and the armistice which followed, rendered the situation of the Duke extremely critical. In the midst of difficulties and dangers, he surmounted and vanquished every obstacle, by that holy enthusiasm which the cause of liberty alone inspires. He and his brave followers have found a home in that land of Liberty, which is so firmly rooted in the hearts of the people, that it can never perish but with the dissolution of the British Empire. By an easy and grateful transition to the proudest feelings of Englishmen, I now proceed to the happy event which unites so many loyal and respectable subjects this day, to render homage to the virtues of a beloved Sovereign. When his Majesty ascended the throne, one of his first Public Acts was to give additional security to the liberty of the subject, by rendering the Judges independent, and we all have the proud satisfaction of knowing and feeling that the meanest Peasant in the kingdom is as secure in his natural rights and civil liberties, as the most opulent and powerful Peer of the realm. His Majesty's first speech from the Throne has invariably been the rule of his conduct, during an eventful reign.—' Born and educated in this country, I glory in the name ' of Briton, and the peculiar happiness of my life will ever consist in ' promoting the prosperity of a people, whose loyalty and warm ' affection to me I consider as the greatest and most permanent ' security of my throne.'—A throne fixed in the hearts and affections of the people, is fixed on the immutable principles of truth and justice,—and whilst we see around us the once happy Nations of Europe deluged in the blood of their citizens, and groaning under the iron grasp of military despotism, we remain secure,—a beacon for the distressed,—a secure asylum for misfortune,—the happy seat of wealth, independence and commerce. In expressing my individual sentiments, I am fully confident that I only repeat the general wish of this company, that we may long enjoy under Divine Providence the government of a Patriotic King over the affections of a free, loyal, and united people." This speech (of which we have only been able to give this rough sketch), was received with unbounded applause and acclamation. In the evening there was a very numerous and most respectable ball. It was truly gratifying to see so many lovely females assembled on such an occasion, to express their affectionate attachment to a beloved king, the father of his people. The " mazy dance " was continued with great glee to a late hour. To perpetuate the recollection of an event so dear to the feelings of Englishmen, liberal subscriptions were raised towards building a School of Industry, and for the relief of the British prisoners in France, The Overseers of the poor of Bishop Wearmouth distributed to upwards of 100 poor widows, 1 oz. of tea, a quarter of a pound of sugar, and three penny-worth of bread each, and to those in the Poor House a plentiful dinner. Lady Milbanke, with her usual munificence, presented a gratuity to each private of the Sunderland Volunteers, to drink his Majesty's health.

WYNYARD.—Sir H. V. Tempest, Bart., had a large ox roasted

and distributed, with bread and beer, to nearly 400 of his neighbours.

---o---

ESSEX

CHELMSFORD.— Thirty fine fat wether sheep, 540 quartern loaves, 600 half-quartern ditto, 500 shillings, and 500 six-pences, for beer, were distributed to upwards of 2000 persons. Meat, bread, and money, were also given to the debtors and felons in gaol, and the prisoners in the house of correction were also plentifully provided for, by order of the Magistrates. The officers of the Royal Westmoreland Militia entertained the wives and children of the men present with the regiment, with a most excellent dinner of roast beef and plum pudding, together with a pint of ale, and a tea and a dance. A subscription from the Colonel, Major, and Adjutant, and the four officers in command of companies, was also made for the men of the regiment; with which the whole were regaled, and the day was spent with that festivity so proud an occasion demanded, and which it was the pride of British soldiers to commemorate. The whole of the officers dined together, and entertained a select party of friends.

BRADFIELD.—By a very handsome subscription of the principal inhabitants of the parish, nearly 700 poor people received a liberal supply of bread, cheese, and strong beer, in which they participated with their families, and joined in the general rejoicings of the day.

BURES.—After attending divine service, 500 of the industrious inhabitants were entertained with an ample dinner of roast beef and plum-pudding, which was received with gratitude and satisfaction visible on every countenance. At the conclusion of this happy meal "God save the King" was sung in full chorus, and this rural company broke up with hearts full of loyalty to their Sovereign, and thankfulness to the donors of the feast. Meat, bread, and beer, were also distributed to 300 persons in Bures Hamlet. The Minister and principal inhabitants afterwards dined together at the Queen's Head Inn.

COLCHESTER.—The morning was ushered in with the ringing of bells, and all descriptions of people hastened to concur in the public observance of the day. At eleven o'clock the Mayor and Corporation walked in procession to St. Mary's Church; the other places of public worship in the town were filled; in all of which appropriate discourses were delivered. A subscription of upwards of 400*l.* including a donation of twenty guineas from each of the Members, had been previously expended in providing nearly 6000 poor, with a comfortable dinner. The brigade of Artillery fired a Royal Salute, the troops in garrison a *feu de joie*, and the first East Essex Cavalry three volleys in honour of the day. A large and most respectable company, consisting of the Mayor and Corporation, R. H.

Davis, Esq., one of the representatives for the Borough, the Clergy, principal inhabitants of the town, and its immediate neighbourhood, the Officers of the First East Essex Cavalry, and the Officers of the third Regiment of Essex Local Militia, dined at the Three Cups Inn, where, under the auspices of the chairman, John Round, Jun., Esq., various apposite and loyal toasts were given. "The King, the reverend Sovereign of a free People," was drank with enthusiasm, amidst cheers of seven times seven, corresponding with the number of years his Majesty had so happily reigned over us; the sentiment of "Long may our beloved Sovereign George the Third continue to reign over a free, loyal, happy, and undivided people," was also favourably received, and followed by the whole company, joining in the national air of "God save the King." The band of the third Regiment of Local Militia attended in the Orchestra, and performed several select pieces, in a pleasing style. Among other festivities of the day, Mr. A. F. Miller, with his accustomed liberality, distributed six puncheons of fine old beer among the populace. An ox of about twenty score, was roasted whole in Mr. Hawkins's timber-yard, of which his workmen, their wives and families, to the number of about 200, partook, with a plentiful supply of beer, &c. The evening concluded with a ball and supper at the White Hart Inn, which was numerously and respectably attended.

GREAT DUNMOW.—The Jubilee was observed in this place, by distributing to upwards of 1200 poor persons, meat, bread, and beer.

HARWICH.—The day was ushered in by the ringing of bells, firing of guns, and colours flying. The Mayor and Corporation met at the Guildhall, and proceeded to Church, where an appropriate sermon was preached by the Rev. W. Whinfield. A subscription was entered into, by which all the poor of the town were relieved. The poor in the Workhouse were regaled with a good dinner. The Volunteers attended divine service, and after firing a *feu de joie*, with the detachment of the York lying there, partook of a cold dinner in tents pitched on the lawn. There were dinners at all the places of public entertainment, which were numerously attended by the Mayor and Corporation, and respectable inhabitants. There was a ball and supper on Thursday evening.

LAWFORD PLACE.—At Lawford Place, the residence of George Bridges, Esq., upwards of 100 poor inhabitants of the parish were regaled with an excellent dinner of beef, mutton, and plain puddings, with a plentiful supply of beer.

MANNINGTREE.—Upwards of 600 lbs. of beef and mutton, 600 six-penny loaves, and 600 pints of strong beer, were distributed among the poor. A number of Gentlemen and respectable Tradesmen, partook of a well-served dinner at the Pacquet Inn. After which, many loyal and constitutional toasts were given, and the day concluded with the utmost harmony and conviviality.

MISTLEY.—The poor were supplied with bread, beef, beer, and coals, by the bounty of F. H. Rigby, Esq., the Rev. J. Watson, and other opulent inhabitants.

ROCHETTS.—Lord St. Vincent gave a grand entertainment, in honour of his Majesty's Accession, at his beautiful seat. The most princely munificence was displayed in the whole of the preparations. The fete consisted of a dinner, ball, and supper. The Prince of Wales was expected at the former, but a sudden attack of the gout having prevented his Royal Highness from attending, Lord Erskine apologised. Previously to the arrival of the company, in front of the house, the lawn, the avenues leading to the latter, the lodge-gates, and a part of the wilderness, (or forest) on the outside of the park-wall, were brilliantly illuminated. It is supposed that 10,000 variegated lamps were used by the King's lamplighter. Opposite the principal front of the mansion there is placed a noble conservatory, which was decorated with one immensely large transparency of the King's arms; and in an appropriate situation, another of the Prince's plume. At the top of each of the columns, or pillars at the lodge-entrances, appeared a variety of devices, and in the wood there were two vast anchors in coloured lamps, the latter served as finger-posts to enable the coachmen to *steer* clear of *shoals*. The visitors entered the outer hall, and thence proceeded to the inner one; wherein their ears were delighted by duets, admirably executed on French horns, by performers of acknowledged celebrity. Proceeding up the grand staircase, the company were ushered by Lord St. Vincent himself into the principal drawing room, wherein the Countess was seated to receive them. About ten o'clock the dancing commenced in the ball room, which was fitted up with much taste; about thirty couple tript "on the light fantastic toe." A supper, the most abundant and costly, about 150 persons partook of, at one o'clock in the morning. The ornamental decorations bore every mark of loyalty and judiciously-blended taste. It was about six o'clock before the party broke up. The Officers of the Prince's Regiment, (the 10th), those belonging to the Duke of Cumberland's (15th), a few attached to the Navy, and others of the Military quartered in the neighbourhood, were present.

ST. OSWYTH.—The Volunteers, of which corps Frederic Nassau, Esq., is Colonel, had a handsome dinner, and every poor person in the parish, to the amount of 600, received two shillings each, from the liberal subscriptions of the inhabitants, to which Mr. Nassau largely contributed. In the evening, Mrs. Nassau gave a ball and supper to the domestics and others, at which her two sons danced till three o'clock in the morning.

WITHAM.—A liberal subscription was raised in the town, to the amount of 95*l.*, with which an allowance was made of 1 lb. of the best wether mutton, 1 lb. of bread, and six-pence in money, for the purchase of beer, to each poor inhabitant, old and young, to the number of near 1400.

GLOCESTERSHIRE.

GLOCESTER.—The festival was ushered in by the ringing of bells at the different Churches; the shops were kept closed; and the places of divine worship exhibited crowded and attentive auditories. The Corporation, preceded by the bands of the city and the Local Militia, went to the Cathedral; and were followed by the troop of Glocester Volunteer Cavalry, the Officers and troops of the Garrison, and the permanent staff Officers, non-commissioned Officers, &c., of the first Royal East Glocester Local Militia. A very excellent discourse was preached by the Rev. Dr. Morgan; and appropriate music was performed on the organ by Mr. Mutlow. After quitting the Church, the military formed in a line in the College Green, and gave three grand and distinct cheers in honour of the happy event. At half-past three, a large party sat down to dinner at the King's Head, where Sir Berkeley William Guise, Bart., presided. A variety of apposite toasts were given, and many loyal and other songs added a zest to the entertainment, which continued to a late hour. The Glocester Volunteer Cavalry dined together at the Upper George; their Captain, Robert Morris, Esq.. M.P., in the chair. The Officers of the 18th, and those of the staff, also dined at the George; and several other dinner parties were held at different Inns in the city. The ball in the evening, at the Bell, was numerously and respectably attended. The collections made in behalf of the poor, including 20*l.* from Captain Morris, and 20*l.* from his troop, amounted to upwards of 228*l.* This sum, with the profit of the ball tickets, (supposed to be 30*l.*) enabled the Committee, after deducting expenses, to allow to more than 4700 deserving persons a shilling each. Roast and boiled beef, pudding and strong beer, were given to upwards of 100 poor in the Workhouse. The Committee for charitable purposes in the county gaol, ordered a good dinner to be provided for all the prisoners confined therein; in addition to which, the debtors received from Mrs. Entwisle, of Cheltenham, a humane and most generous donation.

BADMINTON.—The Duke of Beaufort commemorated the day by distributing meat, bread, potatoes, and beer, in sufficient quantities, to upwards of 1200 poor persons, belonging to his parishes in Glocestershire and Wilts, around his seat at Badminton.

BERKELEY.—In the towns of Berkeley, Dursley, etc., the poor were also ample partakers of the joyous festival.

BITTON.—The Jubilee was celebrated in the parish of Bitton, by a very full attendance at the Church. More than 400 poor persons present received one shilling each. The Gentlemen of the parish then proceeded in procession, attended by a numerous concourse of people, to an ancient barrow in a field. The ladies, gentlemen, etc., having ascended to the top, a circle of more than 200 children was first formed round the barrow, to each of whom was given a small plum cake or biscuit: then the men formed a circle, and his Majesty's

F

health was drank, with full acclamation, in good English **strong** beer, **a hogshead of** which was placed upon the top of the barrow : 400 **loaves of bread** were then distributed.

BRISTOL.—The grand national Jubilee was celebrated in this city, in a manner worthy of the occasion. The morning was ushered in by the ringing of bells ; by a display of flags and standards from the steeples of the Churches, the tops of the public buildings, and the masts of the shipping of all nations in the harbour. In the course of the morning, divine service was performed in the several Churches **and** Meeting-houses, where appropriate sermons were delivered **to** crowded congregations. The Mayor and Corporation attended divine service at the Mayor's Chapel, where an impressive discourse was delivered on the occasion, by the Rev. T. T. Biddulph. About nine o'clock the Volunteer corps of the city and neighbourhood assembled in Queen-square, from whence they proceeded to St. Paul's Church, where **an** excellent and appropriate sermon was delivered by Dr. Small. **After** service the Doctor, attended by the Church-wardens, and the principal inhabitants of his parish, proceeded to **lay** the foundation stone of an Obelisk, to be erected in the centre **of** Portland-square, as a memorial of his Majesty's happy reign. The senior Church-warden, carrying the large plate of brass, with an appropriate inscription, the junior Churchwarden several coins of his Majesty's reign, and medals struck upon the occasion, in a napkin upon **a** gold plate, followed the Doctor, who placed them under the stone, which he struck with a mallet, in a true Masonic manner. He then addressed the audience in nearly the following words : Friends and fellow subjects, It has fallen to my lot to have the honour of laying the Foundation-Stone of an Obelisk, to be erected on this spot, by the voluntary contributions of the loyal inhabitants of this parish, in honour of the best of Kings, and the father of his people, and as a memorial to future ages of the religious and moral virtues of our most gracious and venerable Sovereign Lord George the Third ; who in the 72nd year of his age, commences on this day, the 50th of his reign—a reign replete with anxiety, trouble, and difficulties, such **as** this kingdom never before witnessed, and such as nothing but **his** invincible fortitude, mild government, and paternal watchfulness, could have surmounted. By these, under the blessings of Almighty **God, are** secured to us that freedom and liberty, in the exercise of **our civil** and religious duties, which **our** forefathers purchased with **their** blood, and left **to us** as legacies **ever to** be valued—ever to be defended. May his virtuous example influence the conduct of his Royal Successors, and **may** we never want **a** descendant of the illustrious House of Brunswick to defend our pure religion, to protect our liberty, and to promote the safety, honour, and welfare of the United Kingdom of Great Britain and Ireland. This day, my friends, this memorable day, I shall **ever** esteem as one of the proudest of my life ; and while I cordially return **to** you, my worthy parishioners, grateful thanks for the honour you have now conferred upon me, give me leave to express to these, our fellow citizens, who nobly stand forth against a daring and implacable enemy, in defence of the manifold blessings we enjoy—in defence of every thing that is dear and valuable to us on earth—give me leave to express to them, the high sense we entertain of the honour they now do us, in giving a sanction to these our efforts, and, by their presence, stamping them with dignity and approbation." The ceremony was concluded by firing three volleys over the stone. After which the Volunteers marched to Queen Square, where, about two o'clock, they were joined by the garrison ; and the whole, being drawn up in order, fired a *feu de joie* in honour of the day. This was answered by a salute of fifty rounds from the Bristol Volunteer Artillery, stationed on Durdham Down. The Corporation gave 200 guineas, in augmentation of the subscriptions for the poor in the different parishes, and 2s. 6d. to each poor man and woman in the city Alms-houses ; a cake, a glass of wine, and a new six-pence, were distributed to each of the boys of the City School, and girls of the Red-maid's School.—They also ordered a pound of beef, bread, and potatoes, to each prisoner in Newgate, and a waggon load of coals to be distributed by the keeper amongst the persons under his care. In the Castle Precincts, the sum collected for the relief of the poor, and of the debtors in Newgate, amounted to 71*l*. 19*s*. 6*d*. including 10*l*. received from the Corporation, and 11*l*. 11*s*. 9*d*. collected at Castle Green Meeting,—which enabled the Overseers to afford relief to 781 poor inhabitants of the said precincts and transfer a balance of 21*l*. 11*s*. 9*d*, to the Committee for the release of persons confined in Newgate for debt. The sums collected at the various places of public worship amounted to nearly 1400*l*. and were distributed in various ways to the poor. One of the most striking circumstances in honour of the day, was the erection of a Grand Triumphal Arch, across Corn-street, between St. Werburgh's Church and Mr. Norton's house, the plan of which was originated with Mr. Slade Baker, of Small-street, and Mr. Richardson, Druggist, of Corn-street, and which was constructed with so much judgment and secrecy, that when the streets began to fill on Wednesday morning, it seemed to have risen as if by enchantment during the night. The Arch was begun about eleven o'clock on Tuesday evening, and was finished before eight o'clock on Wednesday morning. It was surmounted by a Crown, over which the British Ensigns waved from each side of the street. Underneath, on one side, the Arch was formed by " Long live the King," and on the other " God save the King,"—The whole festooned with laurel. The Corporation passed under this Arch, on their way to and return from Church in the morning, as did also the Volunteers, in going to and returning from Portland Square. Several medals and devices were displayed on the occasion. The ladies wore dark blue ribbons and hankerchiefs, with Jubilee medals, suspended from their necks. In the evening a divertisement, consisting of loyal and constitutional songs and national airs, was brought forward at the Theatre, and the evening was passed with balls, routs, and festive parties, varying with the taste and circumstances of a free and loyal people. Divine service was performed at the Jewish Synagogue, in Redcliff-street, where a most excellent prayer, written for the occasion by the Rev. Solomon Hirschell, was read by the congregation.

CHARLTON KINGS.—At Charlton Kings, the Jubilee was celebrated by a distribution of bread, meat, coals, and ale, in ample quantities, sufficient to enable 538 of the poorer inhabitants to enjoy the festival, all of whom attended divine service. The bells rang a merry peal, and every one appeared to unite in fervent wishes for an increase of years of happiness to our beloved Sovereign.

CHELTENHAM.—The bells at an early hour began to proclaim the approaching celebration of the national Jubilee. The Royal flag was hoisted on the Church steeple. Divine service was performed, the military were exercised, and the amount of a liberal subscription distributed among the poor. At half-past four o'clock a most respectable company of the principal inhabitants of the town and neighbourhood, together with a considerable number of visitors, sat down to an elegant dinner in the Town-hall; T. B. Delabere, Esq., in the chair. The utmost harmony prevailed during the evening.

CIRENCESTER.—The morning of the Jubilee was ushered in by the ringing of bells, which continued till the time of the service. The Volunteer Infantry and Cavalry paraded at an early hour; after which the Infantry were marched to Church, where an excellent sermon for the occasion was preached by the Rev. Mr. Pye, and appropriate music was performed on the organ. About two o'clock the Infantry were drawn up in the Market-place, and fired three volleys. There were excellent dinners provided at the different Inns, which were numerously attended. In the evening, there was a ball at the King's Head, at which were present nearly all the first families in the town and neighbouroood. A general subscription enabled the poor families of the town to share in the festivities of the day. Previous to divine service, on the day of Jubilee, a distribution took place of 5s. to every poor family in the town, housekeepers, without exception, and 2s. 6d. to every lodger. The whole sum distributed was 213l. 8s.

CLIFTON.—The subscriptions amounted to upwards of £300 by which 747 poor families, consisting of 2513 persons, were enabled to join in the general festivity. All the chimney-sweepers and their masters were invited to the house of Captain Budworth, who entertained them in his garden, with beef and pudding. After the cloth was removed, a plum-cake and six-pence were placed before each happy climber; and they departed, with a promise to repeat their visit on the King's birth day, as long as it shall please God to spare his life.

COTE HOUSE.—The seat of Sir Henry Protheroe. Over the gateways leading to this elegant mansion from Durdham Down, triumphal arches were erected, beautifully decorated with laurel and variegated lamps ; the outside of the house had a very brilliant appearance, having in the centre a Crown and 50, with G. R. on the wings, formed in large letters by coloured glass lamps. Amongst the company invited were the Dukes of Beaufort and Leinster, the Earl and Countess of Berkeley, Gen. Warde, the Officers commanding the different regiments in garrison at Bristol, and most of the principal families in the neighbourhood. In the course of the evening a brilliant display of fire-works was exhibited on the lawn. At one o'clock two large rooms were thrown open for supper, which was of the most splendid and elegant description ; immediately after which Sir Henry proposed the King's health ; when the whole company stood up and sung "God save the King." The dancing was then resumed, and continued with much spirit until the dawn of day.

DODINGTON.—C. Codrington, Esq., gave away a fat ox, divided into suitable quantities, and four quartern loaves of bread, to each poor family round his Mansion at Dodington ; and a day's wages to all his numerous labourers.

FRAMPTON.—At Frampton-upon-Severn, the poor were regaled, the usual village sports were exhibited on the green, and the day was spent with the utmost harmony and regularity.

FROCESTER.—The poor inhabitants of the parish, to the amount of between 2 and 300, after hearing an admirable sermon by the Rev. G. Hayward, Jun., sat down to a dinner of roast and boiled beef, and a quart of strong beer ; and so liberal were the subscriptions, that there was an overplus sufficient to supply each necessitous family, on the following day, with a gallon of rich soup, and a quantity of beef.

LYDNEY.—The steeple rocked with a merry peal : and a liberal subscription having been raised by the Right Hon. Charles Bathurst, and the other householders of the parish, for the use of the poor, the active exertions of those who were preparing the tables for their entertainment increased the interest of the day. After divine service, 140 poor families assembled round the Market-place, and carried each to his joyful cot a good joint of meat, a loaf of bread, and a gallon of cider, given by Mr. Bathurst, whose happy family were spectators of the grateful scene. The respectable inhabitants afterwards retired to the Plume of Feathers, where a good dinner was provided, graced with venison and hare, presented by the hospitable owner of Lydney Park. Care was banished from the table, and while the ruby glass went briskly round, the welkin rang with "three times three," many times repeated, to the health of our venerable Monarch, and prosperity to the Realms of Freedom.

MARSHFIELD.—After a sermon suited to the day, a large quantity of bread was distributed to the poor. What renders the celebration at this place particularly interesting is, that the same eight persons took their parts in the Coronation Anthem on this day, who sang it when our gracious Sovereign was crowned.

MISERDINE CASTLE.—The Jubilee was celebrated at the seat of Sir Edwin Bayntun Sandys, Bart., with every demonstration of loyalty; upwards of 300 poor people were fed with roast and boiled meat, bread, and strong beer, which were served out in **abundance round** large bonfires in the Park.

NEWENT.—Two fine sheep were roasted whole, and two baked, which were divided and distributed to the poor. Money and beer were also given away. There was a dinner of the inhabitants at the Red Lion, and a ball in the evening. **Some very** excellent fire-works were also exhibited.

NEWTON PARK.—Colonel Gore Langton distributed money and provisions amongst the families of his neighbourhood; and his farmers entered into **the spirit** of the day, after **the** same hospitable example set them **by their** worthy landlord.

OLVESTON.—**The Rev.** Mr. Charlton gladdened the hearts **of** 120 of his poor **parishioners in** Olveston, Elberton, &c., **by** distributing amongst them a fine fat ox.

PAINSWICK.—The Jubilee was observed **by a** very general **attendance at divine** service, when an appropriate sermon was preached by **the Rev.** John Fearon, Vicar of the parish, who took his **text** from **the 1st of** Peter, 2nd chap, 17th verse. A very liberal subscription **of £54** 12s. by the inhabitants of the parish, provided 1200 poor per**sons** with 1 lb. of meat each, and bread in proportion to their fami**lies**, which were distributed to them the preceding day, at their own habitations.

PENCOMBE.—The **Rev.** Mr. **Glasse** gave **bread and** money, to every poor person in his parish.

SHIREHAMPTON.—An ox was killed, and given to the poor with a profusion of bread and **ale.** The evening was concluded with a bonfire, **a** display of fireworks, **and** other demonstrations of loyalty.

STAPLETON.—£44 **13s.** were distributed **among the poor,** with preference to the aged.

STROUD.—The inhabitants of this town and neighbourhood subscribed £230 and upwards, by which nearly 5000 of the **poor** were supplied with 5543 lbs. of meat, and 115 bags of potatoes.

TEMPLE GUITING.—The poor were presented with 144 blankets, 40 pair of sheets, 40 shirts, and 56 shifts, in value 144*l*. from the funds of the Sunday Schools of that parish. A dinner was given **by Mrs.** Talbot to the Stow Troop of Cavalry; and the poor inhabit**ants of** the village afterwards partook of the same.

TEWKESBURY.—The Corporation, with the Volunteer Cavalry, attended divine service. Five oxen, with a due share of potatoes and beer, were distributed among upwards of 3000 people. The ball at the Cross Keys, in the evening, was attended by a large and fashionable company, who remained till a late hour. A local medal was presented by a gentleman of the first respectability, who holds a high official situation in the Borough, to the inhabitants of Tewkesbury, and the neighbouring families.

TORTWORTH.—The Tortworth Yeomanry Cavalry met at their head quarters, Kingscote, where they were received by their Commander, the Right Hon. Lord Ducie, who gave them an elegant dinner at Hunter's Tavern.

WOODCHESTER.—Messrs. Paul Wathen and Co. of Woodchester, gave a dinner to about 600 persons employed in their manufactory. In the evening an illumination of their extensive mills, workshops, factories, &c., with bonfires and fire-works, attracted a large concourse of spectators.

WOTTON-UNDER-EDGE.—The inhabitants attended Church, where a discourse, adapted to the festival, was preached by the Rev. P. M. Cornwall, Jun., A.M. Rd. Nelmes, Esq., the Mayor, treated the young gentlemen of the Free Grammar School with cakes, and gave to each boy on the foundation a handsome medal. He likewise sent cakes to the boys at the Blue School; and a shilling to each pensioner in the Hospital, to drink his Majesty's health. A subscription was set on foot immediately after divine service; and the fund established will help to feed the hungry, and clothe the naked, during great part of the winter. The Rev. P. M. Cornwall, Sen., A.M., Master of the Free Grammar School, gave the scholars a dinner of roast and boiled beef, plum-puddings, pies, &c., and Mr. Miles, Master of the Blue School, also regaled his scholars liberally; and Mr. Taylor very hospitably entertained 24 industrious, labouring people, with a substantial dinner, under his own roof.

HAMPSHIRE.

WINCHESTER.—After the clock had struck twelve on Tuesday night, all the bells of the different churches were rung in this city and suburbs, to usher in the happy 50th anniversary of the accession of our beloved Sovereign.—At ten o'clock the inhabitants, military, friendly societies, &c., went in procession from the County Hall to the Cathedral Church. All the procession returned to the airing ground behind the barracks, where the soldiers in barracks and the Winchester Loyal Volunteers fired a *feu de joie*, with cheers of three times three. The sermon was preached by the Rev. Mr. De Grey. The concourse of people was immense. After the ceremony the charity children were regaled with a hearty meal of roast beef, plum pudding, and strong beer; the girls at the Guildhall, and the boys at the school room at St. John's-house. There was an elegant dinner provided at St. John's-house, for above one hundred gentlemen of distinction, where the utmost conviviality prevailed to a late hour. Many excellent songs were sung; at each end of the large room two excellent transparencies were displayed. The evening concluded with every demonstration of joy; the societies, after the procession, regaled themselves at the different inns. A handsome donation of meat, coals, and bread, was distributed to the poor throughout the city and suburbs. Never was a day of more festivity in the memory of the oldest inhabitant.

ALRESFORD.—The 50th Anniversary of his Majesty's accession to the Throne was most loyally commemorated, by ringing of bells, and other demonstrations of joy. The Volunteers assembled on their parade, and marched to church, to attend divine service; afterwards they had a field day, and fired several excellent volleys. A handsome subscription of the principal inhabitants supplied the poor, with a suitable proportion to each, of bread, meat, and strong beer, which made them joyful and happy for the day. In the evening there was a Ball at the Swan Inn, which was well attended, and continued to a late hour.

ANDOVER.—In addition to every festive celebration of the day upwards of £200 was raised by subscription, and given in provisions and money to the poor.

BASINGSTOKE.—Not less than one thousand persons (comprehending the indigent of both sexes, and of all ages) were liberally treated with an amplitude of wholesome viands, accompanied with ten hogsheads of strong beer, a Lord Bolton's seat, at Hackwood. Mr. Chute, Col. Jervoise, Mr. Wither, Mr. Blackburn, Mr. Harwood, and other neighbouring gentlemen, emulated each other on the joyful occasion, in similar acts of liberality. The day was introduced by a ball and cold collation on the preceding night, at which all the neighbouring gentry were present. The religious service of the day was attended by the Mayor and Corporation, the North Hants Cavalry, and Basingstoke Infantry; when an excellent sermon was preached by the Rev. Mr. Russell, curate of Basingstoke; a liberal subscription was raised for the indigent, and the day concluded with a public dinner, at the Town Hall, attended by the Mayor and Corporation, the North Hants Corps, and many of the neighbouring gentlemen, where the utmost harmony and festivity prevailed to a late hour.

BEAULIEU.—After divine service, the Duke of York's New Forest Volunteers fired three volleys, and were dismissed to make room for another display—not so gay, but gratifying to every one possessing a heart to feel—the sight of 600 happy human faces, round tables covered with well dressed beef, mutton, vegetables, and plum pudding, the gentry waiting on them, and rejoicing in their happiness.

BURGHCLERE.—The liberality of D. Chambers, Esq., of Adbury House, was particularly distinguishable; to each of the poor in the parish of Burghclere a gallon loaf was distributed, and a raiment of the most useful kind, to each of the heads of the families.

EMSWORTH.—Very liberal subscriptions were entered into, and above 500 persons were provided with good English fare to perpetuate the day; and the inns had parties at dinner and supper, to celebrate the happy occasion.

FAREHAM.—The subscription enabled 1500 of the poor to be supplied with bread, meat, and beer.

FAWLEY.—Andrew Berkeley Drummond, Esq., gave a fat ox, (above forty score weight), to the poor of the parish, which was roasted whole, on an eligible spot on Ash Down. It was roasted by two o'clock in the afternoon of the 25th, when it was cut out and divided amongst the poor, at tables placed on the Down for the purpose, with 100 gallon loaves, and six hogsheads of good strong beer, raised by a subscription from the gentlemen of the neighbourhood.—The day concluded by singing "God save the King," in full chorus.

GOSPORT.—The inhabitants of Gosport and Alverstoke testified their loyalty and attachment to our beloved Sovereign by every mark of respect and public festivity. A very considerable subscription was raised, and the poor, to the extent of 3000 persons, were most liberally supplied with the best ox beef, bread, and beer. After attending divine service, the Gunners of the Gosport Volunteer Artillery, were regaled with beer, &c., by their Officers and non-commissioned Officers; and the Gosport Battalion of Volunteer Infantry, consisting of four companies, dined in companies at four different taverns, at the expense of their Officers. A dinner was given by some of the respectable tradesmen, in the Market-house, to several hundred persons, where the greatest order and regularity prevailed. There were also dinners at the principal Inns; many convivial toasts, sentiments, and songs, which were written expressly for the occasion, were given, and the day was enjoyed in the utmost harmony and unanimity. In the evening there was a ball at the Crown, attended by upwards of 100 of the most respectable inhabitants of Gosport and its vicinity. "God save the King," was sung in full chorus. A sermon was preached by the Rev. David Bogue, for the benefit of the poor. The learned preacher in an impressive discourse, considered his Majesty's pious example, and moral rectitude: his daily devotions—his strict observance of the sabbath—the liberality of his religious opinions—and his temperance; as deserving the imitation of his audience, and of all classes of persons, and such as were uncommon traits in the character of any King!

HAMBLEDON.—The poor were regaled on the Jubilee day, by Admiral Erasmus Gower. Upwards of 60 persons partook of his bounty.

HAVANT.—The day was ushered in by the ringing of bells; the shops were shut, and divine service was performed at the Parish

Church, where a numerous congregation attended. The sum of £94 19s. was subscribed, and expended in liberal donations of meat, bread, beer, and coals, to 814 poor persons. The inhabitants dined together at the Inns, where the health of our beloved Sovereign was drank with enthusiasm; and in the evening the tower of the Church was illuminated.

HURSLEY LODGE.—Sir W. Heathcote distributed upwards of 100 pairs of blankets, among his poor neighbours.

HURSTBOURNE PARK.—Among the many festivities of the Jubilee, the Earl of Portsmouth gave a fine ox, beef, plum-pudding, and good strong beer, to the poor inhabitants of his Lordship's several adjoining Manors, to the number of 1000 persons, who enjoyed with inexpressible delight their excellent repast, and departed with repeated expressions of the most heartfelt loyalty to their beloved Sovereign, and of grateful acknowledgement to their noble benefactor.

ITCHEN ABBAS.—The whole of the poor of the parish of Itchen were regaled by A. R. Dottin, Esq., of Itchen Abbas. Three sheep, stuffed with potatoes, were roasted whole; puddings, ale, and a tub of punch, were served to all the happy villagers in great abundance, and a sum of money distributed to the poor females. The King's health was drank with three distinct cheers, and several other loyal and patriotic toasts. The festive day concluded by drinking the health of Lord Cathcart, and his Majesty's 2nd Regiment of Life Guards, in which Mr. Dottin had the honour to serve several years.

MAPLEDURHAM HOUSE.—Michael Blount, Esq., entertained all his labourers, with their wives and families, with good old English cheer, and sent 2 lbs. and a half of meat to every widow in the parish.—Mrs. Blount, with her usual goodness, entertained all the widows in the Almshouses.

PORTCHESTER.—A liberal subscription was raised, and upwards of 300 poor people, of all ages, bountifully supplied with bread, meat, and beer. They had besides nine-pence each given.

PORTSMOUTH.—The day was ushered in by the ringing of bells, and by fifty guns being discharged from the Platform battery. An appropriate and most excellent sermon was preached in the parish Church, by the Rev. J. G. Bussel, from the 50th Psalm, and the 14th verse: the Church was fully attended. After divine service at the different places of worship in both towns, collections were made; the amount of which being added to the united subscriptions of the town and Portsea, exceeded the sum of £500. The poor, to the number of from five to six thousand, were regaled, at their own houses, with beef, strong beer, and bread, from the above subscriptions and collections. The prisoners confined for debt in the County Gaol, and those in the Borough Gaol, were released. And the County Hospital also had a handsome donation presented it, from the balance remaining in the hands of the Committee, for the laudable purposes of the Institution. The inmates of the Poorhouses, and Alms-houses, were regaled with roast beef, plum-puddings, and strong beer; and the Portsmouth Institution for "Educating and clothing Poor Children," gave a similar dinner to the children of that charity. The Militia Regiments, under the command of Gen. Whetham, and the Volunteers in the Garrison, marched to South-Sea Beach, forming a very extended line. At one o'clock the Royal William, Admiral Sir Roger Curtis's flagship, commenced a salute of 50 guns, which was a signal for every ship at the port to fire a salute of 21 guns. The troops on the beach then opened a fire of *feu de joie*, until they had expended fifteen rounds of ammunition; the guns at Fort Monkton, South-Sea Castle, Block House Fort, Cumberland Fort, on the Portsea lines, and those on the Gosport lines, were fired in succession, forming one of the grandest scenes ever exhibited. On the cessation of firing, the troops gave three cheers, and marched past the General. Most of the respectable inhabitants dined together in parties, either privately, or at the principal Inns, to celebrate the day. The principal inhabitants of Portsea dined at the Society Hall. The Jews had a grand dinner at their Vestry, having previously distributed meat, bread, and beer, to upwards of 200 necessitous persons. In the evening there was a most superb ball and supper at the Crown, given by the Officers of the Army and Navy, to the principal inhabitants of these towns, Gosport and neighbourhood. Messrs. W. Burridge and Sons, of Portsmouth, distributed three-pence to each of the French prisoners confined on board the prison ships in that harbour, to the amount of 6715; and sixpence to each of the Danish prisoners, being 186. They had printed cards distributed, signifying that the donation was, "In consequence of the humanity shown by Marshal Mortier to the British sick and wounded, after the Battle of Talavera." It was indeed a day entirely devoted to expressions of loyalty, festivity, respect, and affection to our most gracious and beloved king.

PRESTON CANDOVER.—The High Sheriff entertained, in a most liberal manner, upwards of 200 persons who live contiguous to his estate.

SOUTHAMPTON.—At eight o'clock, ten cannons planted before the Custom-House, were fired five rounds, as an announcement of his Majesty's 50th Accession to the throne. Immediately after which the bells rang an admirable touch of 700 changes of grandsire trebles, composing 50 treble leads, being the number of years of the Anniversary. The flags were displayed on the usual places; the Volunteers mustered and went to Church; the different places of worship were well attended, and appropriate discourses delivered. Three excellent *feux de joie* were fired by the Volunteers after service, drawn up before the Audit-House, where the Magistrates were convened. Bread was given to the poor the previous day, and continued daily, till the subscriptions were expended. Messrs. Taylors, builders, Evamy, saddler, and other opulent tradesmen, treated their journeymen to dinners, with plenty of suitable beverage. But the most remarkable treat was given by Messrs. R. and W. Saunders, brewers, in East-street, who distributed ten sheep, and supplied all comers, *ad libitum*, with good strong beer, from a tap in a large cask. Some fire-works concluded the evening, and no injury or complaint ensued. At Cadlands, a large fat ox, the gift of H. Drummond, Esq., was roasted whole, and given to the villagers of Brumley, &c., with plenty of potatoes, bread, &c., and eight hogsheads of best stout, which made them cheerful and happy. On the opposite side of the river, at the village of Weston, Miss Short was not less remarkable for her bounty; she had abundance of good English cheer, such as roast beef, &c., dressed at home, and tables spread on the lawn, where she superintended the joyous assemblage of the place.

SOUTHWICK.—The celebration at the neat little cot of William Sergeant, Esq., in this village, was not exceeded by any.—Mirth and rejoicing on the occasion, was coupled with a liberal donation of beef, plum-pudding, &c., to all the poor inhabitants of the village. After divine service in the morning, the doors of the hospitable cot were thrown open, when about 50 of the villagers entered, and were received by Mr. and Mrs. Sergeant with every mark of familiarity and attention. At twelve o'clock a table, spread in the hall, was covered with roast and boiled beef, mutton, plum-puddings, and suitable vegetables, with plenty of good old ale. At two o'clock, in an adjoining apartment, a handsome dinner, the good old fare of roast beef and plum-puddings, with wines of the best quality, punch, &c., was prepared for the family, and a few friends in the neighbourhood; who vied with each other in making it indeed a day of rejoicing.—After dinner, the ale was served round to the villagers, and grog, or wine, to those who preferred it. Songs and toasts went round in each apartment, and all was joy and gladness. Soon as the day shut in, a most beautiful display of variegated lamps was exhibited in various parts of the garden and grounds, and G. R. surmounted with a Crown, placed in a conspicuous situation, was very attractive. On these being exhibited, "God save the King," and "Rule Britannia," were sung in great style, and chorussed by the whole company. A discharge of rockets, was the signal for the beginning of a display of fireworks. Never was a day spent in greater harmony and festivity. At eleven o'clock the whole of the company retired highly delighted, the villagers bestowing their blessings on the donor and his family for their kind hospitality.

ST. MARY BOURN.—Four fat oxen were distributed to the poor, on the 3d, which would have been on Jubilee day, but that was prevented by the very liberal donation to upwards of 900 people, given by the Right Hon. the Earl of Portsmouth, at his Park at Down Hurstbourn.

SHERBOURN ST. JOHN.— William Chute, Esq., entertained upwards of 400 of the inhabitants with a dinner, consisting of old

English roast beef, plum-pudding, and strong beer, at his seat, the Vine.

TITCHFIELD.—The Loyal Titchfield Light Infantry assembled on parade, at ten o'clock, and marched to Church, where a most excellent and appropriate sermon was preached by the Rev. A. Radcliffe, Vicar. The regiment fell in immediately after service was over, and marched with colours flying to the centre of the town, where they fired three times three volleys, with three cheers between each three volleys, and in which cheering they were most heartily joined by the loyal inhabitants of every description.

———0———

ISLE OF WIGHT.

NEWPORT.—The hour of midnight betwixt the 24th and 25th, was scarcely past, when the inhabitants of the Borough were informed of it by "God save the King," in full chorus, sang through the streets. At dawn of day the bells rang their merriest peal; and soon the streets were filled with cheerful countenances, in their gayest attire. The Corporation, with the Lodge of Free Masons, attended divine service, when an excellent sermon was preached by the Rev. P. Geary, and the Coronation Anthem was sung by a full choir. After divine service the whole congregation hastened to St. James's Square, where, in temporary booths, the poorer inhabitants, to the number of 1800 and upwards, sat down to an excellent dinner, provided for them by the subscriptions of their richer neighbours.—A committee of gentlemen presided. The dinner being over, his Majesty's health was drank, with three times three, by the whole party; the Queen and Royal Family followed, and a more pleasing scene was never viewed. The different Gentlemen of the Island, and the Army and Navy there, dined together at the Sun Inn. About 200 sat down, at four o'clock, to a most sumptuous dinner.—Lord Fitzharris, the Governor of the Island, presided. It need scarcely be added, that "The King," was drank with enthusiasm; that many other loyal and constitutional toasts were given, and that the utmost conviviality and good humour prevailed to a late hour. Captain Foquett, and the Officers and Gentlemen of the Isle of Wight Yeomanry Cavalry, dined at the Bugle Inn; and other parties at the different Inns. When the day shut in, the principal houses in the town were illuminated. The whole town appeared brilliant and handsome till the spectator reached Sir A. Worsley Holmes's, when all was wonder and admiration at this apparently fairy palace. The Mayor released all the prisoners in confinement on trivial charges, and, through the benevolence of Corporation, those in goal for small debts; there was not a heart that did not beat with joy throughout the whole town, nay island, as there was not a parish or place in which the poor were not relieved in some way or other. On the 26th Sir H. Worsley Holmes entertained the Corporation of Newport, and a select party of friends at dinner, and in the evening there was a ball at the Sun Inn, which was attended by all the beauty and fashion in the Island.

CELEBRATION OF THE JUBILEE AT THE ARMY DEPOT.—Early in the morning divine service was performed, and suitable discourse delivered by the Rev. Mr. Sneyd, Chaplain of the Garrison, on the quarter deck of the prison ship in Cowes Harbour, to the persons on board, including such of the prisoners whose offences could not admit of their receiving his Majesty's pardon. The impressive manner in which those unfortunate men were addressed, on this more than interesting occasion, had an evident effect on the minds of even the most hardened offenders; and there can be little doubt but a discourse so applicable in all its bearings to the individuals to whom it was directed, will be the means of converting many of them, so as to make them good soldiers, as well as good subjects, when they join the respective stations at which, in consequence of their former irregularities, they have been destined to serve. At half past eleven, the whole of the garrison at Parkhurst Barracks was drawn out on the parade, and formed into a square, where the General in person, the Officers of the Staff, Military, Medical, and Civil, in their full uniforms, and all the attached Officers belonging to the Depot, attended and heard divine service read by the Garrison Chaplain; who afterwards delivered to them one of the most able discourses that perhaps, ever was addressed to a military congregation. After divine service, the usual compliments being paid by the Officers to their Generals, a *feu de joie* adapted to the occasion, was fired throughout the whole line, the band immediately playing "God save the King;" and the ceremony was concluded by three cheers from the Officers and men, the General taking the lead. These cheers were given in a manner that showed they came from the heart, and were strongly indicative of that respect, affection, and loyalty towards the best of Sovereigns, and that regard for the most inestimable of Constitutions, which it is hoped will ever prevade the British Army. Each soldier, as well as each prisoner at the Ship, received one day's pay in advance; and each soldier's wife had one shilling, and each child six-pence, from a particular fund; out of which a suitable dinner was provided for the occasion, which was conducted with a propriety and decorum that did credit to the establishment. The General, and all the Staff Officers, afterwards dined with Lord Fitzharris and the Gentlemen of the Island, at the Sun Inn, Newport, where the utmost cordiality, and the most unbounded and repeated tests of loyalty and thankfulness for the occasion, distinguished the day; and in the evening the whole of the Barracks at Parkhurst, covering an eminence (as it is well known) a most extensive space of ground, was brilliantly illuminated, so as to be observable from most parts of the Island; while the Staff Officers residing at Newport, vied with each other which could present the most conspicuous testimony of their sense of the occasion.

STEPEHILL—The Right Hon. Earl of Dysart being at his Cottage, Steephill, on the day of the Jubilee, it was celebrated with every demonstration of joy. His Lordship, with his usual beneficence, treated his labourers and dependents with a sumptuous dinner; and to every poor family in the parishes of St. Lawrence and Steephill, was given twelve shillings. The same patriotic loyalty was shown by the Noble Earl, at his Seat, Ham House, in Surrey, where a most excellent dinner was given in his Lordship's magnificent avenue, and a liberal donation of £30 to the subscription for the poor.

———o———

HEREFORDSHIRE.

HEREFORD.—The celebration of the day, sacred to loyalty, was observed in this city with every demonstration of joy and attachment to our venerable Sovereign. At an early hour the bells rang a merry peal, and preparation was every where busy. The Mayor and Corporate Body, the Staffs of the three regiments of Local Militia, with Colonel Matthews and the officers of the different regiments, and Captain Parry's troop of Yeomanry, assembled, and, preceded by the trading companies, with their flags, the band, drums and fifes of the military, went in procession to the Cathedral, where a most excellent sermon was delivered by the Rev. Dr. Cope, one of the Canons Residentiary; the whole again formed after Church, and proceeded to the Castle Green, where three volleys were fired by the staff of the 1st Regiment of Local Militia; after which the procession moved to the Town Hall, when the officers and a large number of gentlemen, with the Reverend Bishop, were regaled by the Mayor with cake and wine, and his Majesty's health drank. A public dinner was afterwards served up at a room belonging to the Corporation, and formerly part of the New Inn, to a large party, amongst whom were the Right Rev. the Bishop of the Diocese, Col. Sir J. G. Cotterell, Bart., M.P., R. P. Scudamore, Esq., M.P., Colonel Matthews, a great number of the gentlemen of the city and neighbourhood, and most of the officers of the regiments of Local Militia.—In the evening a Ball took place at the Hotel, which was numerously attended, and the festive dance did not cease till nearly five o'clock the next morning. The overplus, arising from the sale of tickets, after deducting the expenses of the music, amounted to £31 10s. 9d., which was distributed amongst the poor of the city. The Cavalry dined together at the Royal Oak. At the Green Dragon 233 poor aged men and women were regaled with a plentiful dinner, and their venerable and happy appearance highly gratified a large number of gentlemen and ladies who went to witness their repast.

ALLENSMOOR.—Edmund Pateshall, Esq., distributed mutton, bread, potatoes, and old cider, to about 300 of the neighbouring poor, assembled in his lawn at Allensmoor.

ALMELEY.—The Hon. A. Foley distributed ten guineas to the poor of the parish.

BROCKHAMPTON.—The seat of J. Barneby, Esq., exhibited a most agreeable mixture of benevolence and loyalty; in the morning, 24 poor children, who are clothed and instructed at Mrs. B.'s own expense, had an entertainment provided for them; in the afternoon Mr. B.'s numerous labourers, and the surrounding poor, were regaled with soup, beef, and beer, added to which, each woman received a loaf at her departure.

FOWNHOPE.—After a very impressive discourse from the Rev. J. W. Phillips, a collection was made in the church, amounting to £17 19s. 1½d., and immediately distributed to the poor.

GARNONS.—A splendid feast was given in celebration of the day, at Garnons, the seat of Sir J. G. Cotterell, Bart., one of the Members for this County, to several thousands of the neighbouring peasantry. At five o'clock on the preceding evening, a large ox was set down to roast, in a temporary building erected for the purpose, with more than a bushel of potatoes in his belly, which being ready by one o'clock on Wednesday, was distributed, with great quantities of plum pudding, many other smaller articles of provisions, and five hogsheads of cider, among the crowd who assembled to partake of the bountiful and hospitable fare on the lawn, in front of the Mansion House; every room of which was at the same time full of guests, consisting of the principal tenantry and farmers of the neighbourhood, and their families; here the lively dance was kept up with great spirit. A tar-barrel, mounted on a May-pole, was set on fire, and the house brilliantly illuminated, and it was with reluctance the company separated at a late hour, most highly gratified with the obliging attentions and unbounded hospitality of their kind host and hostess, and their amiable family.

HINTON ST. GEORGE.—Earl Poulett gave a fine ox and eight sheep, with 150 loaves of bread, to the poor in the village, and each received an allowance of 6lb. of meat, a loaf, 60lb. of potatoes, and a gallon of cider.

KINGTON.—The morning was ushered in by the ringing of the Church bells; nearly 300 poor persons assembled at the Market-House, where they each received 3lbs. of beef, a quartern loaf, and 4 lbs. of cheese, which were distributed to them before breakfast; they proceeded in a body to the Church, and in the evening were each regaled with a pint of beer. An elegant entertainment, with wines of the first quality, was provided at the Oxford Arms, where a very numerous company sat down to dinner about five o'clock; Dr. Thomas presided in the chair, who gave, "The King, God bless him, and long may he reign over a free and united people!" which was drank with three times three, amidst thunders of applause, that continued unabated for a considerable time: a great number of other loyal and constitutional toasts were drank, interspersed with many excellent songs. The harmony of the company was kept up with great conviviality till a late hour.

LANROTHAL.—Joseph Price, Esq., of Monmouth, assembled all the poor of the parish, with the workmen and their families employed on his farm, to attend divine worship. After the service was over, they repaired to the Parsonage House, where tables were laid for dinner. Nearly 120 persons, men, women, and children, were regaled with three sheep roasted, and potatoes, with copious libations of cider, in which beverage the health of the Sovereign was drank with such zeal, as made "the welkin resound." When the repast was finished, Mr. Price gave to each of the children a Bible, Prayer Book, Testament, Sellon's Abridgement of the Holy Scriptures, and Mrs. Trimmer's Sunday School Spelling book. Afterwards, every individual in each family had a quartern loaf to take with them to their respective homes.

LEDBURY.—The inhabitants welcomed the day with every sign of loyalty and joy. The morning was spent in rejoicing, and in the evening a very numerous meeting of the inhabitants and neighbourhood sat down to an elegant entertainment, at which the Rev. Dr. Yate presided; who, in addressing them, sketched the blessings we still enjoy contrasted with the rest of Europe, delineated the personal virtues of the Sovereign, and pointed out the necessity of unanimity at the present crisis.

LEOMINSTER.—The Jubilee was hailed with the ringing of bells, and other demonstrations of joy, and at eleven o'clock the Bailiff and Corporation, with the Officers and Staff of the North Herefordshire Local Militia, and a large assemblage of the inhabitants attended divine service, when a sermon was preached by the Rev. Jonathan Williams, A.M. A collection was afterwards made at the Church door, and a subscription, which amounted to upwards of £45 for the benefit of the poor, and at one o'clock the Staff of the Militia fired three volleys. At three o'clock, a numerous party partook of a sumptuous dinner at the Red Lion Inn, after which many loyal and patriotic toasts were drank. In the afternoon there was a ball at the King's Arms Inn, where all the beauty and fashion of the town attended. In the evening some beautiful transparencies were exhibited.

LETTON.—J. Freeman, Esq., gave money to 50 poor families in the parishes of Letton and Winforton, to the amount of one shilling for each individual in every family.

MUCH MARCLE.—Between £60 and £70 was raised by subscription. The morning was ushered in by the ringing of bells, and other demonstrations of joy. After the performance of the prayers ordered for the day, an appropriate and impressive sermon was delivered by the Rev. Kyrle Erule Money, to a very numerous congregation.

From Church all the poor of this large parish, amounting to many hundreds, retired to a neighbouring mole, or tump, and were plentifully fed with beef and cider, and music having been provided, danced with mirth and glee during the remainder of the day.

NORTON CANON.—Col. Whitney gave two sheep, and bread, with a hogshead of cider, to the poor of this place.

STOKE LACY.—The Rev. Dr. Lilly, of Stoke Lacy, distributed a quantity of beef, mutton, and a six-penny loaf each, to the poor in his parish.

ROSS.—A subscription produced nearly £40, for benevolent uses. Early in the morning the bells announced the approaching festival. The Children of the Charity Schools, after attending divine service, returned to their respective Schoolrooms, where they partook of a plentiful dinner of roast beef and plum-pudding. The inmates of the several Hospitals, after attendance at Church, were presented with a pecuniary donation; and the poor of the workhouse were supplied with a comfortable dinner and good ale. The overplus subscription monies were set apart, as the basis of a fund for the purchase of coals, to be sold to the poor at reduced prices during the following winter.

WEOBLEY.—The day was kept in the most joyous manner, and upwards of 150 poor people were treated, by a general subscription, with an excellent dinner of roast beef and plum-pudding; and a proportionate quantity of ale.

———o———

HERTFORDSHIRE.

HERTFORD.—The celebration commenced by merry peals on the bells of All Saints and St. Andrew's Churches. A large and respectable meeting of the Mayor, Corporation, and Inhabitants, took place at the Town-hall, at ten o'clock, when a dutiful and loyal address was unanimously voted. A more numerous congregation than was ever before known, attended divine service in All Saints' Church, where, in addition to the service of the day, were admirably performed on the fine toned organ the Coronation Anthem, and Handel's Hallelujah Chorus, and a very appropriate and impressive sermon was preached by the Rev. M. H. Luscombe, A.M., Head Master of the East India School in the town. A large party dined together at the Town-hall, in which numerous loyal songs were sung, accompanied with many well selected pieces of music by an excellent band. A very large subscription was made, from which nearly 200 poor persons received liberal donations to enable them to join in the festivity of the day, and a surplus of £200, remained for their relief during the winter.

BERKHAMSTEAD.—At eleven o'clock the Church was filled where, after the usual prayers, an excellent and appropriate sermon was preached by the Rev. William Brutton Wroth; after which "God save the King" was sung in full chorus by the whole congregation. Divine service being over, the poorer inhabitants, to the number of about 1500, were regaled with old English fare: the tables reached from the Church to the upper end of the town. How heartfelt must have been the gratification of the noble donors upon seeing so many of their fellow creatures made happy by their generosity, and who might truly be said to sing, with hearts and voices, "God save the King," in universal chorus. The bells were ringing all day, and minute guns were fired from the steeple of the Church. The evening was concluded with a ball for the trades-people.

CHESHUNT.—The morning was ushered in by ringing of bells. Sir A. Hume's Corps of Volunteer Cavalry, commanded by Captain Ludlow, attended divine service, their standard was raised behind the pulpit, supported by Mr. Tassau; there was not a vacant seat in the Church, and numbers crowded the windows from without, who could not gain admittance. The organ opened the service with appropriate music. Psalms, adapted to the occasion, were sung at the proper intervals, and at the close of the sermon, "God save the King," was sung in full chorus.—The service ended, the Rev. W. A. Armstrong, and O. Cromwell and T. Wakefield, Esqrs., distributed alms by subscription to 2200 poor people, who received them with thankful decency, and good order. The overplus was agreed to be paid to the Treasurer of a Charity, established in the parish for the relief of Lying in Women.

RICKMANSWORTH.—A subscription was set on foot, and a large sum raised and distributed in various ways, suitable to the objects of charity, even to those not parishioners resident therein; so that every inhabitant, by an ample allowance of from 2s. 6d. to 10s. in proportion to the number of children, had reason to remember the Jubilee, and to thank God for having preserved so good a King to so late a period, living in the hearts of subjects, over whom he has the happiness to reign. Besides which, every Gentleman Farmer and Tradesman, from the highest to the lowest in circumstances, provided a most substantial repast for their servants of all descriptions. After a numerous attendance at divine worship, the whole parish evinced one animated scene of the most rational enjoyment of unalloyed festivity. The Lord of the Manor's house, (H. F. Whitfield, Esq.), was crowded with visitors of the first respectability; and before his hospitable mansion 100 children partook of a plentiful repast of the most excellent plum-pudding. In the evening there was a brilliant display of fireworks.

ST. ALBANS.—The early ringing of bells announced the auspicious day. After attending divine service, the several parishes in the town distributed bread and meat, in very ample portions, to the poor inhabitants; and having thus gladdened the hearts of the more necessitous, the Mayor, accompanied by the Members for the County and Borough, with nearly 120 of the inhabitants and neighbouring Gentlemen, sat down to an excellent dinner at the Town Hall, where the utmost loyalty, conviviality and harmony, reigned throughout the day. This was succeeded by a ball and supper on the 27th, under the patronage of the Mayor, the profits of which were avowedly to be distributed among the industrious poor of the town; and on no occasion was the hall ever graced with so much beauty and fashion as the present. At twelve o'clock nearly 260 sat down to an elegant supper. After the expenses of the evening were deducted, there remained an overplus of nearly £100, for the poor.

———o———

HUNTINGDONSHIRE.

HUNTINGDONSHIRE.—The day was ushered in with ringing of bells, and a display of flags on the Town Hall and other conspicuous places. An Address to his Majesty was unanimously agreed to. After divine service the Corporation, with a numerous company of gentlemen, partook of an elegant dinner, at the Fountain Inn, and the day was passed in the greatest festivity. In the evening bonfires and fire-works were exhibited, and the whole passed off with the greatest harmony. The poorer classes participated in the general joy, by means of a subscription, amounting to upwards of £270. Each family was allowed a pound of mutton and a half-quartern loaf per head, and a pint of ale for each above the age of twelve, together with a peck of potatoes, a bushel of coals, and a shilling. Half a crown was also given to each journeyman and apprentice in the town who chose to accept it. In short, all were happy.

ST. IVES.—The morning was ushered in by the firing of guns and ringing of the church bells. At ten o'clock the whole population of the town assembled in the following order:—The subscribers to the donation for the poor, in the corn market, each holding a wand of distinction—on their right the poor men, women, and children of the town and different schools, attended by their instructors. The British union flag was elevated at each end of the line; opposite the centre, from the church warden's window, was suspended a blue flag, on which was written in 'large gold letters, on one side, " Fear God, Honour the King;" on the reverse, " St. Ives Jubilee, 25th Oct., 1809. Vivat Rex,"—facing which was a band of music. Part of the royal regiment of North Lincoln Militia drew up on the left of the colours. The ceremony commenced by the vicar, the Rev. Mr. Baines, lowering the colour into the hands of Taylor White, Esq., who elevating it, spoke as follows:—" We receive this flag as a token of our loyalty and attachment to our most gracious Sovereign King George the Third, and as a pledge of our unanimity in celebrating this grand national Jubilee; God save the King." The band immediately struck up that popular air, amidst the earnest, fervent, and joyful shouts of the whole assemblage, who proceeded to church in orderly and solemn procession, the band playing the 104th Psalm. A very animated and loyal discourse was delivered by the vicar, whose text was the 21st verse of the 24th chapter of Proverbs. After service the procession returned, preceded by the military, in the order they went to church, the band playing alternately "God save the King," and "Rule Britannia." After parading the town, they drew up fronting the Crown Inn, where they delivered their colours with three cheers, and dispersed in the highest spirits, the poor (resident as well as strangers), to the enjoyment of the festivity afforded them by the distribution of meat, bread, and beer; half an hour after, the military fired a *feu de joie.* The principal inhabitants dined together at the Crown Inn.

---o---

KENT.

MAIDSTONE.—On the 24th, there was a ball, very fully attended, at the Court Hall, and a distribution of one shilling to each person (from a subscription), to 5,900 men, women, and children. And on the 25th, the poor of the Workhouse were regaled with roast beef, plum-pudding, and ale, and money was given them in addition.—A distribution was also made from the subscription, to the prisoners in the County Gaols and Bridewell. At eight o'clock in the morning, the commencement of the Jubilee was announced by six trumpeters from the Cavalry Depot, at twenty five different parts of the town, headed by 100 Charity boys, with white wands,—by a merry peal of bells, a discharge of cannon, and the Royal Standard and other colours hoisted on the Church and Town Hall. At eleven the Corporation and inhabitants, preceded by a band of music, went in procession to Church, where an excellent and appropriate discourse from the 7th verse of the 21st Psalm, was delivered by the Rev. James Reeve. After divine service, the Military of the Garrison fired a *feu de joie* in the High-street. At three o'clock upwards of 100 of the principal inhabitants (the Mayor in the chair) partook of an elegant dinner in the Town Hall. Captain Turner and his troop of cavalry dined at the Star Inn, and other loyal parties dined at the Haunch of Venison, the Turk's Head, and Castle, and in the evening there was a display of fireworks.

ASHFORD.—A general subscription was entered into by the inhabitants, for the purpose of enabling the poor to celebrate so joyous a day. Upwards of £70 was gathered and laid out in the following manner; one pound of beef, one gallon of potatoes, and one half-quartern loaf, to 800 men, women, and children; besides, a plentiful supply of roast beef, plum-pudding, and beer, was given to every man, woman, and child, in the poor house. At day-break the event was announced by a peal from the bells, which continued with very little intermission the whole day. In the forenoon the inhabitants were particularly forward in testifing their loyalty and attachment to our beloved Sovereign, by assembling in great numbers at the church, where an excellent sermon was delivered by the Rev. J. Nance, A.M., from the 25th chapter of Leviticus, verses 9 and 10. In the afternoon a large party of gentlemen sat down to dinner at the Saracen's Head Inn, R. G. De Lasaux presided ; many appropriate songs and toasts were given, and the greatest mirth and harmony prevailed during the evening. The ball was very numerously attended by all the neighbouring gentry, and kept up till a very late hour.

BROADSTAIRS.—A dinner of roast beef, plum pudding, &c., was provided for the poor at Broadstairs, on a lawn near Muckle's Library, when about 350 partook of this excellent repast, with punch, beer, &c.

At Beduin, Burbage, Collingbourn, Preshute, Raston, Milton, Mildenhall, and other neighbouring places, the opulent inhabitants distinguished themselves equally for their loyalty and generosity, by ample voluntary gifts to their poor neighbours.

CANTERBURY.—At eight o'clock in the morning, a royal salute of 21 rounds of artillery from an eminence in the North Holmes proclaimed the event ; this was followed by the bells of the Cathedral, and other Churches ; at the same moment the bands and trumpets of the Cavalry and other regiments struck up the grand national air of "God save the King," and afterwards paraded the streets playing that, and other national airs, till the hour of divine service. The shops were closed, and the attendance at the Churches was general and spontaneous. The Mayor and Corporation were present at the Cathedral, where an excellent and appropriate discourse was delivered by the Hon. and Rev. H. Hobart, the Vice Dean. At noon the Garrison, with the Yeomanry and Volunteers, were assembled in the Barrack Yard of the Royal Cavalry Barrack, and formed in a hollow square, from right to left, the whole under the command of Lieut.-Gen. Nicoll. At one, while the roar of the guns from the shipping at the Nore and in the Downs, yet vibrated on the ear, a salute of 50 rounds (6-pounders) commenced, and was followed at intervals by an excellent *feu de joie* from the line. The whole closed with three huzzas from the troops and spectators, and accompanied by the respective bands, playing "God save the King." The troops then broke into open column, and passed the General in review order, after which the line was again formed, and the compliment of saluting the General followed, when the troops retired to their respective parades:—previously, however, to this, a ceremony to which the day gave birth, took place ; four deserters were brought into the centre of the square, and informed by the General, that in consequence of the event, their crimes were forgiven, and, he trusted, that this gracious act of Royal mercy would operate so as to induce them to amend their lives in future. At three o'clock in the afternoon, a large portion of the inhabitants met the Mayor at the Guildhall Tavern, to partake of a dinner, at which were also present the Representatives of the City, with many of the neighbouring gentry. The afternoon was passed with that loyalty and harmony such a moment and such an event could not fail to inspire ; and amidst a number of toasts and healths, those of the individuals to whom the city of Canterbury was indebted were not forgotten, and pre-eminently in this place stood that of Richard Milles, Esq., who had for many years ably and honourably represented the city in Parliament, and who also, to use his own words, had the honour to represent it at the time of his Majesty's Accession to the Throne. From the dinner table many of the company adjourned to the Catch Club, where the heartfelt joy of the day was powerfully excited by the exertions of the performers, and particularly by the manner in which the Coronation Anthem was executed. The gaieties of the day concluded by a splendid ball and supper, and it was nearly five o'clock on Thursday morning, before the company separated. The circumstances above told are, however, but a part of the mode of commemorating this eventful day, the completion of the whole was that of hospitality and benevolence. By the princely donations of the Archbishop, the Dean and Chapter, the Mayor and Commonalty, of £50 each : together with twenty guineas by the Representatives of the City, and the liberal subscriptions of the inhabitants, the sum of £666 17s. 6d. was raised and distributed amongst 6300 men, women, and children. Thus ended in Canterbury, a day, which will long be remembered with delight, by the present and succeeding generations. It was a day when every heart was glad, every eye glistened, and every countenance smiled ; for it was a day, when every one had bread on his table, and meat in his pot. It need scarcely be added, that it was a day of universal joy and gratification.

COMBANK.—The Jubilee was celebrated in a way that strongly marked the loyal feelings of its noble possessor, Lord Frederic Campbell. The work-people on his Lordship's estate, consisting of nearly 50, had a comfortable breakfast provided for them, and received a donation of money. After divine service, which was numerously attended, some guns, placed upon a commanding situation, fired fifty rounds. The inhabitants of the parish, amounting to 129 families, then proceeded to Combank, where two oxen had been prepared, and each of them received a piece of beef, proportionate to the size of the family, 5s., and beer to drink the King's health. After expressing the warmest gratitude to their noble benefactor, and giving three hearty huzzas in honour of the day, they returned to their homes. During the morning Lord Frederic Campbell sowed fifty acorns, to commemorate the day and gave directions for their future management. At an early hour in the evening, the children and grand-children of the domestics were indulged with a dance, and when the infantine party had retired to rest, the servants continued the same merry pastime till a late hour. All the boys of the Free School received a shilling each ; and the younger children of the other schools, Jubilee medals and money. Thus, by the sole munificence of this loyal and venerable Nobleman, every inhabitant of the parish of Sunbridge was made happy; and at his request the liberal contributions of the Rev. Dr. Vyse, and Mrs. Porteus, were reserved for the ensuing winter, when Lord F. Campbell declared his intention to make a sufficient addition to it, to furnish the poor with a portion of fuel, and other comforts.

DEAL.—The day of the Jubilee was observed by all the ships in the Downs being dressed out with their colours; the two flagships fired 50 rounds each, and the others a royal salute. The two companies of Bombardiers, under the command of Capts. Underwood and Darby, attended divine service in the morning, and in the evening were regaled with a butt of strong beer, and bread and cheese. The evening passed with many loyal and appropriate toasts, to the satisfaction of a numerous set of spectators.

DOVER.—At sun-rise, 50 pieces of cannon were fired from the different batteries; and at one o'clock a royal salute from the same. The troops of the Garrison were drawn out in line on the beach, and fired a *feu de joie*. In the evening there was a ball in the Assembly Rooms, which had been fitted up in a very tasteful manner, with laurel, variegated lamps, banners, transparencies, &c., and the floor painted. Bread, meat, and beer, in profusion, were distributed to every poor person in the town, a subscription to a large amount having been raised for that purpose. The poor in the different parish houses, were regaled with plenty of roast beef, plum pudding, beer, &c. The benefit arising from the Dover Jubilee Ball, applicable as intended to charitable purposes, was £72 6s. 6d., which, by general consent of the company, was appropriated in equal moieties, viz. one half to the fund for the relief of the wives, widows, or orphans of soldiers within the Dover division of the district; and the other half to a Jubilee Fund, established for the relief of prisoners of war, now in detention and in need, or that may hereafter be taken, belonging to the town or its immediate neighbourhood.

ELTHAM.—Sir Richard Welch, in commemoration of the day, regaled the poor of Eltham, with the old English fare of roast beef, &c., sparing no expense to make them comfortable, and at the same time entertaining a select company of his friends, residing in the neighbourhood, with the greatest hospitality.

FEVERSHAM.—The morning was ushered in by the Church bells, which continued to ring during the whole day with little intermission. In the forenoon Henry Wright, Esq., Mayor, and the rest of the Corporate Body, went in procession to Church, preceded by the children of the Charity and Sunday Schools. Divine service was performed by the Rev. Joshua Dix to more than 2,000 persons; the military of the Garrison at Ospringe Barracks, attended by all their Officers, making a part of the audience. The text was from the introductory sentence of the service for the day. After service the troops of the Ospringe Garrison were drawn up in Court-street, and fired a *feu de joie* with great precision. A company to the amount of nearly 150 persons, including therein, in addition to the inhabitants, many of the garrison, and a large portion of the neighbouring gentry, sat down in the Assembly Room, to dinner provided from the Ship Inn.

FORDWICH.—Anthony Jennings, Esq., Mayor of Fordwich, liberally supplied 20 poor families in that, and the neighbouring parish of Sturry, with beef, and money for bread and beer, to enable them cheerfully to commemorate the day.

GREENWICH HOSPITAL.—The Anniversary of the 50th year of his Majesty's Reign was celebrated at the Royal Hospital for Seamen, at Greenwich, in a manner worthy of that noble Institution. In the forenoon, the Naval Officers, Pensioners and Charity Boys, the sons of seamen, went in procession to the Chapel, where divine service was performed by the Chaplains, after which the whole proceeded to the Painted Hall, where his Majesty's health was drank, and cheered with loud huzzas, from an immense concourse of people. At four o'clock the whole of the Civil and Military Officers of the Hospital, and their families (amounting to 120 persons) sat down to dinner in the upper part of the Painted Hall. After dinner his Majesty's health was drank with enthusiasm, when the bands played the loyal and popular air of "God save the King," and a salute of 50 guns was fired by the Loyal Water Fencibles, from pieces planted on the terrace of the Hospital for that purpose. Several other loyal toasts were drank. At an early hour the company withdrew to the Council Room, and the evening was spent in dancing, &c. The Pensioners were regaled, and their wives and children partook of the provisions, &c., distributed in the parish; the several Officers of the Hospital having subscribed thereto, in common with the parishioners. The east front in King Charles's building, west front of Queen Ann's, the north returns of the Colonades, and the east and west gates of the Hospital, were brilliantly illuminated with variegated lamps, disposed in festoons, crowns, anchors and other emblematical devices. The Hospital was crowded with spectators, and the whole passed off, without the slightest accident, or confusion.

The town of GREENWICH, which has ever been amongst the foremost in demonstrations of its loyalty and attachment to the mildest and most virtuous Sovereign that ever swayed a sceptre, was not deficient on the present occasion. A meeting of the parishioners was called, to determine in what manner they could best celebrate and perpetuate the memory of an event so truly estimable to every Briton; when it was resolved that a collection should be made throughout the parish, to supply the resident poor with bread, meat, potatoes, porter and coals, that they might participate in the general festivities of the Jubilee; and that if a sufficient sum should remain after defraying the expenses of the supply, it should be laid out in erecting Alms Houses for the benefit of poor and aged widows of that parish. A committee was accordingly appointed to carry these resolutions into effect. The sum of £950 was raised by subscription, and the sale of the excellent Sermon preached by the Rev. Mr. Mathew, on the Jubilee day, from Leviticus, chap. 25, verse 10, which he allowed to be printed in aid of those charitable purposes; of which sum £606 16s. 8d., were expended 'in supplying 7027 persons with 1 lb. of bread, 1 lb. of meat, 1 lb. of potatoes, and one peck of coals each; and one quart of porter for every adult, and one pint for every child: the remaining sum, together with what may be still expected, was directed to be disposed of in building four Alms Houses, on a spot of ground belonging to the parish, situated on the south side of the road, leading to Deptford, and near the west end of Queen Elizabeth's Row; the foundation of which was laid the 29th day of December, 1809. In the centre of the Building, is a Stone Tablet, with an inscription, expressive of the occasion, which gave rise to the Establishment.

HYTHE.—The celebration of the Jubilee at this place, was distinguished by the liveliest demonstrations of benevolence and loyalty, a liberal subscription was entered into, for the relief of indigent persons. The number of those whose hearts were gladdened on this occasion with meat, bread, and beer, was upwards of 700 persons. The Mayor and inhabitants dined together at the Guildhall, which was brilliantly illuminated with coloured lamps, and an elegant transparency.

LEIGH.—The Rev. I. Southan, Vicar of Leigh, near Tunbridge, gave two fat bullocks, and 100 gallons of ale, among the poor in his parish, allowing to each in family, 1 lb. of meat, and a pot of ale, the widows to have a double portion.

LITTLEBOURN.—The day was spent in this parish, with the utmost harmony and conviviality. Divine service being over, the inhabitants met at the Anchor, where a dinner was provided for the occasion; after which "The King," was drank, and three times three succeeded. Every individual in the parish partook (by subscription) bountifully of strong beer.

MARGATE.—The Anniversary of his Majesty's Accession was observed with the greatest loyalty and decorum at this place. The morning was ushered in with ringing of bells, and the display of colours from the vessels and principal buildings: among which, two beautiful silk ones graced the turrets of Messrs. T. Cobb's extensive and lofty brewery. The shops were shut, and divine service performed at the different places of worship. The Rev. Sir John Fagg, Rector of Chartham, preached a most loyal and appropriate sermon at St. John's Church, and a collection was made at the doors for the poor, amounting to £40. Collections also for the same purpose were made at the different Chapels; and more than £200 was collected. A royal salute was fired from the pier at one o'clock; and immediately after Church, the eighty children belonging to the Margate Charity School sat down to a dinner provided for them, by subscription, at the Shakspeare Hotel. In the evening there were subscription balls at Kidman's, the Duke's Head, &c.

MEREWORTH.—Lord Le Despencer gave to the poor of Mereworth, two oxen, with bread, and beer in proportion.

THE NORE.—His Majesty's ships at the Nore distinguished themselves by every mark of loyalty. Double allowance was ordered to the men, by the Admiral commanding there. The Heroine fired fifty guns. The royal salute was fired by all the rest of the ships at the Nore, as usual. Their colours were handsomely displayed throughout the day. The Nymphen, Captain Morrill, in the harbour, formed all together an ark of triumph, so well was she decorated, and so ingeniously her flags disposed. When the evening gun fired, the Heroine frigate, commanded by Lieut. Thomas Hewes, returned it by firing of musketry, from divisions of marines. Blue lights at the moment burned at each mast head, and some beautiful rockets sent at the same time into the air, just cleared the smoke, to show an illumination on board the Heroine, by lamps from the bowsprit, and to that of the spanker boom, with all her yard arms and mast heads displaying lights, forming a brilliant sight. All the rest of the ships exhibited splendid fire-works. A large French rocket, taken at Bathz, was thrown at nine o'clock into the air, and added much to the brilliancy of the scene.

RAMSGATE.—The morning was ushered in by the ringing of bells at the parish Church of St. Lawrence, and colours were hoisted by all the ships and vessels in the harbour. The corps of Bombardiers, belonging to the works of the Pier, assembled at ten o'clock, and marched to Church, followed by all the artificers and labourers, in their best and cleanest attire. The inhabitants, and visitors for the most part likewise attended, some the parish Church, others the Chapel, where an excellent sermon was preached by the Rev. Mr. Harvey. A very large collection was made at the doors, for the benefit of the Charity Children, who were neatly dressed on the occasion; and each child presented, by Lady Curtis, with a handsome medal, hung round the neck, by a purple ribbon. At one o'clock, most of the inhabitants and visitors repaired to the beautiful pier, from which they observed and heard the grand salutes from his Majesty's ships in the Downs, and from the several batteries on the coast, and last of all with 50 rounds from the great guns on the pier. The children immediately repaired to the Hall over the Market-place, where tables were spread with roast beef and plum-puddings; each child had afterwards a glass of wine, to drink his Majesty's health; then followed the Pier men, artificers, and labourers, with their wives and children, to a like entertainment, at the King's Head; and by a liberal subscription entered into by the inhabitants and visitors, every poor inhabitant, with his wife and children, had a large allowance of roast beef and plum-pudding, with a sufficient quantity of their natural beverage, strong beer. Much credit is due to Mr. Saunders, the Apothecary, for his great kindness on the occasion. In the evening, the loyal and truly worthy Baronet, Sir W. Curtis, sent down a handsome display of fireworks, which were let off to great advantage at the Pier head, and perfectly to be observed by the surrounding neighbourhood. An elegant ball and supper at the Hotel, closed the festivities of this memorable day, which was one of conviviality and happiness to all ranks of society. In short, there appeared to be but one heart and voice, and those raised to express "God save the King."

RIVER.—The poor in the united parishes in River House, near Dover, consisting of 160 persons, were entertained at dinner with roast beef, plum-pudding, &c. Each man had an allowance of one quart of strong beer, and each woman a pint. The women and children were also served in the afternoon with tea, cream, and cakes. Three hundred poor persons in the parish of River, and 100 persons in the parish of Ewel, were also served with 1 lb. of meat, one pint of beer, and a three-penny loaf each, on this joyful occasion.

SEAL.—At Seal, Lord Camden caused to be distributed to the poor a bullock, with a quantity of bread, and four hogsheads of beer.

SEVENOAKS.—A very large subscription was raised, with which all the poor inhabitants were supplied with beef and bread, after which the Gentlemen of the town and neighbourhood dined together, and passed the day in the greatest harmony.

SITTINGBOURN.—The morning was announced by the ringing of bells. A sermon was preached by the Rev. Thomas Pearce; after divine service, the anthem of "God save the King," was sung by the congregation. The Gentlemen of the town gave a dinner, to upwards of 500 men, women, and children. After the poor were plentifully regaled, the gentlemen dined at the Inn, and closed the happy day with bonfires, and every demonstration of joy.

STAPLEHURST.—The dawn was ushered in by the ringing of bells, and at an early hour, a Committee, appointed to distribute the subscription, divided to the poor families according to their numbers, nearly 600 lb. of fat beef, 300 half-quartern loaves of the best bread, and upwards of 450 pints of what used to be styled an Englishman's native beverage, good strong beer. At eleven o'clock divine service commenced, and an impressive discourse was delivered by the Rev. Thomas Morgan, Chaplain to Lord Hawarden; in the appropriate service of the choir, in Psalms and Anthems of thanksgiving and praise, the national Anthem of "God save great George our King," was sung in full chorus, accompanied by the band. The principal inhabitants assembled at the King's Head Inn, and partook of a dinner in the old English style, consisting of smoking sirloins and plum-puddings, rare British cheer. The glass went jovially round many loyal and constitutional toasts were drank with three times three; several national songs were sung; and after paying the devoirs at the shrine of the rosy god, the company adjourned to a display of fire-works, presented on the occasion by T. Watson, Esq.

ST. PETERS AND BROADSTAIRS.—The inhabitants were not less wanting in their attachment and loyalty to their Sovereign, than the neighbouring parishes; a liberal subscription was opened at Nuckle's and Barfield's Libraries, patronised by Lady Wellington, and several Gentlemen visitors at Broadstairs, to provide a dinner for the poor inhabitants. A subscription was likewise opened at St. Peter's, which was also patronised by Lady Wellington, and liberally supported by the Gentlemen, and most of the principal inhabitants of St. Peter's and Broadstairs, the amount of which far exceeded their expectations.

TUNBRIDGE WELLS.—To the very poorest, the means were given, by a liberal distribution of meat, bread, &c., to take home and dispense the blessing to their families. The principal inhabitants met at the Tavern and dined together, where many loyal and patriotic toasts were given. A display of fire-works was exhibited in the evening; after which the fashionables of the place had a ball and supper at the Assembly Rooms.

WESTERHAM.—The birth place of the immortal Wolfe, 800 of the poor inhabitants, through the liberality and munificence of their more wealthy neighbours, after attending divine service, and hearing a most appropriate and impressive discourse delivered by the Rev. J. Cookesley, from Tim. ii. v. 1, 2, were plentifully supplied with bread and beef, and received six-pence each, to drink his Majesty's health. The children of the Sunday School were also treated, on their return from Church, with bread, cheese and ale, and the poor in the Workhouse were likewise regaled with roast beef, plum-pudding, and porter.

WOOLWICH.—The Jubilee was celebrated by the Royal Artillery, with every characteristic mark of loyalty. The day was ushered in by a discharge of fifty heavy guns, when the Royal Standard was hoisted. The Garrison attended divine service, when the Coronation Anthem was sung by the band of the regiment, with very fine effect. After the Chaplain had read the blessing, "God save the King," was sung in full chorus. At one o'clock, the whole of the troops were under arms, amounting to about 2500 men; a salute of fifty guns was fired from the front, the line presenting arms, and afterwards giving three cheers, the whole marched past the Commandant. The Officers dined together. The time of drinking his Majesty's health was noticed by another salute of fifty guns, and by the discharge of an immense number of very fine rockets sent up into the air by fifties, which had a happy and pleasing effect; the day went off with that harmony and conviviality with which such a remarkable epoch should be celebrated. A liberal subscription was entered into by the Officers, for the relief of the widows, wives, and families of soldiers belonging to the corps, to which Lord Eardley, in his usual kind and benevolent manner, added 100 guineas. A ball was given the following evening, by the Officers to the families in the neighbourhood. All the ladies of the corps wore an elegant scarf, with "Long live the King" in gold or silver embroidery.

YALDING.—The morning was ushered in by the ringing of bells, and a band of music playing "God save the King," and other appropriate pieces. The children belonging to Mr. Williams' School, consisting of about eighty boys, decorated with flowers, &c., at ten o'clock walked in procession to the Church. The first couple of boys carrying in their hands the following words, inscribed in Roman capitals, upon large imperial paper, supported by slender sticks.—1st Couple, *Our Laws are supported.*—4th ditto, *Our Religion is cherished.*—8th ditto, *Our lives are protected.*—12th ditto, *Our children are educated.*—16th ditto, *Our land yieldeth its increase.*—20th ditto, *The hungry are fed.*—24th ditto, *The naked are clothed.*—28th ditto, *The poor have the Gospel preached to them.*—32nd ditto, elevated above the rest and much larger, *For these blessings let the Nation be thankful.*—40th ditto and last, very large, and the boys uncovered, *God save the King.* In this order, the band playing, they proceeded over the bridge to the room appropriated for teaching the children belonging to the Sunday School. There they were met by about eighty children belonging to that admirable institution, preceded by Mr. Thomas Weld, supporting a very large emblematical figure, drawn for the occasion, descriptive of Charity. These were joined by about thirty children belonging to the Poorhouse, and then all immediately moved onwards to the Church, where they heard a very appropriate sermon, by the Rev. Mr. Warde, from 29th chap. Proverbs, and former part of the 2d verse. After divine service, the children again walked in procession to the Sunday School room, where was provided an excellent dinner, consisting principally of roast beef, and plum-puddings.—They were waited upon at dinner by the ladies and gentlemen, who supported the institution. The joy and festivity of the day were supported till very late, and concluded with fire-works and several bonfires.

The following parishes, in this county, celebrated the Jubilee by liberal subscriptions, for the purpose of enabling the poor to enjoy a comfortable day of festivity, and was distributed in meat, beer, and coals, viz., Elnstone, Cranbrooke, Hawkhurst, Lomberhurst, Preston, Wingham, World, and Provender.

———o———

LANCASHIRE.

LANCASTER.—The day was ushered in by the ringing of bells, flags were hoisted on the Church steeples, different parts of the Castle, the Custom-house, and displayed in various parts of the town. The shops were generally shut up. The Corporation went in procession to St. Mary's Church, where an excellent sermon was preached by the Rev. J. Manby, A.M., the Vicar, from Psalm c. v. 3 and 4.—A collection was afterwards made in aid of the charitable fund, which amounted to upwards of £40. Sermons were preached and collections made at most of the other places of public worship in the town. Loyalty and charity were the order of the day. At one o'clock a royal salute was fired on the quay; at which time the committee commenced distributing one shilling each to 860 poor men and women.—There was a ball in the evening at the Assembly Room, and the dance was kept up till an early hour the next morning; the profits arising from which were applied in aid of the fund. His Grace the Duke of Hamilton and Brandon, with his usual liberality, sent thirty guineas to be added to the fund.—The girls of the Charity School, to the number of 48, were treated with tea, by the ladies of Miss Shaw's boarding school; and each of them received a bun and a thimble, and the most deserving received sixpence each.—Mr. Higgin received from Henry Sudell, Esq., of Woodfold Park, the sum of £100, for the debtors in Lancaster Castle, to celebrate his Majesty's enteriring into the 50th year of his reign. An excellent breakfast was provided for them, and, at one o'clock, they all, amounting to 106 persons, sat down to a most sumptuous dinner; an ox was killed for the occasion, and the day was spent with the greatest joy and harmony. Out of the above sum, two poor debtors were discharged, by compromising the debt with their plaintiffs, and restored to their wives and families; several others received different articles of clothing; ten tons of coals were also provided and distributed, and the next morning each person received five shillings.—There were many public dinners in honour of the occasion, where loyal and constitutional toasts were drank. A song written purposely by Mr. Gregson, was given in a capital style, in the Council Chamber at the Town Hall, which was rapturously applauded and encored. In the evening many transparencies were exhibited. A loyal and dutiful Address was voted to his Majesty.

ASHTON-UNDER-LYNE.—At eight o'clock the gentlemen of the town assembled in the Town Hall, when a loyal and affectionate Address was read, and unanimously agreed should be presented to his Majesty. At ten o'clock the Dunkinfield Rifle Corps, commanded by Francis Dunkinfield Astley, Esq., the Constables and Gentlemen of the town, the Lodge of Free Masons, the Orange Society, and part of the 1st regiment of Middleton Local Militia (those on permanent pay), walked in procession to hear divine service, when a most excellent sermon was preached by the Rev. Mr. Hutchinson. After service upwards of 500 poor families were relieved by a distribution of linen, blankets, &c., purchased by a subscription raised in the town, and aided liberally by the Earl of Stamford and Warrington.—At four o'clock about 60 gentlemen sat down to dinner at the Globe Tavern, and a number of appropriate toasts were given, the first of which was the "The King, and may the present Jubilee form a lasting impression on the hearts of his faithful subjects."—The evening was concluded with a ball, which was numerously attended. A true spirit of loyalty pervaded every heart, and the day was spent with the greatest harmony.

ARDWICK.—Messrs. Statham and Son regaled their workmen, one hundred and twenty in number, with plenty of roast beef, plum pudding, ale, and porter.—Messrs. Beswick and Holt feasted their workmen in a truly hospitable and liberal manner; as did also Messrs. Hoyle and Son, of Mayfield.—A lady and gentleman sent a fine leg of mutton and an eighteen penny loaf, to each of nineteen poor families, their tenants, at Garratt.

BOLTON.—Long famed for its loyalty and adherence to the royal cause, in the revolution in 1650, the ringing of bells, discharge of artillery, display of fire-works, public dinners, and other usual demonstrations of civic joy, were not the only testimones of the happiness of its inhabitants. The inhabitants of every rank and description, accompanied by the military then in the town, the masonic lodges, the orange society, the numerous bodies of both sexes and of every age employed in the cotton trade, and other branches of commerce, 40 surviving veterans of the 72nd regiment, companions in arms at the siege of Gibraltar, preceeded by their then Serjeant Bleakley, and the St. George's Sunday School children, amounting to 1100, went in procession, headed by the Boroughreeve, Constables, and other officers of the towns of Great and Little Bolton, to attend divine service. Roast beef, plum pudding, and ale, were afterwards distributed to many thousands of the labouring classes, by the truly patriotic spirit of their employers.

BROWSHOLME.—The seat of Thomas Lister Parker, Esq., the Jubilee was celebrated in the true spirit of ancient hospitality, by a dinner, consisting of a substantial display of roast and boiled beef, plum puddings, &c., &c., to a numerous and respectable tenantry. The health of "the best of Kings" was drank with loud acclamations and three cheers; many other loyal toasts were drank, and the company departed, much pleased with their entertainment. Donations were also given to the poor at Waddington and Whitewell Chapels.

BURY.—All the places of Religious Worship were open, to offer a tribute of thanksgiving to Heaven for its mercies on such a memorable day. The Orangemen marched in procession to St. John's Chapel, where the Rev. H. Unsworth preached an appropriate sermon. About two o'clock, the principal Gentlemen of Bury walked in order through the chief part of the town, accompanied with a band of music, playing "God save the King," to the Union Square, where was distributed about £70, value in ale. An immense multitude attended, and drank his Majesty's health.

CHORLEY.—The day was ushered in by the ringing of bells. All the manufacturing masters gave a treat to their work-people, and injunctions to attend divine service; **which** caused the Church to be more crowded than ever was known by the oldest person living. An **excellent sermon** was preached by the Rev. O. Cooper. There **was a** numerous meeting **at** the Royal Oak, of all the Gentlemen of the town and neighbourhood, Thomas Gillibrand, Esq., **in** the chair, when several loyal toasts were drank. **In** the evening, many of the neighbouring Gentlemen concluded **the festival with a** grand display of fire-works.

CHORLTON.—Mr. James Mason invited **all the poor of both** sexes, upwards of fifty years of age, to dine on **the good old English** fare **of roast** beef and plum-pudding, after divine service. **The sum** of the ages of nine of the youngest among **the** venerable group, amounted to 688. After dinner the young gentlemen **of** Bridge House Academy entertained the villagers with a concert of music, and the loyal airs of "God save the King," and "Rule Britannia." They then returned **to** Mr. Mason's, and were regaled with cakes, strong beer, &c., and the venerable guests passed the afternoon and evening, relating the occurences **of other** times with cheerfulness, comfort, harmony, and decorum. **At night Mr.** Mason gratified his guests and villagers with a grand display **of fire-works.**

DUKINFIELD.—The Rifle Corps **commanded by** F. D. Astley, Esq., were entertained at Dukinfield **Lodge with a** hot dinner, of which all Mr. Astley's workmen **partook.** Fifty poor families at the same time received a donation **of beef and potatoes, and** upwards of 200 colliers **had an** opportunity **of drinking his Majesty's** health. A ball and **fire-works** concluded the **happy day.**

ECCLES.—At ten o'clock on Tuesday night, **an ox** was put down to the **fire to roast,** with shouts from the populace, of "God save the King; **may he live** for ever." At twelve o'clock the Church bells began **to ring.** At half-past ten o'clock, on Wednesday, the Officers of the **Trafford** Local Militia, and the permanents of the regiments, assembled **on the** Green, and were afterwards joined by the Clergy, Church-wardens, principal inhabitants, and the poor from the Workhouse, who went in procession to the Church, where an excellent sermon was given on the occasion by the **Rev.** J. Clowes, **the Vicar.** Afterwards the military fired three excellent volleys. The **Gentlemen** then mounted a stage erected for the purpose, and cut up and distributed the ox to the **poor** inhabitants, with **a** quantity of bread and ale. The poor were **also** regaled with **a** good dinner and ale **in** the Workhouse. After **which** the Clergy and Gentry partook of an excellent dinner provided at the Grape **Inn.** At eight o'clock in the evening, **a grand display** of fire-works **was** exhibited, which ended **with a dance on the Green.**

GORTON.—**The** principal inhabitants assembled at the Sunday School, and went in procession, preceeded by a band of music, and the Sunday Scholars, to the Chapel, where a very animated discourse,

H

was delivered by the Rev. James Gatliff. The scholars **were afterwards** regaled by their worthy Master, Mr. Willan, with **roast beef,** &c., in the School-room.

HALLIWELL.—The workmen of Richard Ainsworth, Esq., to the number of about 500, at their own request, attended their truly patriotic master to Smithill's Chapel, where divine service was performed, and a sermon preached, by the Rev. A. Hadfield, A.M., which gave great satisfaction. After service they assembled in the Quadrangle of the Old Hall, and joined in singing "God save the King," with three times three. They then went to a field where they were to dine ; and were there addressed by Mr. Ainsworth, in very impressive and appropriate terms. They afterwards partook of a very plentiful dinner provided for them by Mr. Ainsworth ; and to the poor of the neighbourhood, who had been invited, soup, meat, and potatoes were distributed. They then voluntarily subscribed about £60, towards the erection and establishment of a Public School, for the benefit chiefly of the poor in the township of Halliwell, in com**memoration** of the Jubilee. The plan had been suggested by Mr. **Ainsworth,** who had previously subscribed, **with** his family, 100 **guineas ;** and most of the ladies and gentlemen **of** the township had given their subscriptions also for the same benevolent purpose. The **day** concluded much to the satisfaction of every one who was **present.**

LATHOM HOUSE.—On Tuesday, two large fat oxen were distributed by E. W. Bootle, Esq., M.P., of Lathom House, among the poor families in the neighbourhood, at the rate of 1 lb. per head, old **and** young. On Wednesday, a bonfire was made at his sole expense, the materials of which were **as** follows :—150 baskets of round coals, —150 ditto slack,—48 cart loads of gorse,—114 ditto wood,—6 ditto turf,—2 ditto wheat straw,—**2** tar barrels. At the lighting of the fire, more than 2000 persons were collected to view it, and strong ale was distributed **to** the populace, to drink his Majesty's health.

LEIGH.—At an early hour, **the** bells ringing " God save **the** King," announced the joyful day ; after that a *feu de joie* was fired, and at ten, a number of respectable loyal subjects assembled at a private room in the Market Place, called the White Hall, when they walked in procession to the parish Church, to hear divine service, when a most excellent and appropriate sermon was preached by the Rev. D. Birket, from the 2nd book of Kings, chap. ii, verse 12. After service, they fired a grand salute of 49 guns, when the members of the White Hall went to dinner ; at four o'clock they walked in procession round the town, and formed a circle in the Market Place, **where** they sang " God save the King," and " Rule Britannia," and **drank** " The King," **with** three times three. The evening was then spent with the utmost spirit and true loyalty, and the whole day was passed with harmony. A grand display of fireworks was exhibited from the top of the White Hall.

LIVERPOOL.—The festivity was announced at an early hour, by the discharge of fifty pieces of artillery from the Fort, the display of flags from the different Churches, the ringing of bells, and other demonstrations of joy. About half-past nine o'clock was exhibited a spectacle which most strongly interested every feeling mind, the liberation of 30 poor prisoners from the horrors of confinement. Divine service followed; and the different places of worship overflowed—never was loyalty so conspicuous, nor piety so sincere; one general sentiment of natural affection seemed to prevail, and it was a glorious spectacle to behold so many of our fellow subjects, addressing themselves in devout supplication to the great Sovereign of the Universe, to bless an aged and virtuous King. Agreeably to the regulations which had been before issued, a procession moved at half-past one, from the Exchange to Great George's Square, in the order of march, six a-breast. It moved along Castle-street, Lord-street, Bold-street, Berry-street, and to Great George's Square. About three o'clock the first stone of a most elegant Equestrian Statue, intended to be raised by public subscription, was laid in the centre of Great George's Square; with the following inscription:—" This Stone, the foundation of a Statue erected by public subscription, in commemoration of the Fiftieth Anniversary of the Accession of our most gracious Majesty King George the Third, to the Throne of these Realms—was laid on the 25th day of October, 1809, by John Clarke, Esq., Mayor of Liverpool." The Military who were stationed round the Square proclaimed the event, amidst the shouts and acclamations of thousands; and the guns at the Fort, and the ships in the river, all of which were decorated with the colours of their respective nations, re-echoed to the neighbouring shores, this lasting memorial of the loyalty and attachment of Liverpool. Various parties, and a public dinner given by the Mayor at the Exchange, and of the Gentlemen of the town, added to the festivity of the day; nor were the lower classes overlooked in the general joy, but were hospitably regaled by the liberality of their employers, or the kindness of their wealthier neighbours. It is to be regretted, that the limits of this publication will not allow of a more detailed account of the public as well as private acts of munificence, with which this loyal city abounded in celebration of the Jubilee. The subscriptions for the liberation of prisoners, and for the erection of the Statue, were noble. In addition to which, a Society was established, for the suppression of cruelty to Brute Animals; the following was the second resolution passed:—
Resolution 2. That we who are now present, agree to form a Society, dating the commencement of it from this day, which has been appointed a day of public Jubilee, to celebrate the entrance of his Majesty George the Third into the 50th year of his reign; conceiving that, amidst the various schemes of benevolence, to which this festival has given rise, we cannot better celebrate it than by setting an example of an Institution, which has been long and pressingly called for.

MANCHESTER.—Very early in the morning a most delightful dawn was cheered by the ringing of bells, and at intervals the firing of guns announced the approaching festival. The warehouses and shops were closed, business was suspended, and every individual was at leisure to join in the pleasures of the day. The Boroughreeve and Constables, with an unusual number of Gentlemen, formed a procession to the Collegiate Church, in which some of the Clergy of that Church joined; a band of music playing "God save the King."—They were also joined by the Volunteer Rifle Corps, commanded by Colonel Taylor, and seven Lodges of Free Masons, in their proper habiliments, with the various emblems of their order. On entering the Church, "God save the King" was given on the organ, and the congregation was immense.—The sermon for the day was preached by the Rev. C. W. Ethelston, one of the Fellows, from the words of the 24th Chap. of Proverbs, the 21st v.—The service of the day was very numerously attended at all the other Churches and Chapels in the town.—After divine service, the Officers of the town proceeded to St. Ann's Square, where a detachment of the 7th regiment of Dragoon Guards was drawn up, and being joined by the Rifle Volunteers they fired a *feu de joie* in honour of the day. A public dinner having been ordered at the Great Room in the Exchange Building, between four and five o'clock, 250 Gentlemen sat down to it.—Conviviality and harmony united this numerous meeting during the enjoyment of several hours, and many incidents evinced the pleasure of the occasion. Numbers of the work-people were treated by their employers; the poor in the Workhouses were remembered; and the Sunday School and other bodies of children were regaled with buns and suitable beverage. Throughout the day the town was a lively scene of festivity amongst the inhabitants in general. In the evening, fireworks were exhibited in four appointed places, and afforded much entertainment to a vast body of spectators.—The roof of Messrs. Philips and Lee's large factory exhibited a splendid Crown, formed of gas lights, which, from the pure flame emitted by that curious preparation, looked beautifully luminous. The factory is lighted with gas, for the general purposes of business. There were fireworks exhibited, in a small degree, by many persons, in different parts of the town. Subscriptions for charitable purposes were made an appropriate and important part of the public proceedings on this extraordinary and most joyful occasion, and they were liberally supported. Messrs. J. and J. Hall regaled their work-people with a barrel of good strong beer, and upwards of 130 veal and pork pies, all stamped with G. R. A loyal and dutiful address to his Majesty was unanimously voted and agreed to.

NEW CHURCH IN ROSSENDALE.—The day was ushered in by ringing the sweet peal of bells of this place, in a most masterly style, which continued all the day, except during divine service, which was devoutly attended. A party of neighbouring Gentlemen and principal inhabitants partook of an elegant dinner; after which the health of our gracious Monarch and the Royal Family, with many other appropriate toasts, were drank. About six o'clock, the company, preceded by a band of music playing "God save the King," marched in procession through New Church, to the hill above the village, where a most brilliant display of fireworks of every description was exhibited; a large frame, supported by three poles, was fixed upon the hill, from which a number of lamps in the form of a Crown, enlivened the whole country, and altogether presented a most beautiful scene.

NEWTON.—After divine service at the Chapel, which was very fully attended, where a most excellent sermon was preached by the Rev. R. Barlow, Master of Winwick School, roast beef, with bread and ale, the gift of Lieut.-Col. Claughton, were distributed to the populace.—Coals were sent to all the poor families in the township, and in the evening bonfires were lighted, and the people again joyfully drank health and long life to our beloved King, in a second bountiful donation of good English beer. A number of the Volunteers attended and fired several volleys in honour of the day.

OLDHAM.—The Staff of the Local Militia, under the command of W. Chippendall, Esq., Captain and Adjutant, fired three volleys and a *feu de joie*, in a most excellent style, and were afterwards treated by the Staff Officers in a manner worthy the occasion. That loyal body of men, the Orange Society, was drawn up with the Staff, and went in procession to Church, and from a thousand to twelve hundred dinners were given on this happy day.

PRESTON.—The morning was ushered in by the ringing of bells, which during the day rung many merry peals. The Mayor and Corporation went in procession to Church to hear divine service; after which the 6th regiment of Foot, together with the Amounderness Local Militia, assembled in the Market-place, and each fired three excellent volleys. At the principal Inns numerous parties of Gentlemen met to dine, and conviviality and harmony reigned every where. Large fires were made in different parts of the streets, numerous fire-works were exhibited, and several beautiful and emblematic transparencies were displayed. Amid the festive scene, the prisoners in the House of Correction of the town, were not forgotten; each of them, consisting of 47 males, and 26 females, was plentifully regaled with bread, cheese, and ale, provided for them by the liberality of several Gentlemen.

PRESTWICK.—The morning was ushered in by the junior ringers, who rang 5,040 changes, in three hours and twenty-nine minutes, in a masterly style. During divine service, several sacred pieces of music were performed, concluding with the Coronation Anthem and "God save the King:" a sermon was preached which did honour to the abilities and loyalty of the Clergyman; afterwards the principal Gentlemen in the neighbourhood, who had subscribed liberally, attended to see an ox roasted, with which from six to seven hundred aged and infirm neighbours were regaled, and who also had plenty of malt liquor.

RAMSBOTTOM.—At the printing works of Messrs. W. Grant and Brothers, all the men, women and children, partook of plenty, whether belonging to the works or not.—At half-past two they assembled at the front of Grant Lodge, where were placed two covered tables, the one with beef, and the other with bread and cheese, and two barrels of strong beer at each end, the whole arranged in the form of a crescent—the people were placed in ranks, and partook of the abundance of provisions, spirits, ale, &c., provided.—Appropriate songs selected for the occasion were then sung, and afterwards the rustic sports of leaping, wrestling, &c., commenced.—At eight in the evening, the band of music played several patriotic airs; dancing then commenced, and continued until twelve at night, amidst the loud acclamations of gratitude and applause.

RIBBY HOUSE.—Joseph Hornby, Esq., with his usual liberality, gave a handsome treat to the whole of the township of Ribby, in commemoration of his Majesty entering on the 50th year of his reign.

ROCHDALE.—A grand miscellaneous concert, by the band of the Hereford Militia, was performed in the parish Church; after which a large sum of money was collected for the benefit of the poor.—Mr. James Howard, a respectable flannel weaver, of Small Bridge, near Rochdale, celebrated the Jubilee by inviting to breakfast 16 of his neighbours, all of whom, (with the exception of one individual,) have for some time received relief from the parish, and whose united ages amounted to 1197 years.

SOUTHPORT.—The morning was ushered in by a numerous display of flags and the firing of cannon. An excellent and very impressive sermon was delivered at the parish Church, by the Rev. Mr. Ford, and a large collection made for supplying raiment to the aged, and religious books to the younger poor of the parish. At one, most of the visitors, and the principal inhabitants of both sexes, met at the Union Parade, when a royal salute was fired, and health to his Majesty was drank by all present. At four o'clock the company re-assembled at the Union Hotel, where they partook of an elegant dinner, after which, many loyal and constitutional toasts and sentiments were given, and the festivity of the day closed by a beautiful display of fire-works.

STONYHURST.—There was great festivity at the Roman Catholic College on the occasion, where High Mass was performed in a most solemn and impressive manner; a grand dinner was given to the young gentlemen, upwards of 200 in number; after which, great rejoicings took place; the students preceded by their preceptors, with flags flying and a band of music, paraded the neighbourhood;

a bonfire of amazing magnitude was lighted in the evening, and the whole of the day was spent in great hilarity and joyous congratulation.

URMSTON.—The cottagers around Mr. Harrison's house, assembled and went to Church to hear a sermon preached by the Rev. Samuel Stephenson, and afterwards returned to his house, where they received one or two loads of potatoes each, according to the number of their families.

WARRINGTON.—Upwards of 850 poor families were provided by a general subscription of the inhabitants, with a plentiful regale of beef and potatoes. A procession of a number of Gentlemen, belonging to the corps of Volunteers, marched to Church, attended by music; and in the evening an excellent dinner was provided at the Trafalgar room, at which John Blackburne, Esq., M.P. for this county, presided. Upwards of 50 Gentlemen of the town and neighbourhood were present. Many appropriate toasts were given from the chair, and the utmost conviviality prevailed.

WALLSUCHES BLEACH WORKS.—The Jubilee was celebrated at the Bleach Works of Messrs. Thomas Ridgway and Sons, near Bolton, in this county, which for benevolence and generosity, deserves to be recorded in the list of noble actions done on the ever to be remembered 25th of October. Very early in the morning, on one of the highest buildings in the Works, were displayed three very large handsome flags, and agreeable to a notice given the evening before, the work-people began to assemble at nine o'clock; at ten, the heads of the different departments in the Works selected their men, and after calling over their names, the whole formed in one line, amounting to upwards of 500. "God save the King," was then sung in a very impressive manner, by a few selected for the purpose. The whole afterwards, (headed by their masters, and accompanied by a band of music, playing the favourite air of "God save the King,") proceeded to Church, where a good and appropriate sermon was preached by the Rev. Samuel Johnson, A.M. After divine service, the women and children had money distributed, to enable them to participate in the general festivity. The men returned to two Public Houses in the village, where excellent dinners were provided, consisting of roast and boiled beef, mutton, potatoes, and pies. After dinner, every man was allowed to drink as much as he pleased, so long as he remained peaceable, and from the report of the men, who were overlookers on the occasion, never was there so large an assembly of people, that conducted themselves with more harmony and good humour; every possible mark of respect to the best of Kings was testified, and they vied with each other in the professions of loyalty and attachment to their Sovereign. The appearance of the men, all habited in their best attire, added not a little to the pleasure of the spectators. What must have been the feelings of their employers, is hard to be described, but it must amply have repaid them for their liberality and generosity.

THE MORAVIANS.—The manner in which the United Brethren, commonly called Moravians, kept the day in their settlement at Fairfield, near Manchester, deserves attention. About six in the morning, a flag was hoisted on the turret of the Chapel, exhibiting in large characters the words "God save the King." At eight, trumpets and other wind instruments, placed in the balcony, announced the festival by playing "God save the King," and other loyal airs. At eleven, public service began, in the course of which, after reading the prescribed form of prayer, and other parts of the Liturgy, an Anthem, consisting of airs and chorusses, being part of the 20th and 21st Psalms, was performed by a good band of vocal and instrumental performers. It was composed expressly for the solemn occasion by the Rev. C. J. La Trobe, and produced a striking effect. The sermon was on the words, "Fear God, honour the King." In the afternoon, the Anthem was repeated in the Chapel, with other appropriate pieces of music from Handel's and other works, closing with the Coronation Anthem; at seven in the evening, there was another service in the Chapel, closing with the Hallelujah in the Messiah; after which, the trumpets and wind instruments in the balcony played for some time "God save the King," and other appropriate tunes. The young people meanwhile had prepared some fire-works in an adjoining field, and by the brightness of the moon, the parties paraded the terrace, the general joy in every countenance displayed the most fervent and untainted loyalty. At the Chapel a collection was made for the poor, and a neighbouring Gentleman feasted a number of poor weavers at the Inn.

---o---

LEICESTERSHIRE.

LEICESTER.—The celebration of the fiftieth anniversary of his Majesty's reign was observed here with a degree of unanimity and public spirit, worthy of a loyal and grateful people. The morning was ushered in with the ringing of bells from all the churches; the day was uncommonly fine, the sun shone in full splendour, and the elements appeared in unison with the joy and exultation that beamed in every countenance. The constituted authorities met previous to divine service, and prepared a congratulatory Address to his Majesty on the occasion. The churches were crowded, and the Reverend Divines, in appropriate discourses, did ample justice to the solemnity of the meeting. After divine service the 4th Dragoon Guards assembled in the Market Place, and fired a *feu de joie* in honour of the day. Sheep were roasted in various streets, and the liberality of the inhabitants (in addition to the munificence of the corporation, who gave £200) enabled every poor person in the town to partake of the general festivity. A very large assemblage of the most respectable inhabitants dined with the Mayor, at the Three Crowns Inn, and the evening concluded with a ball and supper.

ASHBY-DE-LA-ZOUCH.—A handsome collection was made, and with a liberal donation from the Earl of Moira, was distributed to the poor at their homes.

CASTLE DONINGTON.—The Earl of Moira having forwarded a handsome donation, which was liberally supported by the inhabitants at large, all being unanimous (of whatsoever sect or party) in contributing for the laudable purpose of regaling upwards of 1100 persons; the morning was ushered in by the ringing of bells, and the day was spent with the greatest convivialty. After divine service nearly 200 children belonging to the Sunday School, were regaled with cake and wine, provided for that purpose, who sung 'God save the King," "Rule Britannia," &c., and gave huzzas, three times three, on this memorable occasion. Private Parties were general throughout the town, and a public ball concluded the festivity of the day, which terminated with regularity, and the utmost harmony and conviviality.

COSBY.—A subscription was raised, so that every poor man received 1 lb. of meat, six-pennyworth of bread, and a quart of ale; all the children, meat and bread. The principal inhabitants dined, together at the Inn; those above receiving the bounty to the poord roasted a sheep for themselves; the boys made bonfires, and all were loyal and joyous.

FROLESWORTH.—The morning was ushered in with the usual demonstrations of rejoicing, a collection was made, and each poor person received 1 lb. of meat, a six-penny loaf, and a pint of ale, The gentlemen and farmers of the village dined together. In the evening, the principal inhabitants, with their wives, were invited to tea and a cold collation, at the worthy Rector's, where a band of music was stationed, and the conviviality of the evening kept up until a late hour.

HINCKLEY.—The Jubilee was celebrated here with public demonstrations of joy; the day was ushered in with the ringing of bells, and in the course of the morning, every poor person in the town was supplied with money, from the handsome subscriptions made for that purpose. Excellent discourses were delivered at Church, and other places of Public Worship. All the poor in the House of Industry were regaled with roast beef, plum-pudding, and wine, and every Member of the Harmonic Society, with a bottle of wine each, being the very liberal donations of a Lady of Hinckley. The Harmonic Society, together with many others, dined at the Town Hall, which, with the Concert, made the happy day pass away with great festivity. Ale from the Brewery was given away, and in the evening, a ball and supper, at the Bull's Head, was numerously attended; the dancing was kept up till daylight next morning.

HUSBANDS BOSWORTH.—The poor of the parish were regaled with six fat sheep, and a liberal supply of bread and money, accompanied with other demonstrations of joy and congratulation, as a testimony of the sincere and heartfelt loyalty of the inhabitants, for their most gracious Sovereign, and much beloved Monarch, on **the ever memorable occasion** of his having entered the 50th **year** of **his reign.**

MARKET HARBOROUGH.—The joyous day **was** celebrated in this town, in a manner worthy of its loyalty, its attachment to the **house** of Brunswick, and its esteem for the personal virtues and **worth of** our revered Monarch. Upwards of £120 collected among **the** principal inhabitants, was appropriated solely to the relief and comfort of the indigent, and little tradesmen with large families. Nearly a ton weight of beef and mutton, 800 shilling loaves, and £20 in money, were distributed to each individual, men, women, and children, amounting to 800 persons, and money reserved for 20 tons of coals, for the winter. At four o'clock, upwards of 40 of the most respectable parishoners assembled in the Town Hall. W. F. Major, Esq., **took** the **chair, and after a neat and** appropriate address, proposed **the health of the** King, **with three** times three, which was drank **with** enthusiastic applause. **The Queen, &c., &c.** A band of music played "God save the King," **accompanied with all the** voices present; the glass circulated freely, **and the evening was spent** with the greatest hilarity. Parties of **women drank tea in the** public streets, and in the countenances and conduct **of the** poor throughout **the** day, loyalty, satisfaction, and thankfulness, were strikingly evident.

ROTHLEY.—The Jubilee was celebrated with great splendour, and with every demonstration of loyalty and patriotic joy. The dawn **of** that auspicious day was ushered in by **the** ringers with a merry **peal.** A sermon was preached in **the** parish Church to **a** numerous auditory, from Psalm 48, v. 12, 13, and 14. After divine service, the members of the Friendly Society walked in procession to the Temple, with their staves and flag, preceded by a band of music, playing "God save the King." The loyalty and hospitality of Mr. Babbington were conspicuous on this occasion; upwards of 700 persons, men, women, and children, sat down to dinner on the Temple Lawn, where they were plentifully regaled with plum-pudding, mutton, and ale.—After dinner, the popular air of "God save the King," was sung in full chorus, and the company returned home with loud acclamations of loyalty to their King, and of gratitude to the worthy Lord of the Manor. The entertainment on the lawn being ended, a select party of Mr. Babbington's tenants, and respectable Yeomen in the parish of Rothley, with their families, (about 70 in number) sat down to a sumptuous dinner at the Temple, where every thing was conducted in the **true** spirit of Old English hospitality.

WILLESLEY.—Sir Charles Hastings, Bart., gave a dinner, &c., to upwards of 400 persons residing in Willesley and Packington, and principally consisting of his own tenantry. The whole of the day was marked by the utmost good humour, conviviality, and loyal enthusiasm.

LINCOLNSHIRE

LINCOLN.—In the morning the bells ushered in the day with a joyful peal; at nine o'clock, the Mayor and Corporation breakfasted together at the Rein Deer Inn, and from thence proceeded to St. Peter's Church, where an excellent and appropriate discourse was preached on the occasion by the Rev. Mr. Swan, from 1st Timothy, c. ii, v. 1, 2. The loyal Lincoln Volunteers, Cavalry and Infantry, attended divine service at the same place, as did also the Benefit Societies, and the Female Society, accompanied by the honorary Members of that useful Institution. After divine service, the Volunteer Infantry fired a *feu de joie* in honour of the occasion. A most liberal subscription was made in the different parishes, so that the poor were likewise enabled to rejoice, and celebrate the entrance of his Majesty into the 50th year of his Reign. The dinner at the Inn was more numerously attended than was ever remembered on any former occasion. After the cloth was withdrawn, his worship the Mayor, who presided, supported by Lord Mexborough, and Richard Ellison, Esq., the City Members, gave "The King, and God bless him," with three times three, "The Queen, and Royal Family," with three times three, "The Army and Navy," with three times three. "God save the King," was sung, accompanied by all present, in full chorus. Many other loyal and patriotic songs and toasts were sung and given, and the evening was spent in the utmost harmony. A ball and cold collation was given at the Assembly Room, which was respectably attended, and the dancing kept up till an early hour the ensuing morning.

BELTON, &c.—Lord Brownlow gave to the parish of Belton £20, to Faldingworth £15, and £5 to Snelland, for the purpose of celebrating the Jubilee. At Faldingworth, this money, added to the collection made from the principal inhabitants, was given in bread, at the church on Sunday. On Wednesday, all the farmers' wives, indeed all the females in the parish, were treated with tea, and afterwards regaled with plenty of good ale. During the course of the evening, the ladies sung "God save the King," in full chorus, "Rule Britannia," and a number of other songs, and seemed to contend with each other in tokens of loyalty.

COLEBY.—A subscription was entered into for the poor, in commemoration of the happy period. A most excellent sermon was preached by the Rev. M. Sharar, from Psalm 147. After the service was over, which was attended by almost every inhabitant, the poor were desired to walk up to the Altar, and each person, from the aged parent, to the child at the breast, received a three-penny white loaf, baked that day, in celebration of that happy period, which was both gratefully and thankfully received by 168 persons.

GRIMSBY.—The morning was ushered in by the ringing of bells, displaying of flags on the top of the Church, &c. At eight o'clock, the Rev. Mr. Smellie, with the children of his Sunday School, each with a shoulder sash of the letters G. R. 50, preceded by the Volunteer band, paraded through the principal streets. At ten, the Mayor, Aldermen, and Common Council Men, met at the Queen's Head, where, with the Officers of the Corps, they partook of a cold collation, from whence they proceeded to Church in the following order :— Mayor, Aldermen, and Common Council Men, in their robes.—The Members of the different Benefit Societies, with their respective colours ond the procession closed by the Volunteer Infantry. The Mayor and Officers of the Corporation, dined with the Officers of the Volunteer Corps, at the Ship Inn, their head quarters, and the Volunteers, and each Member of the Club, received one shilling, to drink his Majesty's health. Other parties were formed at the different Inns, and the rejoicings closed with a grand ball at the Granby Inn.

HEIGINGTON AND WASHINGBORO'.—In the morning, a very excellent and appropriate discourse was delivered by the Rev. Mr. Massingberd. A very handsome collection was made, and five fat sheep were distributed to the poor, and a hogshead of ale given to drink his Majesty's health. The women were likewise regaled with tea. A select party of Gentleman partook of an excellent dinner, at the Talbot Inn, when several loyal and appropriate toasts were given, and the day was spent with the greatest harmony.

KIRTON.—The day was ushered in with the ringing of bells, and other demonstrations of joy. A subscription was raised by the respectable inhabitants of the town, for the poor, when 70 poor men were accommodated with roast beef and plum-pudding, and a quart of ale a man, to drink his Majesty's health. Two shillings a-piece were also given to the poor widows.

SPILSBY.—A subscription was entered into, and the Volunteers were treated with a dinner, as also the Sunday School children, with a plum-cake and a glass of wine each, to drink his Majesty's health. A most excellent sermon was preached by the Rev. E. Walls on the occasion.

STAMFORD.—The day was ushered in by the ringing of bells. The places of divine worship were all well attended. Numerous parties dined at the Inns in the town ; and in the evening, a ball was attended by a respectable company of about 200 persons. "God save the King," was sung in full chorus by all present, and the mirth of the assembly maintained until a late hour. A subscription of £130, was raised, and one shilling given to every person (man, woman, or child), who chose to accept it.

MIDDLESEX.

(See London).

BRENTFORD.—The Rev. Sir Robert Peat preached a most admirable and energetic sermon, from the words, "Fear God, honour the King." The text was expounded with clear sentiments, and particularly expressive of his loyalty and attachment to the best of Sovereigns, whose piety he noticed as being unparalleled, and worthy the imitation of all his subjects. In a very impressive manner he pointed out the innumerable blessings and happiness of this country, in these most awful times. After divine service, Sir Robert, in a most loyal manner, gave at the Parsonage, to the Brentford Charity Children, beef and plum-pudding, and they cordially joined him in drinking, " Long life and health to his Majesty."

CHELSEA.—The Children of the Royal Military Asylum, about 1200 in number, of both sexes, after divine service, were drawn up in a long extended line, in front of that noble building, and gave a general salute, and three cheers in honour of the day. From thence they marched, in military order, to their respective halls, where a good dinner of roast beef and plum-pudding awaited them, and twopence placed by the side of each plate, to be spent as they pleased. Before and after dinner they sung "God save the King;" and the effect produced from upwards of a thousand voices, resounding through the different Halls, was grand and affecting. They then returned in the same order, cakes were distributed, three more huzzas succeeded, and the afternoon was spent in the truest hilarity and most innocent merriment. The fineness of the day, the military dress of the children, the joy that lighted up their little countenances, afforded a spectacle which our gracious Sovereign himself might have contemplated with pleasure. This noble Institution was brought to its present perfect state, under the auspices and personal inspection of his Royal Highness the Duke of York.

CHELSEA FARM.—Lord Cremorne's Seat was a scene of festivity and joy. A discharge of fifty pieces of artillery, placed on the terrace towards the Thames, announced the rising of the sun. At one o'clock, the Queen's Royal Volunteers, with their full band, assembled on Battersea Bridge. The commissioned Officers displayed a cockade of garter blue ribbon, given them by Viscountess Cremorne, with the following inscription in gold letters;—"*The 50th year of George the Third, ever the Father of his people.*" Oct. 25th, 1809. A *jeu de joie* was fired by them, which was returned by a second discharge of fifty brass pieces of artillery from his Lordship's grounds, where 50 of the Charity Children, patronised by her Ladyship, were assembled, and sung in full chorus " God save the King," after which they were provided with a bountiful dinner. And in addition to his Lordship's munificence, 50 poor families in Chelsea were supplied each with 3 lbs. of beef, a half-peck loaf, vegetables, and two shillings in money, to celebrate the day. A sum of £20 was distributed amongst the poor parishioners. In the evening his Lordship's house was illuminated in a most superb and brilliant manner.

CHRIST CHURCH.—The morning of the 25th was ushered in

by the ringing of bells, and the joyful demonstrations of the people. The Volunteer Corps commanded by Major Meyrick, assembled at an early hour on the parade, whence they were marched in three divisions to different houses, where the Mayor, with a liberality that does him the highest credit, entertained them with a breakfast; they then returned to the parade, where they fired a *feu de joie*, after which they proceeded to the Church, where a sermon was preached by the Rev. West Wheldale, the Rector, to a large congregation. After the sermon the parochial Officers retired to the vestry, and by a well-directed distribution of 1700 quartern loaves, besides the relief of money in peculiar cases, gladdened the hearts of the lower order of the inhabitants of this populous manufacturing parish. In the course of the day, the Rector, Major Meyrick, William Hale, Esq., Treasurer, and the principal inhabitants, dined together, when, as may be suposed, his Majesty's health, "Long live the King," and a number of toasts expressive of veneration and love for our Sovereign, the Queen, and their august Family, were drank, and every expression of joy exhibited which could mark the thanks of a people, grateful for the protection they have received during his Majesty's reign.

EDMONTON.—William Mellish, Esq., Member for the county, ordered three oxen and some sheep to be prepared at his seat, at Bush Hill, to regale the poor of his neighbourhood, and this was distributed on the evening of the 24th, giving the best shares to those who had the most numerous families. And in the same spirit, many of the principal gentry issued liberal donations to their poorer neighbours. On the 25th, the ringers at day break fixed on the Church Tower the colours belonging to the late Association, and frequently in the course of the day repeated their merry peals. A very numerous congregation assembled at the house of prayer. An appropriate hymn preceded the sermon. The Preacher chose for his text, 1st Samuel, 10th chap. 24th verse, and the service ended with two verses of the favourite national song, "God save the King," sung by all present. A collection was made on the preceding Sunday of £29. 13s. 6d. for the purpose of giving to the aged inhabitants of the Almshouses, and the boys and girls of the Charity Schools, 157 in number, a Jubilee dinner. The surplus was distributed in medals to the children and donations to the poor who attended Church. Mr. Mellish feasted his labourers, and many others, in one of his large barns, fitted up for the occasion, and in the evening amused them with a bonfire, and lighted up his house; some of the neighbourhood also illuminated. In the hamlet of Southgate, the sum of £70 was laid out in bread and meat, and given to the poor of that district. And a collection was made by the inhabitants at large, amounting to £213 18s. which is now applied to the relief and comfort of the poor, by supplying them with fuel, at reduced prices during the winter, and to be understood by them, as more immediately emanating from those principles of gratitude to God, loyalty to our King, and love to our country, which have been universally expressed throughout the Empire upon the celebration of the Jubilee.

GREENFORD.—A subscription was raised by the Ladies and Gentlemen, for the purpose of giving a dinner to the labouring people, to which most of the principal Farmers in the parish cheerfully contributed their guinea. The girls belonging to the Charity School were given white aprons to appear in at Church, and to wear afterwards on Sundays. The Church was scarcely ever remembered to be so full. No labourer lost his day's wages, by not working for his master. After divine service, they all repaired to a barn and yard, fitted up for the occasion, and were abundantly regaled with roast and boiled beef, meat pies, plum-puddings, and plenty of vegetables and strong beer. Every child was admitted above five years of age, the younger ones were taken care of by women who could not attend the public dinner, but who were paid accordingly. It is difficult to say which party appeared the most pleased and happy, the donors or receivers; after singing "God save the King," and "Rule Britannia," they all dispersed quietly, and orderly, to their respective homes.

HADLEY.—At the village of Hadley, near Barnet, the day was ushered in by the ringing of bells, &c. The Church was crowded with persons of all ranks and conditions. The sermon was short, and well adapted to the occasion, and the uncommon degree of quietness and silence, in so numerous a congregation, was certainly a strong mark of the attention paid to it. From the Church, all parties proceeded to the spot where the poor had been invited to dine by the Church Wardens, who had taken the trouble of calling at every house, and taking down the number of each family who wished to partake of this convivial dinner, provided by a subscription among their more opulent neighbours. In one room were seen seated upwards of 400 persons, not the least noise was heard, each grown person was supplied with meat and a mug of table beer. After grace, the Ladies and Gentlemen of the village, who had dispersed themselves at the different tables for that purpose, began to carve for their guests. The walls of the room were covered with appropriate sentences, expressive of loyal and religious sentiments on this singular and interesting occasion. The pillars which supported the room above, were decorated with branches of oak and laurel, enlivened with flowers, and nothing was wanting that could give cheerfulness and delight to the guests, or to those who witnessed their happy countenances. There were in another room close to this greatone, nearly 100 persons, equally well supplied with provisions in every respect, and the remainder sat down to tables in the same place, but not under cover. A most respectable looking man, with locks as white as snow, when "God save the King," was sung, stood uncovered, and raised his voice in so devotional a manner, that the tears trickled down his cheeks in rapture whilst he sang. This gentleman was formerly a Member of one of our Universities. Between four and five o'clock, the King's health was again drank with three times three; in less than a quarter of an hour, they dispersed without the least symptom of disorder or riot, though there were at one time not less than 500 spectators on the spot. There remained a sufficient quantity of meat, bread and ale, to supply next day 27 poor families with a good dinner.

HAMPTON.—By the liberal contributions of the inhabitants, aided by the private benefactions of charitable individuals, upwards of 1100 poor persons were relieved with meat, bread, beer and coals. Early in the morning the flag was displayed on the Church tower, the bells rang a merry peal, and with small intermission continued ringing the whole of the day. Divine service commenced at the usual hour in the morning. After the prayers, an excellent appropriate discourse was preached by the Rev. Dr. Morgan, from 118th Psalm, and 24th verse. Te Deum, Jubilate Deo, and Handel's Coronation Anthem, were performed by the choir, and after the sermon the hymn of "God save the King" was sung, in which the congregation joined. The poor persons who partook of the charitable donations attended the celebration of the service, and never was any Church more crowded, or a congregation more attentive. After service many of the respectable inhabitants of the parish dined together at the Bell Inn, on the old English fare of roast beef and plum-pudding. Many loyal toasts were sung, and the day was devoted to harmony and conviviality. The poor in the parish Workhouse were regaled by their Officers, with an excellent dinner and strong beer. Among the acts of private munificence on this happy festival, must be enumerated, that of Mrs. Ryley Williams, and other Ladies of the Hamlet of Hampton Wick, who jointly contributed to entertain 100 poor children with a plentiful repast. Lady Albinia Cumberland gave an elegant dejeune to a select party of Nobility and Gentry at her apartments, in Hampton-Court-Palace. There was a grand subscription ball and supper at the Hoy Inn, Hampton-Court, which was honoured by the presence of his Royal Highness the Duke of Clarence, and attended by nearly 400 of the Nobility, Gentry, and respectable inhabitants of Hampton and its vicinity. A military band attended, and performed several admirable pieces of music; and a grand display of fire-works was made in the course of the evening.

HAREFIELD.—The glorious day was observed in the most splendid manner on the common, numerous tables groaned with the weight of a plentiful repast of all descriptions, suitable to the occasion, enough for the whole parish without distinction, from which no stranger was excluded. An excellent band of music from Pinner attended; and the cannon from the Mines Royal Copper Mill, was fired at intervals during the whole day. G. Speddings, Esq., one of the proprietors of these extensive Works, provided his numerous workmen and their families, (some hundreds) with plenty of hard cash for the occasion.

HIGHGATE.—A sum was collected, which afforded a distribution of five shillings to every labouring and every poor person, and two shillings for each child. The spirited little band of Volunteers, after attending divine service, paraded the village, indulging in frequent huzzas, and their music playing, "God save the King, Rule Britannia," &c. They were hospitably regaled at the Castle Bowling Green. Mr. Prickett's and Mr. Mainwaring's splendid illuminations were the most conspicuous. To the credit of the poor, all was harmony, gentleness, and joy.

PADDINGTON.—This small parish showed its loyalty on the happy occasion of the Jubilee, by distributing 25 sheep, 350 quartern loaves, and 700 candles, amongst 340 families, besides a dinner to nearly 70 children belonging to their Charity School; the above purchased from a subscription collected by the Officers from house to house.

RATCLIFF.— A public subscription was entered into by the inhabitants, to enable the poorer families of that place to participate in the general joy, occasioned by the happy extension of the reign of our good and gracious Sovereign to the 50th Anniversary of his Accession to the Throne. 2796 lbs. of beef, 662 quartern loaves 1120 pots of porter, with two tons and a half of potatoes, were distributed to 500 families, consisting of upwards of 2500 individuals. The children of the Charity School were also regaled with plum-puddings and roast beef, and a donation of six-pence each.

SHADWELL.—The Hon. Thomas Bowes entertained his numerous tenantry with roast beef, plum-pudding, porter, and a little English gin after dinner; nearly 800 partook of his benevolence. The Treasurer and Trustees of the Charity School entertained the Charity Children and the old women of the Almshouses, and the poor in the Workhouse were made happy.

SHADWELL MARKET.—Mr. Thomas Ashfield, the proprietor of this flourishing Market, with a spirit of loyalty to our beloved Sovereign, gave to his tenantry of Shadwell Market, his promised ox, and entertained the whole of the market people, at the White Lion Tavern, Shadwell Market, with roast beef, plum pudding, porter and punch. Mr. Ashfield also provided an excellent band of music.

SOUTHGATE.—Few places evinced more substantial marks of loyalty and affection than the village of Southgate: a liberal subscription was entered into by its inhabitants, which was judiciously expended in furnishing provisions to the labouring class, and providing an entertainment for the children of the Charity School. After attending divine service, when an excellent sermon was preached by the Rev. Thomas Winbolt, M.A., Minister of the Chapel,

I

120 children were entertained with true English hospitality at the Schoolhouse, where the Ladies and Gentlemen of Southgate presided; and a lasting impression could not fail to be produced upon the minds of the children of those blessings which were derived under the mild sway of our beloved Sovereign, and our present happy Constitution.

SOUTH MIMS.—The Rev. Mr. North delivered an excellent and appropriate discourse. The solemnity was rendered truly impressive by a select choir, which performed the national and sublime Anthem of "God save the King," accompanied by the vocal powers of the congregation. The lower classes of society, 600, partook of a plentiful dinner of roast beef, plum-pudding, and strong beer. The hilarity of the scene terminated by the firing of 50 rounds of cannon, fire-works, and other recreations.

UXBRIDGE.—At the suggestion of the **Rev.** Mr. Pike, several leading gentlemen of Uxbridge collected an ample subscription, by which they were enabled to give a substantial dinner to each poor **inhabitant** throughout the **town—viz., 1 lb. of** bread, **with** 1 lb. of meat and a pot of ale to each man, woman and child. Furthermore a distribution was made of 10 chaldron of coals (about 365 bushels), **to** the relief of 114 persons! The truly British hospitality of Daniel Scott Norton, Esq., ought not to be passed over in silence. A company of 145 persons, comprehending the tradesmen of Uxbridge, **and the** men attached to Mr. Norton's extensive Brewery, were regaled in the Brewhouse on the English fare of roast beef, plum-pudding and ale. His Majesty's health was drank in ancient beverage, in addition to which forty gallons of punch were provided by their **liberal** host. The soldiery quartered in the town shared in the feelings **of** the day, and voluntarily mustering before Mr. Norton's door, complimented him with a discharge of three volleys over the Brewery; they were not suffered to depart without partaking of his hospitality. In short, the day was unequalled in Uxbridge for universal happiness and congratulation, and was concluded in the most orderly **and** cheerful **manner.**

MONMOUTHSHIRE.

MONMOUTH.—Lord Arthur Somerset joined with Sir C. Morgan, **his** worthy colleague in the representation of the County of Monmouth, **the** humane and liberal plan of liberating all the debtors in the County **Gaol, whose** debts amounted to £248. A letter was received from **the Duke** of Beaufort, apologising for his absence from Monmouth, by **a previous** engagement at Bristol; but that he had ordered some of **the best deer** in his park at Badminton to be selected and sent for the entertainment. His Grace also gave ten guineas, and Lord Charles Somerset five guineas, to the collection for the poor, which, added to the Corporation subscription, and that of the town at large, amounted to £70, which was distributed by the Committee to gladden the hearts of the indigent.

CHEPSTOW.—The day was announced by the ringing of bells and firing of cannon; and a very large subscription having been made for the poor, early in the morning between 20 and 30 fat sheep, with a suitable quantity of bread, were distributed, affording plentiful meals for the day for themselves and families; and a considerable surplus of money remained to be laid out in the purchase of blankets for the poor. Capt. Lewis, with his troop of cavalry, and the Military and Naval Gentlemen in the uniforms, attended divine service. At one o'clock a royal salute was fired from the ships in the harbour. The cavalry having invited the Gentlemen of the town and neighbourhood to partake of a splendid dinner at the Beaufort Arms, at their expense, between 70 and 80 persons sat down, and the feasting and festivity were kept up to a late hour.

NEWPORT.—Sir Charles Morgan gave an elegant dinner in honour of the day, to his military and other friends, and a ball in the evening to the ladies, both which were attended by numerous and genteel parties; and the worthy Baronet's liberality was the subject of much admiration and praise.

---o---

NORFOLK.

NORWICH.—The Jubilee was celebrated with great splendour and every demonstration of heartfelt joy in this city. At an early hour flags were flying from the Churches and Houses, guns were firing, and bells were ringing. At ten o'clock the Corporation went in procession, with all the pomp of the city regalia, to hear divine service at the Cathhedral. Nearly 1,200 Freemen, principally of the labouring classes of the citizens, met in the Market, and attended the Mayor, Aldermen and Commons to Church. When it is considered how much this city has suffered in its trade by the war, there can scarcely be produced a more striking instance of the loyal and patriotic disposition of its inhabitants, than this voluntary congress of this class of men. The sermon was very appropriate and impressive, and the congregation was exceedingly numerous. At one o'clock, the Garrison was drawn out upon the Castle ditches, where they fired a *feu de joie*, royal salute, and general salute. The firing over, the troops filed off, and the Court resumed their progress to the Hall, where the Officers of the several corps went by invitation from the Mayor, to partake of some refreshments. The Corporation being assembled, Mr. Steward Alderson addressed the Mayor, in the name of the Worshipful the Aldermen and the worthy Commons, in a speech fraught with sentiments of loyalty and attachment to our aged and venerable King, the epithets by which the learned Steward distinguished the Sovereign. "It was not," he said, "even in the romance of the loyalty which all classes of Englishmen felt in common, to hope for a second occasion to commemorate such an event as that of the present day. With the record of the day would be handed down the name of the Mayor," to whose particular liberality, and general merits in the exercise of his important office the Steward paid a just eulogium, which concluded his address. Mr. Harmer, the Speaker of the Commons, as the representative of that body, in a short speech, expressed his entire coincidence in the sentiments of the Steward, to which the Mayor replied nearly in the following words :—" Mr. Steward, Mr. Speaker, and Gentlemen, I am very sensible of the honour you have done me, although unable to express my thanks ; and I am equally sensible that a roast beef dinner, when weighed in the scale against my deficiencies in office, will be found light in the balance. Permit me, Gentlemen, to congratulate you, for I consider that we are here assembled on no common occasion, to celebrate no comment event ; but we are met to testify our joy and thankfulness that it has pleased Providence to permit a good and virtuous King to enter this day on the 50th year of his reign ; to express our attachment to the excellent form of government over which he presides, and our admiration of that glorious Constitution to which I look up as the basis of our strength in war, and our security in peace, as the rock on which all our liberties are founded ; and having stood the test for ages, I hope will be transmitted to posterity, uncorrupted by faction, unshaken by violence, and untarnished by time." At five o'clock, the company, invited by the Mayor to partake of a roast beef dinner, assembled at St. Andrew's Hall ; and soon after the joyful note of preparation was given, by the drum and fife playing " O the roast beef of old England," at the head of a royal baron of beef, weighing 172 lbs. surmounted with the Union flag, which was brought in by four grenadiers, who carried it twice round, and then placed it at top of the hall. The company seated themselves at three tables, which extended the whole length of the middle aisle, which was brilliantly lighted up with chandeliers, &c.

On the baron of beef being placed under the picture of Lord Nelson, the curtains were drawn up, and the transparencies exhibited, which were placed in front of the gallery. They consisted of a likeness of our beloved Monarch, in a gold-coloured frame, one half of which was painted with oak leaves and acorns, and the other half with laurel leaves ; round the frame, on a dark blue ribbon, was inscribed, in large gold letters, " *The 50th year of King George III.*" On each side was an allegorical transparency in chiara scuro—the one of Britannia seated on a rock, with a lion at her feet, and with ships at a distance pointing to the portrait of our beloved Monarch, and exhibiting a scroll with this inscription, " *The effusions of a Nation's love*," and on the other side was Neptune, seated in his car, and pointing to the inscription round his Majesty's portrait ; upon the whole, the effect was good, and did credit to the different artists who painted them. The moment this interesting design burst upon the sight, the excellent band of the Wiltshire Militia, stationed in the gallery, struck up "God save the King," Amongst the Nobility and Gentry who were thus hospitably entertained by the Chief Magistrate of the city (to the number of 341) were—Lord Bishop of Norwich, Viscount Primrose, Lord Bayning, Hon. George Herbert, Sir Thomas Beevor, Sir Thomas Durant, Sir Edward Berry, the Dean of Norwich, &c., &c. The cloth drawn, and the desert served, the Mayor gave "The King," which was received with such applause as would proceed from a settled, principled, and proved attachment to the august Head of our venerable Constitution. A Gentleman sang "God save the King," with additional stanzas, and the company rose and gave the hearty English three times three cheers. The Mayor then proceeded to give the following toasts, the band playing appropriate airs between each :—The Prince of Wales—The Queen and Royal Family—the great Rock of Strength, the British Constitution—may the affections of Englishmen increase with the years of the King—the Army of the Empire—the Navy of the Empire, and success to the wooden walls of old England—the Lieutenant of the County—the Sheriff of the County—the Lord Bishop and Clergy of the Diocese—the Mayor of Norwich, by the Bishop—the Members for the County—the Members for the City—the immortal memory of the Right Hon. William Pitt, &c.

The harmony and conviviality of the party were now, like the occasion, fixed and established. Of the previous arrangement, and general conduct of this happy day, it is impossible to speak in terms exceeding its merit, but that merit must be given to the person who entirely deserved it, namely Thomas Back, Jun., Esq., the Mayor of Norwich. When the Court, by indecision, division, or difference of opinion, declined to take any efficient step for the promotion of that object, which the event has shown was common to all ; the Mayor, by his munificence, hospitality, decided conduct, and judicious arrangement, gave that time to the Jubilee rejoicing which will attract to him, as a public character, the thanks and the regard of every man who loves the establishment of his country. So general, indeed, was the wish to verify the worthy Steward's assertion, "To hand down his name and office, together with the records of the Commemoration," that before the company separated, the following proposals were unanimously agreed to :—"Resolved, That as a testimony of respect for the worthy Chief Magistrate, Thomas Back, Jun., Esq., and particularly for his conduct on this glorious day of the Jubilee—We, whose Names are hereunto subscribed, do request that he will sit for his Picture, to any Artist he may think proper, and permit it to be placed in this Hall. Dated St. Andrew's Hall, Oct. 25th, 1809." The names were those of the most respectable personages in the city of Norwich. Let it not be imagined that the higher ranks were alone regaled on this propitious day, a just tribute must be paid to the many, who by their bounty and exertions, made the cottages of industry, and the huts of poverty, the abodes of plenty and mirth. Subscriptions were made throughout the city, to enable the lower classes of the community to take partake in the enjoyment of the festival. The sums collected at the various places of divine worship allowed of bread, meat, ale, soup, or money, to be distributed as the directors chose, to every poor person who was in need, throughout the numerous and respectable parishes, in addition to which the Freemen in the Orange and Purple Interest received 2s. 6d., and two quarts of beer each. The Volunteers of the city had each of them handsome donations from their Officers. The poor women in the Hospital, in the Rose Lane, had a liberal supply of beef, bread, pudding, and beer. The people in the Workhouse had beef and plum-pudding for dinner, the children a three-penny plum cake each, from St. Peter's Mancroft, and every person had six-pence given by the Mayor. The poor of the parish of Thorpe were amply regaled by means of a subscription amongst the other inhabitants, two of whom added a sheep to their liberal share. The prisoners in Bridewell had a plentiful dinner of roast beef and plum-pudding, and a quart of beer each, given by the Mayor. The debtors and felons in the Castle had from the High Sheriff a plentiful dinner of roast beef and plum-pudding, and one pint of ale each. One Crown Debtor was discharged from the County Gaol, and one from Ipswich, free of all fees. Thus ended in the loyal city of Norwich a day of rejoicing for thousands.

BRACON.—The celebration of the 25th began by a full attendance at Church. After service, "God save the King" was sung in the Church; and the band of music played the same from Church, before the carriage of the worthy possessors of the Hall, who proceeded to that hospitable mansion, where, at one o'clock, the tables were plentifully covered for the comfort of the poor. In the afternoon, the parishioners assembled on the green, where a booth had been previously erected. On an acorn, at the top, was "Oct. 25th, 1809," and "God save the King" on the extended leaves. Here the barrels of beer, and bushels of cakes, which were to be given away, were stationed. At three o'clock, a royal salute was fired, and afterwards, from an elevation in the booth, Mr. Berney, uncovered, gave "The King—God bless him!" with three times three, and a discharge of fifty pieces, the band playing "God save the King," then "The Queen and Royal Family, and long may they flourish." (Three times three, a royal salute, and "Rule Britannia.")—"The Bishop of Norwich, and may the parish of Bracon ever remember his goodness to them, and his good advice!" (Three times three, and seven pieces.) The villagers then gave "Mr. Berney's health, and long may he live to support the King and Constitution!" The acclamations of "Old England for ever," and "Berney for ever," with singing, dancing, and good humour, continued till night closed the gay scene.

FAKENHAM.—Due respect for the many blessings this country has enjoyed through his Majesty's long reign was shown at Fakenham, by the ringing of bells, and the performance of divine service at the accustomed hour; nor were the poor of the parish forgotten, but to every poor family money was given for a dinner, in proportion to the number of each.

HONINGHAM.—The service appointed for that day, with **the additional** prayer, was read, and an excellent sermon, adapted to the occasion, preached at Honingham, by the Minister of the parish. The Church was crowded. Captain Townshend's corps of Volunteers afterwards fired a *feu de joie*, and in the evening several barrels of beer were given to the inhabitants of Honingham, and the adjoining villages; subscriptions for that purpose having been made by **the principal** persons in those parishes.

KETTERINGHAM.—The Anniversary of his Majesty's **Accession was celebrated at** Ketteringham Hall, the seat of Mrs. Atkyns, **in the most loyal** manner. After attending divine service, **upwards of** 200 persons, decorated with blue ribbons, having upon them **the motto** " God save the King," and preceded by a band of music, went in procession to the Hall, which was adorned with branches of oak and other ensigns of loyalty. The tables in all the rooms were abundantly spread in the good old English style. A few friends, the tenants, and the poor, partook of the hospitality of the Lady of the Mansion. In order to perpetuate the remembrance of the event, an oak was planted in a conspicuous place in the park, that posterity might have an object which would recall to their memory the happy occasion of their meeting.

ORMESBY, &c.—A liberal subscription having been entered into by the united parishes of Ormesby, St. Margaret, St. Michael, and Scratby, for the purpose of regaling the poor of each parish:—each man, woman, and child, to the number of 408, had 1 lb. of beef, a three-penny loaf, and a quart of ale each.

WALSINGHAM ABBEY.—The day was ushered in by the ringing of bells; when, after attending divine service, and hearing an appropriate **sermon on** the occasion, by the Rev. J. Lee Warner, **the** numerous poor, by a general contribution of Great and Little Walsingham, and the adjoining parish of Houghton, were regaled **by an ox** roasted whole, two sheep, and plenty of strong beer, and plum-pudding.

WELLS.—A liberal subscription afforded the means of celebrating **and** commemorating the happy event by the lower classes of a numerous population, after an appropriate discourse, most emphatically delivered by the Rev. Valentine Hill, the Rector. The bells ushered in the morn and rang during the day. The Volunteer Infantry, commanded by Capt. Bloom, fired three volleys, accompanied by a royal salute of artillery. The principal inhabitants dined at the Fleece Inn, where loyalty and a love for the King and Country were eminently conspicuous.

YARMOUTH.—The **morning was** ushered in with the ringing and firing of bells. At half past ten, divine service commenced, and never were the places of public worship more thronged than on this occasion. At one, the ships in the roads fired a royal salute, and the Berkshire Militia three excellent *feu de joie*. In the evening the ball was numerously and fashionably attended. The Ladies forming the Committee of the School of Industry, provided every child a comfortable garment, marked with the letters G. R. Medals appropriate for the occasion were presented them by one of the Ladies: with these they attended divine service; after which they partook of a most excellent dinner, at the School, of roast beef and plum-pudding.—A liberal present of a Testament, for each child, was sent by an unknown friend to the Charity. The poor of the town were likewise regaled with roast beef, plum-pudding, and strong beer.

NORTHAMPTONSHIRE.

NORTHAMPTON.—The extraordinary and joyful event of our revered Sovereign entering upon the 50th year of his reign, was celebrated by the inhabitants of this place with the most lively demonstrations of loyalty and attachment, and with a unanimity and public spirit worthy of a grateful people. The morning was ushered in with ringing of bells in the different churches. The Mayor and Corporation, with the Northampton Volunteer Cavalry, went in procession to All Saints' Church, which was unusually crowded. After divine service detachments of the 23d and 48th regiments, stationed here, assembled in the Market-square, and fired three excellent volleys in honour of the day. Soon after one o'clock the populace were gratified with the distribution of an ox, which had been roasting in the Market-square from an early hour of the preceding evening. Several thousands of loaves, and a number of hogsheads of ale, were also given to the assembled multitude. Sheep were likewise roasted in different parts of the town, and many hundreds regaled at tables in the streets. About three o'clock upwards of 200 of the most respectable inhabitants of the town dined at the George Inn, where the Mayor and Bailiffs presided, who were honoured with the company of the Right Hon. the Earl of Northampton, Lord Compton, and the Officers of the 23d and 48th regiments. The Danish, Dutch, and French Officers, on their parole, were also of the party, by invitation, and appeared highly delighted with the entertainment. The health of the King, &c., with several loyal and constitutional toasts, suitable to the day, were given with unbounded applause, and the greatest satisfaction was manifested by the company. In the evening an immense concourse of people, preceded by a numerous band of music, paraded the streets, singing the favourite air of "God save the King," with additional verses adapted to the occasion. About eight the ball commenced at the George Inn, when the company assembled was more numerous than was ever witnessed on any former occurrence. From the liberal donations of the Right Hon. the Earl of Northampton, the

Right Hon. Spencer Perceval, Chancellor of the Exchequer, W. Hanbury, Esq., of Kelmarsh, the Corporation of the borough, and the contributions of the inhabitants, a sum little short of £700, was appropriated to the purpose of supplying the wants and making glad the heart of every necessitous individual throughout the town. Upwards of 6000 men, women, and children of the town, prisoners of all descriptions in the gaols, soldiers in the town and barracks, including non-commissioned officers and privates, as also their wives and children, received 2s. 3d. each; and all the inferior prisoners of war, Danes, Dutch, and French, 5s. each.

ASTROP WELLS.—On this happy event, the Rev. Wm. S. Willes, after divine service, distributed 800 tickets for bread and meat to the poor of his parish; and in the evening gave an elegant supper and ball to 150 of his tenants and neighbours. Every demonstration of joy was manifested on this memorable day; nothing could exceed the loyalty and harmony of the evening, and every praise is due to Mr. and Mrs. Willes for their hospitable and splendid entertainment.

BLISWORTH.—The morning was ushered in with the ringing of bells, a flag was displayed at the top of the church, and a fat sheep roasted whole. A great number of women were provided with cake and tea in the street, and at five o'clock the sheep was distributed among the poor people, with bread and beer, in equal portions to each family. A supper was afterwards provided at the Grafton Arms, where several of the respectable inhabitants assembled, and harmony and convivial mirth crowned the festivity of the day.

BOUGHTON.—Capt. Howard Vyse, M.P., presented all his tenants with a dinner; and the principal inhabitants of the village having raised a very liberal subscription, purchased a fat ox, which was distributed in pieces to every poor family, with plenty of bread and beer. In the evening there was a large bonfire, with fire-works and music; a quantity of ale was also given away, and the evening was concluded with the greatest harmony.

BRADDEN.—A liberal subscription was entered into by the inhabitants, on the 25th, which was appropriated in purchasing wearing apparel for the poor of the parish.

BRAYFIELD.—S. Farrer, Esq., gladdened the hearts of all the poor with plenty of beef, stout, ale, &c., and spared nothing that could contribute in any measure to the festivity of the day.

BROCKHALL.—T. R. Thornton, Esq., gave an elegant and sumptuous dinner to his tenantry, and the whole of the inhabitants of the village, which was followed by a ball in the evening, accompanied with every demonstration of loyalty and respect for our venerable Sovereign.

CULWORTH.—The morning was ushered in with the ringing of bells, and a band playing "God save the King," round the village.

A liberal subscription was likewise made by the principal inhabitants, for the purpose of supplying the poor with a quantity of meat, which was accordingly done, by distributing upwards of 100 stone of **beef**, in equal proportions, to every poor family in the parish.

DAVENTRY.—The day was observed by all ranks of people as **a** day of Jubilee and public rejoicing. The Bailiff, Burgesses, **and** Commonalty, in their formalities, and the principal inhabitants, attended divine service; after which it was unanimously agreed to present a dutiful Address to his Majesty. The poor, to the number **of** upwards of 1300, **were** regaled with beef and a proportionate quantity of bread and ale, **for** which a liberal subscription had been previously raised.

HANNINGTON.—Every poor person in the parish was invited by the principal farmers to dine in the village street, where they were served with a plentiful dinner of mutton, beef, and plum-pudding, of which they partook with a cheerfulness that evinced their gratitude for the opportunity afforded them of thus feasting together upon so memorable an occasion. Tea was also provided for them by the principal farmers' wives; after which every individual was presented with a two-penny Jubilee cake, when the greater part of them repaired **to** their respective homes. About eight o'clock the more respectable inhabitants (who had been instrumental in promoting the general festivity of the day, by their attendance on the poor, &c.) sat down to **a** supper of roast beef and plum-pudding, provided at the Mill Stone public house, and spent the remainder of the evening with **the** utmost hilarity.

HARDINGSTONE.—The inhabitants of this village collected upwards of £60, which was distributed the ensuing Christmas, by the vicar, in provisions, blankets, &c., to the poor of the parish.

HIGHAM FERRERS.—The Mayor and Corporation of the borough, after attending divine service, met at the Town Hall, with their neighbours, and partook of an extremely good dinner, provided by the Mayor. Many loyal toasts were drank, great good humour and conviviality prevailed, and the general sentiment of the day testified the loyalty and true attachment the inhabitants of that ancient and respectable borough **bear** to their venerable **and much** beloved Monarch. A very liberal subscription was made for **the poor**, which was distributed according to the extent of their families.

KETTERING.—Nearly £300 having been collected, part of it was expended in giving meat and bread to all the poor and working people in the town (upwards of 200), with a small sum of money to each family; the residue to be applied to the reduction of coals during the ensuing winter. Joy and festivity were never more conspicuous than on this happy occasion, while the temperance that distinguished the day paid an affecting and sincere homage to the virtues of our aged and beloved Sovereign. The Kettering Volunteers were also assembled, who, after firing three excellent volleys, joined with the band in singing the favourite national ode of "God save the King."

OUNDLE.—The morning was ushered in by ringing of bells; and a very liberal subscription having been previously entered into by all ranks who could afford it, to enable those who could not—to join in the festivities of the day, a committee distributed bread, beer, and meat, in the proportion of a loaf (of ninepence value), and one pound of meat, to every person, two quarts of beer to a man, one quart to a woman, and half a pint to each child; and nearly 500 persons of different ages were thus supplied. After attending divine service, at three o'clock a very large party of ladies and gentlemen sat down to an excellent dinner at the Talbot Inn, and in the evening there was an assembly, when the merry dance was kept up till four o'clock on Thursday morning; and the whole passed off with that harmony and good humour which will ever reflect credit on the town and neighbourhood.

OVERSTONE.—An ox, given by J. Kipling, Esq., was divided into portions, and, together with bread and money, distributed to every poor family in the parish.

PETERBOROUGH.—The Jubilee was celebrated in a manner well suited to the loyalty of that ancient city. Throughout the day joy beamed on every countenance; and loyalty and harmony went hand in hand. At dawn, the harmonious peal of bells at the Cathedral and parish Church proclaimed the arrival of the happy day; afterwards beef and bread were distributed to upwards of 1800 persons, amongst whom the prisoners were not forgotten. At nine o'clock, a most elegant breakfast was given at the Talbot Inn, by the Captains of three troops of Yeomanry, to the Members of that respectable Corps, at which the Clergy, Gentry, and Officers of the Volunteers, were also present. At eleven o'clock, the military, preceded by their band of music, and accompanied by a vast concourse of people, marched to the parish Church, where one of the most appropriate and impressive discourses that was ever heard within its walls, was delivered, with peculiar energy, by the Rev. the Archdeacon of Northampton, from the text, "Honour the King." Divine service being ended, the Yeomanry and Volunteers were drawn up in the Market-place, and the latter fired six volleys. At two o'clock, the Children belonging to the Sunday Schools, in number about 170, and the poor in the Workhouse, were regaled with roast beef and plum-pudding. At three o'clock, about 80 of the principal inhabitants sat down so a sumptuous dinner at the Angel Inn. As soon as the cloth was removed, "The King," with three times three, was drank with enthusiasm, and immediately after Handel's Coronation Anthem was sung with great effect by the choristers of the Cathedral. Many loyal and constitutional toasts were drank, and songs sung, and the company separated at a late hour, earnestly wishing for a long continuance of the already protracted life of the best of Kings.

THRAPSTON.—The day was celebrated by the ringing of bells, and other demonstrations of joy. A subscription (having for its object the comfort of the poor) was opened, and the produce was disposed of on the Jubilee day, in the distribution of beef, bread, beer, and coals, to all those who chose to accept them. Flags were suspended from the battlements of the Church, and the day was spent with the utmost festivity and good humour.

TITFIELD.—The poor of this parish were liberally supplied with an abundance of bread, meat, and beer, which was distributed according to the number of their families.

TOWCESTER.—The inhabitants were happy in celebrating this joyous event, in the true old style of English hospitality. The plan of arrangement was suggested by Gilbert Flesher, Esq., and cordially supported by all the opulent inhabitants of the place. The festivity gave complete satisfaction to every individual, and afforded a display of loyalty truly worthy of Britons. Having ascertained the probable expense of entertaining the poor inhabitants of the parish, upwards of 1000 in number, with roast beef, plum-pudding, and a proper quantity of ale, it was agreed that the Market-hill appeared to be the best adapted for the festal scene; which was accordingly announced by the town crier in the open market on Tuesday, when the presence of the poor inhabitants, men, women, and children, was requested on the memorable occasion, and each person was desired to bring a knife and fork, plate and mug. The auspicious morn was ushered in by the chimes of the Church playing "God save the King," and the bells ringing fifty rounds—a flag was streaming from the Church tower, and every demonstration of loyalty and gladness was exhibited by the populace. The inhabitants and Volunteers went in procession to attend divine service, when an excellent sermon was preached on the occasion. Immediately after, the Volunteers paraded the streets, displaying a Jubilee flag, and their band performing several appropriate airs. At a quarter before one, preparation for dinner was announced by the Church bell; and at one the provisions, which had been dressed at the houses of several of the inhabitants, who also furnished table linen, &c., were placed on the festal board, and several barrels of ale disposed of at proper distances; when upwards of 70 of the principals persons of the place took their stations for carving, &c., while several ladies arranged themselves at convenient parts of the table, whose condescension and kind assistance greatly enhanced the comforts of the day. With such order and regularity was the whole conducted, that even the most infirm, as well as parents with infants in their arms, were not subject to the least inconvenience, notwithstanding 1,200 persons were assembled. An extraordinary fine lamb was roasted and served up whole on the occasion. After the company was properly placed, Mr. Flesher addressed them on the happy cause of their having met together in so novel a manner. He recommended that the fragments after dinner should be conveyed to his house, so that no waste might accrue; by this arrangement upwards of 150 poor families were next day furnished with a comfortable meal. During dinner the band played "God save the King,"

"Rule Britannia," "O the roast beef of Old England," &c. His Majesty's health was drank, when the air rung with huzzas of three times three, the band playing "God save the King." After dismissing the table, the whole assembly stood up, and accompanied by several ladies and gentlemen at the windows of the surrounding houses, sung with the utmost fervour the favourite ode of "God save the King," with additional verses suitable for the day, 500 of which had previously been distributed among the populace. A hundred couple of the poor people dined in the turnpike road ; every stranger passing through the place was invited to partake of the general festivity, and in short, the true spirit of the Jubilee, as recorded in the 25th chap. of Leviticus, was duly observed in the Towcester celebration of the same. Upwards of 50 gentlemen afterwards adjourned to the Saracen's Head Inn, where a handsome entertainment was provided. Mr. Flesher gave the King's health, which was drank with three times three, when the appropriate song of "God save the King," was again sung by all present, accompanied by the band. The Queen and Royal Family, and many loyal and constitutional toasts, were given in the course of the evening; and the whole was conducted with the utmost harmony and festivity. The day was concluded with an assembly, at the Talbot Inn, which was numerously attended, and the company did not separate till an early hour on Thursday morning. A charity was established here in commemoration of the happy event by Mr. Flesher, who, as an experiment, placed three guineas in the hands of a respectable butcher, and tickets were distributed among the poor, entitling each individual to an allowance of three-pence per pound for a certain quantity of meat specified in the ticket, whenever it was most suitable to their circumstances or inclinations to become purchasers. Upon a minute inquiry it was found that this small sum had assisted in supplying upwards of 700 men, women and children with food. Mr. Flesher recommends the plan of this charity to the notice of the Parish Officers throughout the Kingdom, and is of opinion that, if it were generally and judiciously adopted amongst the deserving poor, it would have a tendency to promote industry and morality, and would lessen, if not render altogether unnecessary, the poor's rate. The following are the additional stanzas, which were sung to "God save the King":

ADDITIONAL STANZAS.

O grant that he may see
Friendship and unity
   Always increase !
O may his sceptre's sway
All loyal souls obey !
Join hearts and voice, huzza !
   God save the King !

And, since preserv'd to see
This joyful Jubilee
   Through the land ring,

O hear Britannia's prayer,
Her Sov'reign's life to spare!
Heav'n make him still your care
    Long live the King!

Still may his mild command
Govern this favour'd land
    Years yet to come!
And when his days shall cease,
Heav'n close his eyes in peace!
Death grant a kind release
    To **our** good king!

But distant be that day
May **all the** subjects pray
    Of George our King!
Happy would England be,
Could we live to see
Another Jubilee!
    God save the King!

Still raise a grateful song,
That Heave'n had spar'd so long
    Our belov'd King!
When 'tis the Will Divine,
He should his crown resign,
May he in glory shine!
    God save the King!

WALGRAVE.—The morning was ushered in by ringing of bells; every poor person received a shilling from the Rev. Mr. Stockdale, Curate of Walgrave, and upwards of 400 inhabitants were presented with a Jubilee loaf each, provided from a subscription raised by the Rev. Mr. S. and the respectable farmers; a fat sheep was roasted whole. After divine service a great number walked in procession from the Church to the green, with music playing "God save the King." At two o'clock the Rev. Mr. Stockdale, the Rev. Mr. Payne (dissenting Minister of the place), Mr. and Mrs. Smith (who **were** the representatives of their Majesties at Walgrave, at the time of their Coronation), with most of the farmers of the parish, sat down to an excellent dinner of roast beef and plum-pudding, at Sir William Langham's Arms; **after** dinner several loyal toasts were given, and the healths of Mr. **and Mrs.** Smith were likewise severally **drank. After** three the sheep was cut up and distributed, with a **large quantity** of vegetables and bread, and a barrel of ale. Upwards **of 300 persons afterwards** drank tea upon the green, when several of **the farmers and** others with firelocks, preceded by Mr. Smith, **marched through** the village and fired several volleys in **honour** of **the day.** There was a ball in the **evening,** which was kept up till midnight.

WELLINGBOROUGH.—The morning was ushered in with ring**ing** of bells; **a** handsome subscription, which had been raised for **the** occasion, was distributed **to** afford the poor inhabitants of the town the means of participating in the festivities of the day. A very fine ox, given by Charles Hill, Esq., was roasted whole, and, with a considerable quantitity of ale, was distributed to the populace. The ox, with his horns gilded, and G. R. in golden letters on his forehead, was drawn round the town in a carriage, attended by a number of Gentlemen with a band of music, and, on being placed before the fire, "God save the King" was sung in full chorus. A handsome dinner was provided at the Hind Inn, which was numerously and respectably attended. Mr. Hill was called to the chair, and on his rising to propose the first toast, he addressed the company in an appropriate speech, in which he begged to impress upon their minds that it was his anxious desire, and was also the wish of every gentleman with whom he had communicated upon the subject, that the commemoration of this memorable event should be considered totally unconnected with any political occurrences ; that it should be considered not as a public expression of their approbation of any political measure, but as an expression of the unfeigned loyalty and sincere attachment of the inhabitants of the town of Wellingborough to the person of our most gracious Sovereign ; and after observing upon the baneful effects of the French Revolution, the internal peace this country had enjoyed during the long Reign of his Majesty, the excellence of our Constitution, and the enviable state of this country, contrasted with other kingdoms in Europe, the Chairman paid a high and just compliment to the inhabitants of the town for the alacrity with which his proposal for celebrating the occasion was received, to the liberality and generosity with which they had so abundantly subscribed for the relief of their indigent neighbours, and particularly to the gentlemen composing the committee for distributing the funds, and for their great attention and indefatigable perseverance ; after which the King's health was drank with three times three. Many constitutional toasts were given in the course of the evening ; Mr. Hill's health, who supported the chair with so much ability and conviviality, was also drank, with three times three, and the whole was conducted with the greatest harmony and festivity.

WEST HADDON.—The morning was ushered in by ringing of bells. About 100 stone of beef were distributed among the poorer inhabitants. In the afternoon ale was given to nearly 700 persons, who very cheerfully and heartily drank the healsh of the best of Sovereigns. In the evening there was a brilliant display of fireworks, and the whole was conducted with the most perfect harmony and good humour.

NORTHUMBERLAND.

NEWCASTLE.—The day was ushered by the ringing of bells, the corporation flag was hoisted on the old Castle, and flags were also displayed upon some of the churches, and by the ships in the river.

In lieu of illuminations, a subscription was made for the foundation of a public school, upon the plan of Mr. Lancaster and Dr. Bell; £600 were speedily contributed, and it is supposed will be considerably increased. Another subscription was humanely commenced among the ladies and gentlemen for the liberation of debtors, and such prisoners in the gaol whose situations admitted them to partake of this honourable and charitable institution. In aid of this subscription the Corporation gave 50 guineas, and the Members 30 guineas. The first act of charity performed was the liberation of six debtors and four prisoners from the gaol. They were severally admonished, and advised to attend divine service, and presented with half-a-guinea, to procure a good dinner, and drink his Majesty's health. Three guineas were given to the gaoler, to provide a dinner for the remaining prisoners. Six prisoners were also liberated by the Mayor from the House of Correction, and the rest partook of a good dinner. The Mayor, Magistrates and Military, attended divine service; an excellent and appropriate sermon was preached by the Vicar, from Hebrews, chap. 3, v. 4. After service the military proceeded to the Town Moor, where they were drawn up in line, and after the Royal Artillery had fired a royal salute of 21 guns, gave three excellent volleys in honour of the day. At five o'clock the Mayor, the Members for the town, the Sheriff, Lieut. Gen. Dundas and his staff, Sir Charles Miles Lambert Monck, and others, to the number of 87, dined at Loftus's. The band of the associated Volunteer Infantry attended, and the non-commissioned officers and privates received 3s. each from the officers' fund to drink the King's Health. In the evening there was a ball and supper at the Assembly Rooms, which was attended by 281 ladies and gentlemen. Three hundred children belonging to the different charity schools were provided with most excellent dinners, and received 6d. each. 500 of the poor of the parish of St. Nicholas had a dinner of beef and plum pudding, and a quart of ale each. A similar act of charity was also performed at the Gateshead poor house, and the poor, who are regularly relieved by the congregation in Hanover-square, had, on this occasion, each an allowance of a loaf of bread, 3 lbs. of beef, 2 oz. of tea, ½ lb. of sugar, and a bottle of porter. The Newcastle Volunteers dined together at Embleton's, on the Quay Side. The Corporation, besides (the £50 subscribed towards the release of debtors, and 5s distributed to each of the inhabitants of the Freeman's Hospital, in lieu of a dinner), voted towards the establishment of a general school a sum adequate to the completion of it. The Trustees of St. Nicholas's Charity School presented 2s. 6d. each to the children, and 10s. 6d. to the master and mistress. The Commercial Travellers gave £5 to the school fund. By the hospitality of Major Anderson, and a few other benevolent burgesses of the town, the poor members of the Freeman's Hospital dined together on the green before the house, and were plentifully supplied with beef and plum pudding, ale, wine, &c. The decent and orderly appearance of sixty venerable persons, whose hearts were made glad on this joyous occasion, afforded a **sublime** gratification to a number of spectators; and this interesting **scene** closed with one general shout of blessings on the friends of the poor. Each female was furnished with a royal blue ribbon and a new white apron by Mrs. Major Anderson. Sir C. Heron, Bart., distributed to 50 poor housekeepers in Gallowgate, 7 lb. of beef, and twelvepenny loaf each. A gold cup was on this day presented by the South Tyne **Legion**, to Col. Burdon, their commanding officer, who drank out of it his Majesty's health, with three times three; after which the **corps was** marched to the **lawn** adjoining his house, and partook of **a good dinner** and plenty of strong beer. The officers, and a large party of visitors, were entertained by Col. Burdon with a sumptuous **dinner at** the Queen's Head, where the evening was spent with **the utmost** harmony and conviviality.

ALNWICK.—The morning **was** ushered in by the **ringing of** bells, and the *reveille* by the drums of the Northumberland regiment of Local Militia, and by the bugles of the Percy Volunteers, **who** were stationed on the turrets over the great gates of the Castle, from the saluting battery of which a gun was fired at sun-rise, and the flag hoisted. Before noon the brigade of artillery, the detachment of 17 rifle wall-pieces, three troops of **cavalry** with the ancient standards of the family), and nine companies of **riflemen**, being the northern half of the corps of Percy tenantry, **marched into** Alnwick Castle, where refreshments were provided for **them; after** which they took post on the battlements, towers, **and top of** the castle. Immediately after divine service the salute commenced with 7 guns from the artillery, which was followed by all the wall pieces, and a *feu de joie* from the cavalry drawn up under the castle, and afterwards from the riflemen on the walls and top of the castle, which was succeeded by three cheers, and then a flourish from the bugles **in the** flag tower. This was twice repeated, completing the royal salute of 21 guns; after which the troops and companies returned immediately to their several places of muster, where dinners were provided for them. The Officers of the corps on duty at Alnwick, dined with **their** Colonel, Earl Percy, at the castle; where they were **most elegantly** and hospitably entertained, and "God save the King" was **sung in** full chorus after his Majesty's health **was** drank. Jubilee **medals,** in honour of the day, **were** delivered **to all the officers and serjeants** of this corps, **which consists of above 1500 men, paid for by his grace the** Duke of Northumberland. **At the town hall in the evening there was a** ball, which **was** numerously attended.

BERWICK-UPON-TWEED.—The morning **was** ushered **in** by **ringing of bells, and** pleasure brightened every countenance; the **Mayor and Magistrates,** attended by **Colonel Allan,** one of the representatives, **and a great** many gentlemen, **went** in procession to church. After prayers **an** excellent discourse, **most** appropriate for the occasion, **was** delivered by Mr. Barnes, the Vicar. After divine service the cannon were **fired** from the ramparts, **and** the troops fired a *feu*

K

de joie. But the most interesting scene followed : Col. A. having by hand bills invited all the boys in the town to come to the Town Hall, to eat roast beef and plum-pudding, and to drink the King's health, about 700 fine youths sat down to dinner in the outer and inner hall. The table was abundantly supplied with roast beef and potatoes, succeeded by plum-pudding, bread and cheese, and apples; each boy had his mug, and was supplied with good London porter, from barrels in the adjoining room. After dinner Col. Allan addressed the boys, and gave " The King's health, and God bless him," which was drank by all present with three times three cheers, the hall resounding with the shrill voices of the boys calling out " God save the King—Long live the King, and Allan for ever." The boys were all led into the hall by the masters of the respective schools, and had scarlet and white ribbons in their hats, (Col. Allan's colours). The charity school, and the poor boys in the workhouse were not forgotten. The masters and other persons purposely attended to preserve order, and to help the boys. It was with difficulty that people could be prevented from crowding into the hall. Many ladies and gentlemen outside, to witness so novel and interesting a scene, with difficulty forced their way in, and were highly gratified. The streets and the windows of the houses were crowded with company. After dinner the boys were led away by their masters in the order in which they came, and the hall was cleared to prepare for the evening, Col. Allan having invited all the burgesses, with their wives and daughters, to a supper and a dance. At four o'clock the Mayor and a large company of gentlemen dined together at the Red Lion Inn. Among other toasts, the health of Col. Allan, who had contributed greatly to the festivity of the day, was drank with three times three cheers. At an early hour he left the company, and went to the Town Hall, where there was about a thousand people assembled; he was greeted with the loudest and repeated cheers and shouts of " Allan for ever." The band of the Forfarshire Militia was in the outer hall, and some excellent violins in the inner hall. Col. A. went down a dance in each room, and it was a scene of the utmost gaiety and happiness. Supper was laid in the adjoining Committee-room, and within the crowd was exceedingly great; the utmost harmony prevailed; the hall was illuminated, and the streets were again crowded with groups of people, and the windows of the houses near the Town Hall were filled with company. Col. A. had sent money to the different clergymen, to distribute in small sums to the poor, that they might also be happy, at least on that day, and bless their good King. He also sent money to each of the debtors in the gaol.

HEXHAM.—A collection was made at the Church on the Jubilee day, which was presented to the Bible Society at Newcastle, by the Rev. Mr. Hedley.

MORPETH.—The day was celebrated here with great festivity and joy. The Bailiffs and Aldermen walked to Church in procession, where an appropriate sermon was preached by the Rev. Mr. Ekins. At three o'clock the Bailiffs, &c., met at the Queen's Head, and spent the evening in the greatest harmony. A handsome present was sent by the company to the prisoners in the gaol and house of correction. Between 60 and 70 of the Brethren of the Venerable Bede's Lodge of Free Masons, sat down to an elegant dinner in their Lodge Room, which was illuminated with 100 variegated lamps.

NORTH SHIELDS.—A general subscription was raised through the town, for the School of Industry. The poor inhabitants in the parish Workhouse received from John Scott, Esq., one of the Magistrates for Castle Ward, a barrel of ale; and from the Overseers of the poor roast beef and plum-pudding, in honour of the same day. The Volunteers fired three excellent volleys.

TYNEMOUTH.—The prisoners in the House of Correction received each from the Managers of Dockwray Square a good dinner and a pint of beer on the Jubilee occasion.

---o---

NOTTINGHAMSHIRE.

NOTTINGHAM.—The demonstrations of attachment to the person of the Sovereign were never more general, nor has there ever been an occasion where the practice of the moral duties was carried to a greater extent. In the morning the Corporate Body of the town breakfasted together, and afterwards proceeded in their formalities to Church; all the military in the town were also assembled, together with the Staff of the Local Militia, and the troops from the Barracks, and marched to the same place. About two o'clock the military again assembled, and fired a *feu de joie* in honour of the day, which was followed by three cheers. The spectacle closed by the troops passing in review, when they were dismissed. A subscription was immediately set on foot for the soldiery, by two or three highly respectable characters, and the sum of £50 collected, which amounted to one shilling each man, and was distributed among them, to drink his Majesty's health. Public dinners were provided in almost every quarter of the town, which were numerously attended, and in Barker Gate a sheep was roasted whole, and distributed to the poor. Several Gentlemen afterwards dined together at the Shoulder of Mutton public house, where the health of the King was drank with acclamations, and many other toasts of a loyal nature. The festivities of the day were no where interrupted by party squabbles or dissentions—all was gaiety and joy. In the evening, there was a ball at the assembly rooms.

KELHAM.—At the seat of John Manners Suttons, Esq., an ox and two sheep were roasted whole on the lawn, 120 quartern loaves, with a quantity of plum-pudding and potatoes, were served up in large baskets to regale the poor of the parishes of Kelham, Avesham, and Rolleston. Five hogsheads of ale completed this old English repast

His Majesty's health was drank with three times three, and the two bands of music which attended struck up "God save the King," which was sung by the whole people present; old and young danced upon the green, until sun-set, when they all retired peaceably to their respective homes. The gazing crowd, collected chiefly from Newark, who were quietly amusing themselves with looking on, were then invited forward to partake, and drink his Majesty's health, which they did with enthusiastic shouts of loyalty. The laudable conduct of the farmers of Kelham, Avesham, and Rolleston, must not pass by unnoticed—they paid the day's wages to their labourers, but forbad them to work, and by a generous subscription, every family, with their children, received one shilling each, and the widows received three shillings each.

SEVERTON HALL.—At the seat of the Dowager Mrs. Thornton, the poor of the parish were regaled with roast beef and plum pudding, plenty of ale, and each person in the parish received a shilling from this Lady's bounty.

STOKE HOUSE.—At the seat of John Handley, Esq., two sheep were roasted whole for the poor of the parish, and they were also regaled with plum-pudding, bread and cheese, and plenty of ale.

At Retford, Worksop, Mansfield, and almost every town and village' rejoicings and thanksgivings took place—loyalty and philanthropy reigned in every breast—the hungry were fed, and the aged and widows' hearts made to sing for joy.

―――――o―――――

OXFORDSHIRE.

OXFORD.—The day was ushered in by the ringing of bells, and a display of flags in different parts of the University and City. The Vice-Chancellor, Heads of Houses, Noblemen, and other members of the University, attended divine service at St. Mary's Church, where an excellent sermon was preached by the Rev. Mr. Mount, Fellow of Corpus Christi College; and the Mayor and Corporation, accompanied by the regiment of Oxford Loyal Volunteers, proceeded to St. Martin's Church, where an appropriate discourse was delivered by the Rev. Mr. Green, Vice-Principal of Magdalen Hall. In the course of each service the Coronation Anthem was performed. The Volunteers marched to the Parks, were they fired three volleys in honour of the day, and afterwards dined together, in much harmony, at the Wheat Sheaf, St. Aldate's. A very liberal subscription in the University and city, for the poor, enabled the Committee to afford relief to nearly 7000 persons within the city and suburbs. The prisoners in the County Gaol were regaled with roast beef and plum-pudding, by the benevolence of the Rev. Dr. Cooke, President of Corpus Christi College. The subscription for liberating the debtors was fully adequate to that purpose. On account of the entertainment at Sherbourne, the

Earl of Macclesfield's, the Jubilee ball, which was to have taken place on the 25th, was postponed till the following Wednesday, on which day the city of Oxford was crowded with all the rank and beauty of the county. The Earl of Abingdon and Sir C. Pegge gave grand dinners, in honour of the day, to select parties, who afterwards proceeded to the ball. The number of tickets issued was 400, at one guinea each. The profits were most laudably offered for the relief of the prisoners confined for small debts. This elegant entertainment took place at the Town Hall, the decorations of which were very splendid. A transparency, representing our beloved Sovereign, painted and presented to the Stewards by Miss Burton, attracted universal admiration. The ball was opened at ten, with the Jubilee, by Lord F. Spencer, and Lady C. Bertie, and the merry dance was kept up with great spirit till nearly two, when supper was announced, after which several loyal songs were introduced, particularly some additional stanzas to "God save the King," composed for the occasion, and given with great effect by Sir C. Pegge, which were loudly encored. Dancing was renewed after supper, and continued till nearly five.

BANBURY.—On the auspicious day Mr. and Mrs. ———, of Banbury with their seven children, planted a grove of oaks, in the centre of which was placed a large cubical stone, bearing the following inscription:—*This Grove was planted October 25, 1809, by* ———, *and their seven children, to commemorate the 50th Anniversary of the Accession of George the Third."*

Hæc olim meminisse juvabit.

What nobler honours, on this festive day,
Could Britain to a much-lov'd Sovereign pay?
A prouder monument could grandeur rear;
Or piety an offering more sincere?
When, as each little patriot grasp'd the tree,
The pray'rs of innocence were breath'd for thee,
(Nor shall such pray'rs in vain to Heav'n ascend)
For thee—Great George, their Father, King, and Friend:
And every breeze that murmurs through the grove
Proclaims at once their Loyalty and Love.

BLECHINGDON.—Upwards of 300 persons, in the parish, were regaled with a fat ox, given by A. Annesly, Esq., and a proportionate quantity of bread and strong beer, furnished by a subscription of the principal inhabitants of that parish.

BLENHEIM.—His Grace the Duke of Marlborough distributed beef and bread to upwards of 5000 poor in the neighbourhood o Blenheim.

CROWSLEY PARK.—John Atkyns Wright, Esq., treated all the poor inhabitants of Shiplake, amounting to upwards of 200 persons, with roast beef, plum-pudding, and strong beer, at his Seat at Crowsley Park, near Henley.

CULHAM COURT.—The Hon. Frederic West, in honour of the

day, decorated a large Barge in a most beautiful and tasteful manner, with various appropriate emblems of loyalty, which was **drawn** from his Seat, Culham Court, to Henley Bridge, by six gray horses, richly **caparisoned with** leopard spotted **cloth** and royal purple, and was **filled by the** neighbouring Ladies **and** Gentlemen, attended by a Band **of music. On** landing they walked **to a tent erected** for the purpose **in the meadow,** where an elegant **cold** collation was provided, con**sisting of** every delicacy in **season, the** music playing the whole time. **After** staying about two hours, **the** company departed, highly pleased **and** delighted at the **novelty and** splendour of the scene, and the polite attention shown **them. The** joyous occasion of this well-concerted and elegant entertainment, with **one** of the most extraordinary beautiful and delightful **days** that ever was witnessed **in** October, drew together several thousands of spectators from the surrounding country to view **so signal** a display of generous hospitality, all of whom appeared **highly** gratified. The Wargrave Rangers, and a part of the Berks **Local** Militia, kept the ground, and the former Corps dined **together in a** neighbouring tent. Fifty poor men walked by the side **of the horses** that drew the Barge, **in new** clothes, with a medallion **of his Majesty** affixed, which, to the **admirer** of benevolent and **generous actions,** added not a little **to** the pleasure **of** the scene.

HAMBLEDON.—The poor of Hambledon, near Henley, consisting of upwards of 1200 persons, were supplied with meat, bread, and beer, on occasion of the Jubilee.

HENLEY.—The inhabitants of Henley and Remenham subscribed £130. to treat the poor residing in those places with a good dinner of baked and boiled **beef, plum-pudding, and strong beer,** in Mr. Orme's Spinning Manufactory, **Henley.** Upwards of 700 persons dined, who all conducted themselves **in a decent** and orderly manner, and after drinking his Majesty's health, and singing "God save the King," went home well satisfied and thankful. The remainder of the subscription was given **away on** Friday, **to** upwards of 1600 persons, in meat, soup, and **bread.** All the poor in the Workhouse **were** also treated with baked beef, plum-pudding, and strong beer; **and** John Atkyns Wright, Esq., Recorder of Henley, sent every person in Henley Alms Houses, **a good** joint of meat, a loaf of bread, and **a** shilling. —Most of the farmers **in** Henley, Remenham, Harpsden, and the neighbourhood, also **gave the** same dinner to **the** labourers.

HIRTHINGTON.—The Seat of Sir **Henry** Dashwood, Bart., Miss Dashwood **gave** beef, bread, and beer, to above 300 poor, besides her own **School,** who were entertained in honour of the day.

SHERBORNE CASTLE.—The **Jubilee** was celebrated with great splendour at Sherborne Castle, the **seat** of the Earl of Macclesfield. In the morning all the poor inhabitants of that parish, and of Stoke and Clare, together with all the workmen employed by his Lordship, received 2 lbs. of beef for every person in their family; and after divine service, a proportionate quantity of strong beer. In the evening there was a numerous assemblage of all the neighbouring families for a ball, when the front of the Castle was illuminated with G. R. Fifty Years, in large letters of lamps. There was also an exhibition of fireworks, in the concluding blaze of which appeared *George III. Fifty Years King and Father of his People.* At one o'clock the company sat down to a magnificent supper; after which the dance was resumed, and kept up with great spirit till a late hour in the morning.

TEW LODGE.—The Seat of G. F. Stratton, Esq. The Jubilee and harvest-home were celebrated at Tew Lodge, near Enstone, in the following manner:—Nearly 100 labourers who had assisted in getting in the harvest, or worked at the extensve building and machinery now erecting on the farm, sat down in the large barn to an abundant dinner, succeeded by excellent ale and music; they were waited on during dinner by the various tradesmen and mechanics, their masters, and by the Farm Steward, and other upper servants and pupils of Mr. Louden, whose intention it was (according to the Roman custom) to have been head-waiter himself, had he not been severely indisposed at the time. Dancing commenced at seven o'clock, and was kept up with appropriate spirit till an early hour next day. The remains of the feast were distributed among the poor of the parish of Great Tew.

THAME.—At a meeting held at the Town Hall, Thame, on the 19th, a subscription was entered into for the purpose of enabling the poor of that parish to celebrate our beloved Sovereign's Accession to the Throne; and on the 25th 1400 poor persons were rendered happy by a distribution of 1 lb. of mutton, a three-penny loaf, and three pence to each individual, to drink his Majesty's health. On the same day, a most excellent and appropriate sermon was preached by the Rev. T. Lee. The principal inhabitants to the number of 50, afterwards assembled to old English fare, roast beef and plum-pudding, when his Majesty's health was drank with enthusiastic ardour, and "God save the King" was echoed by every voice, accompained by a full band, and the evening passed with the utmost conviviality.

WHITHAM.—At Whitham, the Seat of the Earl of Abingdon, and at Middleton, the Earl of Jersey, the noble owners displayed their loyalty; the children of Jersey School were entertained with a dinner in honour of the Jubilee.

WOODSTOCK.—A liberal subscription was entered into by the inhabitants of Woodstock, and meat, bread, and beer, and a number of blankets, distributed to every poor family within that Borough. The Mayor and Corporation, the Oxfordshire Yeomanry, and the Woodstock Volunteers, attended divine service at the Church. A *feu de joie* was afterwards fired in Blenheim Park, accompanied by a discharge of 21 cannon from a battery erected for that purpose. The Corporation afterwards dined at the Bear Inn, where a handsome entertainment was provided for them by their Recorder.

RUTLANDSHIRE.

OAKHAM.—The poor of Oakham, by a liberal subscription of the inhabitants (to which Colonel Noel very handsomely contributed), were regaled with 80 stone of beef, 200 loaves of bread, and a quantity of ale, distributed to every one deemed a proper object of such bounty. The principal inhabitants, with some friends from the neighbourhood, dined together at the George Inn. After dinner Col. Noel proposed that a Dispensary for the poor of Oakham and Barleythorpe be established, to be supported by benefactions and annual subscriptions, and that it be named the Royal Jubilee Oakham Dispensary, in honour and commemoration of the day. The proposal was unanimously approved, and a subscription book opened. Col. Noel declared his intention, and the intention of his son, Mr. Charles Noel, to give each a benefaction of 100 guineas, and also an annual subscription of five guineas.

BURLEY-ON-THE-HILL.—The Earl of Winchelsea gave an entertainment at his seat of Burley-on-the-Hill, near Oakham. His Lordship being absent he ordered a most plentiful repast to be prepared for his tenants and labourers of the town of Oakham, and for the whole village of Burley. Tables were spread in the house with the good old English fare in the most liberal manner, when upwards of 500 sat down to partake of his Lordship's hospitality. The health of the King, with repeated cheers, followed by those of the Earl of Winchelsea, and of his mother, Lady Charlotte Finch, were drank with enthusiasm. The merry dance followed immediately after the dinner, and continued to a late hour, when the company retired to their homes, full of grateful respect to their beloved Monarch, and to their noble landlord.

MARKET OVERTON.—At Market Overton and Edmondthorpe considerable sums of money were subscribed for the poor. In the latter place the clergyman gave five guineas for a calf, and Charles Manners, Esq., gave half a hogshead of ale, a round of beef, a quantity of mutton, and ten shillings to the women for tea. The respectable farmers gave ale, provisions, and money to the poorer inhabitants, and the day was spent most jovially.

UPPINGHAM.—By a subscription, beef, bread, ale, and money were bounteously dispensed to all those whose circumstances made the present acceptable; and the day was observed with the utmost loyalty.

———o———

SHROPSHIRE.

SHREWSBURY.—The auspicious day was ushered in so early as four o'clock by ringing of bells, which continued with little intermission through the day. Persons of all ranks crowded the streets at an early hour, some ready to join in the pleasures of the day, others anxiously waiting the hour of attendance on public worship, that they might pour out their thanks to the Great Disposer of Events, for the long reign of a Patriot King. About eleven o'clock, the Mayor and Body Corporate, preceded by the different incorporated companies, with their ensigns and banners, and a band of music, proceeded from the Guildhall to St. Chad's Church, where a sermon was preached to a very crowded audience, by the Rev. Mr. Nunn, from Neh. ii, 3, and the service concluded with the national anthem of "God save the King."—The Shrewsbury Yeomanry mustered strong on the occasion, and attended at St. Julian's, where a highly appropriate discourse was delivered by their chaplain, the Rev. H. Owen, to a very numerous congregation. The different recruiting parties in the town also attended divine service; and, on this interesting occasion, the parochial churches, the chapels, and the meeting houses of dissenters of every description in the town, were fully attended; and the discourses delivered in all of them such as tended to promote in an eminent degree the objects of the day. On the return of the party of the 53d from church, they were assembled in the Square, and fired a *feu de joie*, and then cheered. The Yeomanry afterwards met in the Square, under the command of Captain Lloyd, where they waited a considerable time for the return of the Mayor from St. Chad's. Soon after his arrival, the music struck up "God save the King," the troops fired a *feu de joie*, and concluded with three times three cheers. Colonel Lethbridge gave a military dinner to the officers in the town. The dinner parties at the inns were numerous; and many respectable persons treated their labourers and mechanics, together with their wives and children, in a very liberal and hospitable manner. The inmates of the House of Industry were indulged with roast meat, and a portion of good beer to drink the health of their King. The children at some of the charity schools partook of buns, coffee, &c., and the best boy and girl at the schools founded by the late Mr. Allatt had each a Jubilee medal presented to them, which they wore through the day. In short, the day passed as it was intended—the tears of the widowed matron and unprotected child were dried up—the victim of penury has been cheered—and means have been adopted for the release of the debtor, and the relief of the subject of disease. Thus, while it has gratified the characteristic loyalty of the inhabitants of this town, it has given to their beneficence an ample scope and sure direction. The doors of some of the principal inhabitants were ornamented with laurel, to which were attached mottos and devices. The barges on the river were decorated with laurel, flags, and pendants; the firing of cannon and muskets, with every other customary demonstration of popular satisfaction (except illumination) were abundantly displayed; and at night, fire-works were exhibited from the gardens of Mr. Benyon, Mr. Lloyd, and Dr. Evans; and bonfires were observed on many of the distant hills in the county.—The subscription for the poor amounted to nearly £500.

ADDERLEY HALL.—The seat of Sir Corbet Corbet, Bart. The ringing of the bells, and display of a large flag on the tower of the church, ushered in the morning. Divine service was performed at ten o'clock before the largest congregation ever assembled there, and an excellent and most appropriate sermon on the occasion, preached by the Rev. Mr. Judgson. After service ended, a Royal Salute of 21 guns was fired from an eminence in the front of the park at Adderley, and dinner immediately served up to upwards of 100 children, educated at the Adderley School—the military band playing "God save the King." At two the labourers and their wives and children, to the number of 150, had a plentiful banquet in the riding house: when this was finished, Sir Corbet, after a short and impressive speech, drank the King's health, with three times three, which was followed by "God save the King," played by the full band, and sung by the company present. While the band and attending servants retired to another room to dine, the labourers had a plentiful supply of excellent ale. All the tenants' wives and daughters were invited to tea at the Hall at six, and a very handsome display of fire-works took place at seven and continued till eight. The cannon were again fired, when the female party adjourned from the hall to a very handsome suite of rooms over the riding-house. Joined by the tenants, &c., the festive dance now commenced, and continued, with the intermission only of a very handsome supper, till a late hour in the morning.

ALBRIGHTON.—All the poorer inhabitants of this parish were feasted by the more opulent, who liberally subscribed for the occasion; and more than 600 persons, old and young, received 1 lb. of meat and 1 lb. of bread per head. The Royal Oak Volunteers, consisting of 120 men, of the parishes of Donington, Albrighton, and Boningale, met, and fired a *feu de joie*, went to Church, and afterwards dined together. All hearts and voices sang "God save the King."

BISHOP's CASTLE.—Thirty pounds were given by the Members for the Borough, and the Earl of Powis, to which the inhabitants at large subscribed, and distributed the whole to the poor and needy.

BRIDGNORTH.—The morning was ushered in by the firing of cannon and ringing of bells; which were only suspended during the time of divine service, and at short intervals the rest of the day. A very handsome subscription having been previously collected for the poor, was distributed among them; and at twelve o'clock, the Bailiffs and Corporation in their gowns, the Free Masons in the Insignia of their Order, and the Morfe Loyal Volunteers in their full uniform, proceeded in one continued procession, accompanied by the worthy Members for the Borough, Thomas Whitmore, and Isaac Hawkins Browne, Esqs., the principal inhabitants of the town and neighbourhood, to the Church of St. Mary, where the service of the day was performed, and an appropriate sermon preached by the Rev. Thomas

Dethick. It was delivered from the heart with an energy of which he appeared from every corporeal symptom incapable, being scarcely recovered from a long illness; it was universally admired, and listened to with the deepest silence, by a very crowded and attentive congregation. The discourse was masterly, and contained some highly wrought encomiums upon the King for his religious principles, moral conduct, and readiness to sacrifice every personal interest for the Protestant Religion, and security of the Established Church. After the service was concluded, the Volunteers marched to Highstreet, where having fired three excellent volleys, they filed off by companies to different Inns, and were regaled with true English fare, provided for them at the expense of Colonel Whitmore, and the other Officers of the Corps; the Colonel also presented the town with some splendid fire-works. Sumptuous dinners were served at the Castle and Crown Forts; when the circling glass passed rapidly to loyal toasts and songs, rapturously applauded, and enthusiastically cheered. There was a ball in the evening at the Town Hall, under the patronage of the Bailiffs, Benjamin Gates, and Francis Moore, Esqs., which was numerously and genteelly attended; the profits arising from which were added to the Charitable Fund. Dancing was kept up to a late hour, when the company dispersed, expressing themselves highly gratified by a day, in which all ranks seemed animated by one idea of loyalty; and which they had passed, not only with joyful conviviality, but with perfect harmony.

BROSELEY.—The morning was ushered in with a discharge of cannon, at five o'clock. A subscription for the poor had been previously arranged. The Rector, the Rev. Thomas Forester, also supplied six fat sheep and two barons of beef; and after divine service, upwards of 800 people were supplied with roast and boiled beef, vegetables, and one quart of ale each. The principal inhabitants sat down to a sumptuous dinner at the Town Hall, which in the evening was most splendidly illuminated.

COALBROOK DALE.— At the Porcelain Manufactory of Messrs. John Rose and Co. six fat sheep were roasted whole for the entertainment of their numerous artists and work people in celebrating the Jubilee, and two hogsheads of good Shropshire ale given to drink the King's health.

DONINGTON.—A sum of money was raised by subscription, and expended in the purchase of bread and meat, which were distributed to the poor of the parish, at the neighbouring town of Shiffnal, each family receiving a quantity proportioned to the number of which it consisted, and a considerable sum was left to admit of a further distribution the ensuing Christmas. Divine service was performed in the Church, which was numerously attended.

ELLESMERE.—The Jubilee was celebrated here in a very impressive manner. In the course of a few hours, on the Monday, near

£100, was subscribed by the inhabitants; and on Wednesday above 200 poor people were regaled in the Town Hall, whilst their wives and families enjoyed themselves at home, with money distributed for that purpose. A sum was also appropriated to find the poor in coals during the winter. A procession to Church took place, and afterwards a large number of the inhabitants sat down to an excellent dinner at the Bridgwater Arms, and the glass was circulated in harmony till a late hour, when the company separated, having first of all voted their unanimous thanks to Mr. Rogers, for his sumptuous dinner, excellent wines, and great attention paid his friends, not only on that day, but on **every former occasion.**

GREAT NESS.—The western division of the Hundred of Pimhill Light Horse Volunteers, celebrated the Jubilee in the neighbourhood of Nesscliffe, with an observance of religious and military duties in the morning, and the remainder of the day in festivities, elegantly and liberally adapted to the occasion.—A most excellent sermon was preached at Great Ness, by the Rev. Geo. Martin, from 1 Peter, chap. 2. v. 17.—After which the corps was hospitably received at the Hall, by their worthy Lieutenant, John Edwards, Esq., they next proceeded to a field beautifully situated on the south side of Nesscliffe-hill, and had the honour to be reviewed by General Despard; and afterwards dined at Nesscliffe with the General, and their honorary members, in a room fitted up for this occasion, with much taste, by the ladies of the neighbourhood.—The day following was dedicated to the charitable distribution of a most bountiful donation of provisions and money, in the neighbourhood: and at Boreatton Hall, an ox was killed, and dealt out, and blankets were also given to the really deserving poor.

HALES OWEN.—Besides the usual demonstrations of loyalty and joy, a liberal subscription was made for the poor, at a public meeting convened by the High Bailiff, with which five fat cows were purchased, and distributed to nearly 600 families in that town and neighbourhood.

LINLEY.—At the hospitable mansion of R. Moore, Esq., all the tenants and their families were invited to a dinner, at which their respected landlord presided, and who with his amiable family enjoyed the sight of the youthful dancers in the evening. Two fat sheep were roasted, and, with plenty of ale, distributed to his work-men, and the neighbouring poor of the parishes of More and Shelve. On the hills above the hall, bonfires were kindled, and the noise of cannon was echoed by the rocks and woods: fire-works were displayed at night. Nor were the rejoicings of the industrious poor confined to that day only; for the generous master ordered to some families a bushel, and to others half a bushel of wheat, according to the number of children. A party of the surrounding gentry dined together on the succeeding day.

LUDLOW.—The Bailiffs, Corporation, and a very numerous body

of gentlemen and tradesmen, went in procession to Church; and parties dined at the principal Inns.

NEWPORT.—In this town, and the adjoining parishes on the confines of this county and Staffordshire, subscriptions were appropriated to the relief of the poor; oxen and sheep roasted; plenty of good ale; firing of cannon; bonfires; the Military Yeomanry were on duty in their neighbourhood; the loyal corps of Cavalry Troop of the Batchacre Legion, commanded by Richard Whitworth, Esq., Lieut.-Colonel, who marched a gallant set of horsemen to the town of Newport, and fired a *feu de joie*; the Troop in their way to the camp had the honour of being regaled, and drinking the King's health, at the hospitable mansion of Thomas Barrow, Esq., of Chetwynd Hall.

OSWESTRY.—The Magistrates went in procession to Church; the Cavalry assembled and fired in honour of the day, and by a happy concurrence, the lamps newly put up, were for the first time lighted on the 25th. The generous subscriptions of the inhabitants afforded a dinner, in the Town Hall, to the children of the Sunday Schools. The ball at the Cross Foxes was well attended.—At Whittington, about 170 children were regaled by the Worthy Rector, the Rev. Mr. Lloyd.

SHIFFNALL.—The inhabitants of this place were among the first to propose and among the first to celebrate with rational rejoicing, the festivities of this extraordinary day.

WHITCHURCH.—After a very excellent sermon at the Church, the sum of £29 18s. was collected. Contributions to a large amount were also added by the inhabitants; the whole to be appropriated to purchase coals for the poor in winter.

———o———

SOMERSETSHIRE.

BATH.—The festivity was ushered in by the ringing of bells, and display of flags on the different churches. At eleven o'clock, the Mayor and Corporation, accompanied by the Bath Volunteer regiment of Infantry, the young gentlemen of the Grammar School, the children of the Charity Schools, and the Friendly Societies, (33 in number, containing 2487 members, each Society distinguished by its particular banners and colours) went in grand procession to the Abbey Church, where an admirable sermon was preached by the Rev. Mr. Marshall. Part of the Societies went to Walcot Church, where an equally excellent discourse was delivered by the Rev. Mr. Barry. Collections were made at the doors of both Churches, for the benevolent purpose of releasing the debtors in the County Gaol. On returning to the Hall, cakes and wine were given to the juvenile part of the procession. The Volunteers marched to the Crescent Field, where they fired a *feu de joie*; and the members of the Friendly Societies departed to their respective club-rooms, in which they dined together in much harmony; each man received towards his expences 1s. 6d. from the public subscription for that purpose. The children of the Blue Coat Charity School, about 120 in number, sat down in their School-room to a plentiful dinner of roast beef and plum-pudding, provided at the expense of a highly respected and loyal Gentleman, a resident of that city. Between 2 and 300 persons, including the children of the Sunday School, were regaled by Mr. Jay, and the Managers of the Argyle Chapel, in their Vestry-Room, &c., with a dinner of beef, mutton, and plum-pudding. The Sheriffs, George Crook, and George Lye, Esqrs., generously opened the prison doors of the city, and released every debtor that was confined at *their own costs*. The Mayor and Corporation, the Clergy, and a select party dined at the White Hart. In the evening there was a ball at the Town Hall. Jubilee Medals, with ribbons having suitable mottos in gold letters, were generally worn.

BRUTON.—Early in the morning, the ringing of bells announced the approaching festival. At six o'clock commenced a plentiful and judicious distribution of beef, bread, and strong beer, to every poor family in the parish, provided by a very liberal subscription of its inhabitants. The Volunteers, accompanied by their fellow-townsmen, marched to Church, and heard an appropriate sermon by the Rev. Mr. Cosens; after which, the Volunteers proceeding to their field, went through various evolutions, and fired a *feu de joie*, to the great satisfaction of Captain Dampier, who very ably did the honours of a Field Officer.—Admiral Goldesbrough gave an elegant entertainment to his friends, and treated them with some of his old and excellent Port and Madeira.—The dinner given by the Burton Officers to the whole corps, was very numerously attended, and the most perfect harmony prevailed. Every one enjoyed the festivities of the day with great propriety and moderation; and they afterwards retired to their respective homes, in peace and good order.

COMBHAY.—The tenants of John Leigh, Esq., as well as the families of the labouring poor, were plentifully supplied with meat and strong beer.

COURT HOUSE.—The day was celebrated with every demonstration of joy at Court House, the residence of Mr. Thomas Winter. In the morning, fifty of his labourers, with their families, were regaled with toast and cider, when they afterwards proceeded to the parish Church of Bishops Lydeard in procession, headed by an excellent band of music, playing the national air of "God save the King." From thence they returned to the Mansion-house, at the approach of which, a grand Triumphal Arch was erected, encircled with wreaths of laurel and oak, with the motto "REX," in yellow letters. A royal salute, with ten fowling pieces, was fired five times over it. A sumptuous repast, composed of roast beef and plum-pudding, was provided, and about 250 persons of both sexes sat down to dinner. After the cloths were removed, the donor and every person present drank his Majesty's health in a bumper of that wholesome old English beverage, provincially styled "October." In the evening the company retired about a mile distance, to the pleasure grounds and gothic tower at Watt's Place, belonging to John Winter, Esq., situated on a lofty eminence, commanding an extensive view of the vale of Taunton Dean, and adjacent country, on the summit of which, two bonfires of immense size were lighted up,—a fat sheep roasted whole,—the tower windows and battlements brilliantly illuminated,—and a fine display of fire-works was exhibited to upwards of 1000 spectators, who testified their joy for their beloved Monarch with repeated huzzas. About ten o'clock the populace returned to their respective homes.

CROWCOMBE COURT.—J. Barnard, Esq., gave a fat heifer to the poor, with strong beer, &c., in sufficient plenty.

DUNSTER CASTLE,—The Seat of J. F. Luttrell, Esq. The doors were thrown open to the poor, and the respected owner gave a fat bullock and a hogshead of beer to the inhabitants of Dunster, and the like donation to the poor of Minehead, as well as several sums of money to the neighbouring parishes.

FROME.—The day was ushered in by the ringing of bells, and by flags and streamers waving from the steeple. To gladden the hearts of the aged and sick poor, a subscription had previously been made, upwards of £100, to be distributed in beef, bread, and money, to such poor as were of the age of his Majesty or upwards, or lay oppressed by the hand of sickness. Of the former class there were about 300 who received 4½ lbs. of beef, a quartern loaf, and a shilling each; the remainder of the subscription was distributed among the sick and poor families of the town. A numerous congregation attended divine service at the Church, where a very appropriate sermon was preached by the Vicar. At one, the Volunteer Cavalry and Infantry fired three volleys; the Officers afterward dined together in high cordiality, and many loyal and constitutional toasts were drank. The day was concluded with bonfires and fire-works.

HORSINGTON.—Mr. Thomas Bailward, of Horsington, entertained a large number of persons; and at Hadspen House, the seat of Henry Hobhouse, Esq., all the inhabitants of the neighbouring village were regaled with plenty of beef and plum-pudding, and dismissed with a liberal distribution of clothes. After the lower classes had been thus sent joyfully to their houses, all the Gentry of the environs assembled at Ansford Inn, where a very elegant supper was provided under the conduct of several Gentlemen, and dancing was kept up till a late hour of the morning.

KEYNSHAM.—Every poor family was relieved by a distribution of 2 lbs. of mutton to each poor man and woman, and 1 lb. to each child ; 22 sheep were killed for the occasion. Upwards **of 500 persons, consisting** of all the respectable inhabitants, and Four **Clubs in the parish,** assembled at Mr. Gurner's, the Lamb and Lark, and proceeded to Church. The Rev. Mr. Cocking preached an excellent sermon, **and** they afterwards regaled themselves with moderation at the above mentioned Inn.

LONG ASHTON.—The parishioners **of Long** Ashton invited **every** inhabitant, male and female, that had attained their 50th year, **to** partake of a good old English dinner, of roast beef and plum-pudding, properly moistened with Sir John Barleycorn's best stingo. Immediately after divine service, in which the blessings and duties of the auspicious day were most impressively enforced by the Vicar, about 120 persons walked in procession from the Church to the Angel Inn, and sat down to the plentiful **meal** which was provided for, and served up to them, by the Gentlemen of the parish. After having been abundantly, but temperately regaled, they again attended their Minister, Church-warden, and the other Gentlemen, to the Church, **where** every person received **a** shilling loaf of bread ; and **money** was liberally given **to all the** inhabitants, who would **accept the same,** in proportion **to the** number of their respective families.

NETTLECOMBE.—Sir J. Trevelyan, Bart., **liberally regaled the poor of his parish.**

NEWTON PARK.—Col. Gore Langton distributed money and provisions amongst the families **of** his neighbourhood, and his farmers entered into the spirit of the day, after the same hospitable example set them by their worthy landlord.

NORTH PETHERTON,—Near Bridgwater. **Not** fewer than 400 **families were supplied with beef,** bread, &c., after the delivery of **which, a procession took** place **to** attend divine service at Church, and **an appropriate sermon** by the Rev. Mr. George. In the afternoon **an excellent dinner** was provided at the George Inn in that town, and **the day closed in** harmony, friendship, and festivity.

ORCHARDLEIGH,—The Seat of —— Champness. The Union Flag was displayed by break of day. After the family had attended the service of the Church, 50 poor persons were regaled with excellent meat, &c. ; **in the** evening a most magnificent bonfire, accompanied by a display of sky-rockets and discharges **of** artillery, illumined the whole country around. **At** nine o'clock music summoned the different groups to **the** Mansion, when upwards of 50 persons, consisting solely of the **tenantry,** their wives, sons and daughters, sat down to a plentiful supper, composed of old English fare, and after drinking his Majesty's health, with three times three, **and** imploring every blessing on him, **the** merry pipe and harp were introduced, and each loyal youth singled out his partner in the dance, till day break summoned them to their different avocations. Nothing could exceed the regularity and decorum of the whole of this rustic fete.

SANDHILL PARK.—The Seat of S. J. Lethbridge, Bart., was appropriated to the reception of the poor of the neighbourhood, who were sumptuously regaled with old English fare, beef, plum-pudding, and strong beer. The Baronet, his Son, one of the Representatives of Somerset, many ladies, and between 2 and 300 of their tenantry, dined together in the Mansion, and enjoyed themselves till a late hour.

TAUNTON DEAN.—Every individual, high or low, rich or poor, contributed his share of gratitude and acknowledgments due to the revered Monarch of this happy Island. The day was ushered in by a general ringing of bells, discharges of artillery, musketry, &c. Divine service was universally attended, and the Churches were thronged. After which each parish, generally speaking, entertained its own poor, by feeding and in many instances clothing them, under the directions of the various Clergymen and Magistrates, who resided in that part of the country. In many places sumptuous and hospitable entertainments were made by the different gentlemen at their Seats. At Taunton a most sumptuous dinner was provided, which was attended by at least 80 Gentlemen of the town and neighbourhood. Mr. Lethbridge, one of the County Members, presided, supported by the leading characters of this populous County. An elegant ball, fire-works, and every other demonstration of festivity and joy, completed the evening. In the course of the morning a meeting of the inhabitants of Taunton was convened, and, to their honour be it named, within a quarter of hour, a sum not less than £1200 was subscribed for the purpose of endowing an Infirmary, for the lower classes of the neighbourhood.

TELLISFORD.—Every poor person received a loaf of bread and ne pound and a quarter of excellent beef.

TWERTON,—Near Bath. Four sheep were roasted and given to the poor, with a proportionate quantity of bread and beer, the donation of the Rev. Dr. Fothergill, Mr. Nash, and the opulent farmers; and a subscription for the like purpose, and the same liberality, were displayed at Saltford.

WELLINGTON.—Every house was brilliantly illuminated; the poorer inhabitants were generously supplied with candles at the expense of Thomas Eyton, Esq., whose house was eminently splendid, and the motto, "Fear God, Honour the King," was formed of variegated lamps. There was also a display of fire-works. The subscription to a large amount was appropriated to purchasing four oxen, and the beef was given in quantities proportionate to the number in each family. But a more lasting memorial than these was executed through the exertions of the Rev. John Eyton, namely, the establishment of a school.

L

YEOVIL.—G. B. Prowse, Esq., fed nearly 200 poor families, and clothed many. Messrs. Watts provided a dinner and strong beer, with which 250 were regaled in the Market House. Forty poor persons were treated with a dinner at the house of Mr. Andrews, mercer. Capital cider was rolled out by hogsheads by Mr. Collins, Mr. Watts, Mr. Wellington, Mr. Cox, and others. The manufacturers made all their work people rejoice. There was a brilliant display of fire-works, and in the evening a ball. Two squadrons of the East Somerset Yeomanry Cavalry, commanded by Major White, were, at the invitation of John Phelips, Esq., assembled in front of Montacute House, and fired three volleys with the utmost precision. They were entertained in that spacious mansion with an excellent dinner, in the genuine style of English hospitality, and retired under a strong impression of the polite attention and liberal hospitality of their respected host.

At the parishes of Trent, Merston Magna, Rimpton, West Camel, and most others in the neighbourhood of Yeovil, in the county of Somerset, the day was ushered in with the ringing of bells, and other demonstrations of joy, in testimony of their loyalty to the best of Kings. The public service was well attended in the several churches, where appropriate discourses were delivered by the clergy, and the poor of all descriptions were afterwards regaled with a liberality suited to the occasion, and in the old English style, with roast beef and plum pudding. It was indeed to the poor of these parishes, a day of jubilee, of comfort and satisfaction, the remembrance of which will be gratefully handed down to the latest posterity.

———o———

STAFFORDSHIRE.

STAFFORD.—A very liberal subscription for the poor of Stafford and Forebridge, extended to upwards of 600 families. A select circle of ladies gave an excellent dinner to the poor of the Workhouse and Alms-houses, and attended themselves, with the Mayor of the town, (F. Hughes, Esq.) to carve, wait at table, &c. A band of music, at sunrise, assembled on the battlements of the church, and played "God save the King." A public breakfast, at the Swan, given by the Mayor, commenced the festivities of the day; after which the body corporate went in procession to church, where an excellent sermon was preached by the Rev. E. Dickinson, B.D. The public dinner at the George was filled as soon as advertised. F. Hughes, Esq. (Mayor) in the chair, W. Horton, Esq., Vice. The President prefaced the toast of "The King," with an eulogy on his character. It was given in three times three, with all the ardour which human voices and human hearts could give it. "God save the King" was then sung in full chorus, with additional verses for the occasion. The dinner at the Vine was well attended; and loyalty and harmony out-lived the night. The ball, under the patronage and taste of Mrs. Shapland

Swiny, and Captain Swiny and F. Hughes, Esq., Stewards, was crowded with fashion. The gay scene was continued till the morning, and closed with " God save the King," in full chorus, by all the ladies and gentlemen present.

ARMITAGE.—Thomas Lister, Esq., with his usual generosity, gave every poor family in the parish of Armitage, two quartern loaves each, on the occasion.

BERKSWICH.—In addition to a large quantity of beef given by the Rev. Richard Levett, the poor families were treated with a good dinner and ale, by subscription. In the evening, a may-pole, erected at his Majesty's Coronation, was lighted up, and upwards of 40 couple of villagers enjoyed themselves in dancing.

BLITHFIELD.—Lord Bagot entertained all his labourers and the poor of his parish of Blithfield, men, women, and children, upwards of 200, with roast beef and plum-pudding, ale, &c. The fineness of the day, and the whole scene of it, was as gratifying to the heart as it was honourable to the glorious occasion.

BROCKTON HALL.—The loyal Berkswich Volunteer Infantry, commanded by Captain Chetwynd, paraded in the afternoon, at Brockton Hall, and after exercising for some time, and firing a *feu de joie* in honour of the day, they were regaled with a barrel of excellent strong beer, by Sir George Chetwynd, who also distributed a sum of money amongst the poor in the village and neighbourhood of Brockton.

BURSLEM.—A public dinner at the Town Hall, was attended by about sixty gentlemen, at which John Davenport, Esq., of New Port, presided. The cloth being removed, the health of his Majesty was proposed by the President, which he prefaced by an elegant speech, wherein he observed he was sure the toast he meant to give would be drank with the greatest enthusiasm.—That the reign of the King had been marked with signal benefits to the country, and must be considered, under all circumstances, more prosperous than any that had preceeded it. It might be said that errors had been committed, and in all human institution errors must be looked for—but he would leave it to the company present to say whether under all our burthens and misfortunes, the prosperity and opulence of the country had not risen to an unprecedented pitch. Agriculture, under the direct encouragemen of his Majesty, had been improved beyond calculation ; and arts and commerce had flourished in a manner unknown before. But above all, this country enjoyed a blessing, which, he was sorry to say, the other nations of Europe were at this moment strangers—he meant Freedom, which under our happy constitution, we had hitherto preserved ; while all the nations around us had fallen victims to the worst military despotism.—(*great applause*). It would, he said, be superfluous to observe upon the religious and moral character of our beloved Sovereign, as his virtues had been one of the subjects of an elegant discourse delivered that morning by the worthy minister on his right hand, (the Rev. Mr. Salt), and he would therefore spare himself the trouble of going further into those subjects, and of trying the patience of the company—but would give them " The King, and long life to him," which was drank with enthusiastic applause. "The Queen and Royal Family" was the next toast; afterwards, " The Prince of Wales," &c., &c. The evening was spent with the greatest loyalty and conviviality. The outside of the Town Hall was tastefully and brilliantly illuminated with near by 2000 lamps made for the occasion; busts of the King and Queen, and other transparencies, were displayed in the windows. The letters G. R. with the crown between them, supported by the number 50, and displayed by variegated lamps, adorned one end of the Hall, the other end having the Prince's Plume, embellished in the same manner.

CANNOCK.—Upwards of 500 poor people sat down to a sumptuous dinner on the Bowling Green; and the evening concluded with dancing on the green, a ball at the Inn, bonfires, &c. Festivities were prolonged through the following day. Six hundred dined upon roast beef and mutton, with plum-pudding. Lord Paget contributed £30.

CHEADLE.—The inhabitants of this town subscribed a sum sufficient to provide 500 of the poor with a comfortable meal. The servants were likewise treated with a ball by their respective employers, as an additional means of rejoicing on this memorable occasion. There was also an assembly of the principal inhabitants of the town and its vicinity, who, after dancing until a late hour, partook of an elegant collation provided for the purpose. In the course of the day the bells were rung in honour of occasion; and in the evening there were bonfires and a grand display of fire-works. All ranks seemed to vie with each other in manifesting their attachment to the King

ECCLESHALL.—In the morning of the 25th, two fat cows, which were purchased by subscription, were cut up and distributed amongst the poor, (consisted of upwards of 160 families), of this town and neighbourhood, together with a portion of bread and money, according the number in each family. The principal inhabitants, headed by the Minister, and all the poor who were relieved, afterwards went in procession from the Town Hall to church, and were preceded by a band of music playing " God save the King." After hearing a most excellent sermon, adapted to the occasion, from the Vicar, they returned in the same order. The paupers in the poor-house were likewise regaled by the liberality of the inhabitants. The morning was ushered in by the ringing of bells, which continued at intervals the whole day. " God save the King" was again sung in the evening, in all the principal parts of the town, and the whole concluded with the utmost unanimity.

ENDON.—A liberal subscription was raised by the inhabitants, for the purpose of regaling their poor neighbours with a plentiful supply of good boiled beef, bread, &c., &c., with plenty of good ale. The evening concluded with festivity and hilarity.

FENTON POTTERIES.—The respectable house of Messrs. Bourne, Baker and Bourne, of Fenton Potteries, gave to 300 of their servants, 300 loaves of bread, 300 lbs. of beef, and 300 quarts of ale. They all appeared in the centre of the Manufactory in a decent respectable manner, attended by a band of music. After dinner, and drinking long life to our good old King, and being fully satisfied with the kind liberality of their employers, each departed (benefited by this example of loyalty and generosity in their patrons) comfortably and happy to their repective homes.

FORTON.—John Fenton Boughey, Esq., gave to the poor of the parish of Forton, a fat cow ; and the inhabitants of that parish collected about £20, and gave it away in bread at the same time.

HANBURY.—Great numbers of the poor in the parish of Hanbury, Needwood Forest, were regaled with beef and ale, by the voluntary contributions of their neighbours. The worthy Vicar (the Rev. Mr. Bailey) and his wife, with their usual goodness, dressed all the meat at their own house.

LEEK.—Many of the inhabitants of the town went round to the houses of the poor, and gave food according to the number of each family, and left tickets for a suitable quantity of ale : the Volunteers fired three volleys, and ale was given among them and the assembled populace. A numerous party of Gentlemen dined at the George Inn, with the utmost joy and festivity.

LICHFIELD.—The celebration of the Jubilee in the city of Lichfield commenced at the instant that the clock of the Cathedral announced the termination of the 24th of October. The principal Gentleman of the town, accompanied by a band of music, and by crowds of loyal subjects of every denomination, paraded the different streets, singing the national anthem of "God save the King," amidst the cheers of the numerous spectators, while the bells of the Cathedral, and of the several parish Churches, bore ample testimony to the loyalty of this ancient city. A liberal subscription for the poor had been previously made, and a truly handsome donation of beef, bread, vegetables and money, was made on the Tuesday afternoon, to those whose circumstances needed such assistance, and who by the gratitude and loyalty they evinced, fully repaid the bounty of their benefactors. Considered as a depot for French Prisoners of War, it was peculiarly desirable, that Lichfield should be pre-eminently distinguished on this memorable occasion, and how truly gratifying must it have proved to every Briton present, to witness the unanimity that prevailed through this happy day. The inhabitants of Lichfield proved to the subjects of France, that, the Throne of the English King is fixed on the immoveable basis of his People's Love ! ! ! Although the Churches were well attended, the Cathedral shone most conspicuous, from the combined circumstances of the solemnity of the services, and the brilliancy of the congregation. The whole Collegiate Body moved in procession from the house of Archdeacon Vyse, to the Cathedral, chaunting the 100th Psalm,— the effect of this was indescribably sublime, and the tears of hundreds of spectators spoke, most forcibly, the feelings of their hearts. On their entrance into the Cathedral, the Coronation Anthem was given with great effect, and after a most impressive and suitable sermon from Dr. Vyse, the congregation dispersed, imploring Heaven to prolong and to bless the life of their beloved Monarch.

LONGDON.—The Earl and Countess of Uxbridge gave £100 to be distributed to the poor of Longdon and Cannock, by the Minister and Church-Wardens. The inhabitants testified their joy, by making a bonfire on the very high hill of Ladderege, and regaling upwards of 300 persons plentifully with ale and bread and cheese; and the evening concluded with the utmost demonstrations of joy.

NEWCASTLE.—The morning was ushered in by the ringing of bells, and the lighting up of bonfires in various parts of the town.— A band of music playing "God save the King," paraded the streets, attended by the different Friendly Societies; after which they went to Church, preceded by the Body Corporate, accompanied by J. Macdonald, Esq., one of the Members of the Borough, and many other Gentlemen. The Friendly Societies made a contribution for their superannuated class, to each of whom they gave six shillings, to cheer their hearts on the joyful occasion. An excellent and impressive sermon was preached by the Rev. Clement Leigh, to a very numerous congregation; the principal inhabitants afterwards dined together at the Inns.

NEW LODGE.—Robert Harper, Esq., gave a waggon load of wood, to be burnt on the hill at Hanbury, and an equal quantity at Tutbury, and the two corresponding fires on these two eminences were seen at a great distance.

PATTINGHAM.—This small place appeared by no means proportionably small in its exertions to celebrate this joyous day in such a manner, as that all the inhabitants might partake in its celebration. The morning was ushered in by ringing of bells; and the weather being uncommonly fine, enabled 600 men, women, and children of the poorer residents, (after having attended divine service), to sit down to table out of doors, with all the regularity of a private party; when they were regaled with beef and ale; after having stood up and drank the health of their beloved Sovereign, and joined in the popular song of "God save the King," the remains of the oxen were distributed among them, in quantities, from 4 to 6 lbs. each family, according to its number, and all retired grateful and well satisfied. The persons who had so amply provided for their more indigent neighbours, after enjoying the cheering scene, sat down to dinner at the Pigot's Arms, and finished the day with the jovial conviviality of loyal and true-hearted Britons.

PENKRIDGE.—The parishioners made a subscription for treating the poor; when 1 lb. of bread, 1 lb. of beef, and three pints of ale, to each man, three half-pints to each woman, and half a pint to each child, were given to nearly 1000 persons, and a considerable sum remained to be distributed amongst such poor persons as the Committee of the subscribers should direct. The gentlemen dined at the Littleton's Arms, and several loyal songs and appropriate toasts were given. Sir Edward Littleton went through the duties of the chair, at Penkridge, with a degree of vivacity seldom equalled; and on the following day, when he gave a ball, which was attended by upwards of 100 persons, he remained in the room till half past two in the morning. He was the life and soul of every rejoicing given in his own neighbourhood on the joyful occasion. It might be a difficult task to find in all his Majesty's dominions, a similar instance, in a man who was, like Sir Edward Littleton, a Captain during the Rebellion of 1745.

RONTON. After an appropriate sermon, the congregation assembled at a small distance from the Church, and drank "The King! God bless him, and may he live long to reign over us." This being done, the poor received assistance, from a subscription, and returned home, blessing their good old King, and thanking their neighbours for their liberality.

RUDGE HALL.—Thomas Boycot, Esq., roasted a sheep, and gave plenty of ale to the poor of the Hamlet.

RUGELEY.—The day of Jubilee was celebrated here in a manner becoming true and loyal subjects: it was ushered in with ringing of bells, firing of cannon, and the military band paraded round the town, playing, "God save the King."—The Volunteers attended Church, where a most excellent sermon was preached by the Rev. C. Inge, to a numerous audience. They afterwards dined together at the Town Hall, where several appropriate and suitable toasts and songs were given. Tables were placed in different parts of the town, decorated with upwards of three hundred weight of beef, (in the true old English style) 8 fat sheep, plum-puddings, &c., &c., for all the poor in the town and neighbourhood; a pint of ale was given to each person, to drink health and long life to his Majesty, with three times three; after which there was a dance in the open air, where high and low, rich and poor, intermixed with each other; and the day concluded with the greatest conviviality and good order.

SEDGLEY.—The subscriptions for the poor were marked by a munificence that was in the highest degree honourable to the Gentlemen in the neighbourhood.

STOKE-UPON-TRENT.—The Jubilee was celebrated with every demonstration of joy by Josiah Spode, Esq., at Stoke-upon-Trent. The servants mustered at his extensive Manufactory, from whence they went to Church, where a most impressive sermon was preached by the Rev. W. Robinson, the Rector, to a very crowded congregation. Mr. Spode, attended by about thirty Gentlemen of the neighbourhood, and the servants two and two, to the number of 600, paraded up to the Mount, the residence of Mr. Spode, the music playing "God save the King." When they arrived at the Mount, the servants each drank the health of our good old King, in a pint of ale, and sang "God save the King" in full chorus, the whole of the spectators, not less than 3000, joining heartily in the song. The Gentlemen were entertained with a cold collation in the house; here the good old King's health was drank with three times three, besides numbers of loyal and appropriate toasts.—Afterwards each servant had a pint more of ale, a loaf of bread and a shilling; they then paraded down to the Manufactory, and sang "God save the King," with the two additional verses, as before. Mr. Spode then claimed silence, and in a very handsome manner thanked his servants and the spectators for their attendance, and the good order they had preserved; they were then dismissed, and went comfortable and happy to their homes.

WESTON.—Amongst other liberal donations in the various parts of this county, was that at Weston, the seat of the Right Hon. Lord Bradford; his Lordship and family attended divine service appointed for the day, to enjoy the heartfelt satisfaction, in the sight of a numerous assembly of the poor, amounting to 200 people, who were entertained with every thing they could wish for, by his Lordship, at nine tables. Yet this hospitable feast was but a trifle to that which on the following day contributed to the domestic comfort of many families, who retired to their homes, with the fragments that were left of an ox, several sheep, and six bushels of flour, baked into bread. Two hogsheads of excellent ale were drank, and all were rendered perfectly happy, and cheerfully joined in the loud and loyal toast of "God bless the King," given by the hospitable benefactor.

WOLVERHAMPTON.—The dinners at the Lion and Swan were crowded by the principal people of the town and neighbourhood. At the Lion (T. Giffard, Jun., Esq., president, and F. Holyoak, Esq.) a dinner consisting of every rarity of the season, was served up to about 100 people. A buck was given by Lord Dudley; and game and fruit of every kind by Sir John Wrottesley, Bart., who was present. The 25th being the birthday of the Hon. Baronet, he was cheered on the occasion with additional eclat. Sir John was dressed in the uniform of his regiment of Staffordshire Local Militia, as were all the Officers of the Corps, who were likewise present. Some excellent patriotic toasts and songs were given; and a meeting of more unanimity, loyalty and mirth, never assembled. The dinner at the Swan was equally well conducted; it was influenced by the same spirit, and marked by the same patriotic devotion. The ball at the Theatre in the evening, patronised by the taste of Lady Caroline Wrottesley, could not fail of being well attended. The pit was boarded over, and upwards of 300 Ladies and Gentlemen were present; a throng distinguished not less by beauty and fashion, than order and cheerfulness. Different subscriptions were made in the town for benevolent purposes; and charity and mirth divided the day.

UTTOXETER.—A very liberal subscription having been collected, it was judiciously distributed amongst the poor (amounting in number to more than 1600) in beef, bread, potatoes, and money. In the morning a very excellent sermon was preached on the occasion, by the Rev. J. Stubbs. The poor, at the House of Industry, were regaled with roast beef and plum-pudding, and each person who had attained the age of his Majesty, was allowed a quart of ale, to drink his health, and wish him long to reign.

―――――0―――――

SUFFOLK.

BURY.—The Jubilee Day was observed in Bury by the ringing of bells, and colours flying; a subscription was opened for the poor, and in the evening there was a ball at the Guildhall. It being fair time, the town was extremely full of company. The Earl of Bristol's donation to the parishes of Bury (consisting of 400 pair of blankets and 100 women's cloth cloaks) was distributed to the poor.

ALDBOROUGH.—The very splendid manner in which the Jubilee was celebrated in this place, by the most Noble the Marquis of Salisbury, will ever be a striking instance of his Lordship's loyalty and liberality. His Lordship at his own expense during the whole of this auspicious day, seemed resolved, by every means he could devise, to diffuse joy throughout the town, and to gladden the hearts of all descriptions of its inhabitants. Never was there such a day seen at Aldborough! The town, from one end to the other, from six in the morning till past four the next morning, exhibited one continued series of mirth and gladness.—The morning was ushered in by the ringing of bells, and other demonstrations of joy, which were kept up during the whole day, except during divine service; flags were flying in all directions; the ships in the port and off the place, were dressed in their colours; his Lordship's band paraded the streets, repeatedly playing "God save the King," and other loyal and patriotic tunes. At one o'clock, a royal salute of 21 guns was fired from his Lordship's battery on the terrace in front of his house, after which a *feu de joie* was given by the Volunteers. Houses were opened by his Lordship during the whole of the day, containing refreshments for any of the inhabitants of the town or country who were disposed to partake of them; dancing, and other amusements, in a temporary room erected by his Lordship for the purpose, were kept up with much spirit till a late hour. At eight o'clock there was a most beautiful display of fire-works from his Lordship's gardens, succeeded by a very grand illumination, and appropriate transparencies painted for the occasion. At nine o'clock a large company assembled at his Lordship's house, to partake of various entertainments prepared for them. The rooms were decorated with **banners** and other **Royal** emblems. A most elegant supper was served **up at** one o'clock, **with** the choicest **viands** of the season, **to which** upwards of 70 persons **sat down.** Many loyal toasts were **given,** which **were** followed by **the** song of "God save the King," in full chorus by all the company. Dancing was then resumed, and kept up with great spirit till four o'clock in the morning. His Lordship distributed 1 lb. of beef, with beer, **to** every poor person, **man,** woman, and child, in the town ; beer to all the artificers, and to the detachments from different regiments in the district, employed **on his** Majesty's works here ; to the Volunteers of the town, to the **Sea** Fencibles, and to the crews of all the ships in the port. In short, **every** individual shared his Lordship's bounty **on** this joyful occasion ; **nor was** his Lordship's munificence confined to this place ; he regaled his regiment at Ipswich with beer, and all their wives and children with a dinner, besides contributing largely in different **parts of** the county of Hertford and elsewhere, to celebrate this joyous **event.**

BECCLES.—**A** liberal subscription **was** made by the inhabitants, and added to £50 from the Corporation, and three guineas from the **Apollo Lodge** of Free Masons, for the purpose of providing the poor **with the** comforts of a good meal, to cheer their hearts on **the** 50th **Anniversary** of the King's Accession to the Throne.

BRANDON.—**James Denton,** Esq., of Brandon, regaled **57** poor **widows and others, at his own house,** with roast beef, plum-pudding, and strong ale.

HELMINGHAM.—The Helmingham **V**olunteers, upwards of 500 strong, commanded by the Right Hon. **the Earl** of Dysart, met, and proceeded **to** Helmingham Church, where an appropriate sermon was preached **on the** occasion, **by** the Rev. Edmund Bellman, Chaplain to the Regiment ; **after** which, they formed **in** line, and fired a *feu de joie* in honour **of** the day. His Lordship, with his usual loyalty and generosity, gave **each** of the privates half-a-crown to drink his Majesty's health. An excellent dinner was also provided for the Officers. Many loyal **and** constitutional toasts were drank, and the day spent with the greatest harmony. His Lordship's loyalty and beneficence stopped not here, for at the same time that the Officers and Volunteers were regaling themselves ; the poor old men, women, and children, of Helmingham, and the adjoining parishes, had reason to feel and remember the day as a Jubilee indeed, his Lordship having **given** £100 to be distributed amongst them for that purpose.

IPSWICH.—Early in the morning **the** joyful event was announced by the ringing **of** bells and firing of guns. The shops were closely shut up, and flags **were** displayed from the steeples and from many houses. A Great Court was held in the forenoon, when a congratulatory address **to** his Majesty was unanimously agreed to. After which the Corporation went in regalia to St. Mary's Tower Church, where an excellent discourse was delivered by the Rev. Mr. Howorth, who took his text from 91st Psalm, 14th and two following verses. An appropriate sermon was also preached at St. Clement's Church, before the Free Masons, by the Rev. Dr. Wallis. At noon, Gen. Burgoyne's Brigade attended divine service, on the parade ground, near the New Barracks, after which the 3rd Light Dragoons of the King's German Legion, the 3rd West York, the Northumberland and Hertford Militias, with the Ipswich Loyal Volunteers, fired a *feu de joie* in honour of the day. The troops afterwards passed the General in open order, officers saluting and bands playing. The regiments then marched to their respective barracks, and each soldier was allowed 1s. to drink the King's health. At five o'clock nearly 100 of the principal Gentlemen of the town and neighbourhood sat down to an elegant dinner at the Bear and Crown Tavern. Many loyal and constitutional toasts were given, and some excellent songs; and much harmony and hilarity prevailed throughout. About 100 officers of the garrison dined at the Coffee-house, Generals Loftus and Sir Montague Burgoyne presiding. There were also public dinners at many of the Inns. It might truly be called a Jubilee day, for the poor as well as the rich had their hearts made glad on this occasion. The soldiers' wives, their children, and persons residing here, who belong to parishes out of the town, all partook of the general festival. The parish of St. Lawrence having not above 7 poor resident families (and not more than 110 poor persons belonging to it), very generously raised £40 12s. which was paid into the hands of E. Bacon, Esq., the Treasurer, to be appropriated to the relief of the poor in general. The Free Masons sent a donation of £5 to the Committee in St. Clement's parish, for the same benevolent purpose. J. Bleaden and A. H. Steward, Esqrs., of Stoke Hall, had 3 sheep roasted on the occasion, and upwards of 100 poor persons sat down to dinner, and had 1s. each given to them. What remained was afterwards distributed among them. The prisoners in the Borough Gaol had a dinner of roast beef and plum puddings, ordered them by the Magistrates. The ball and supper at the Coffee House, on Thursday evening, was very fashionably attended; 170 ladies and gentlemen were present. Medallions were very general both at the dinner and the ball. The visiting Magistrates of the county gaol in this town, humanely ordered each person confined therein, a pound and a half of beef and a quart of porter. The gentlemen of the Tower parish gave the debtors in the above prison one guinea on the same occasion.

LAVENHAM.—The inhabitants celebrated the anniversary in the most loyal and handsome manner; contributing very cheerfully and liberally to the comforts of the poor, and spending the day in the utmost conviviality.

MELTON.—The poor in the House of Industry, to the number of 240, were regaled (in the true old English style) with plum puddings, roast beef, and strong beer; and likewise the out-poor of the above parish had a quantity of bread and beer distributed to them, in proportion to the number of their families.

NEDGING.—In commemorating the Jubilee, the principal inhabitants of Nedging began a subscription for the benevolent purpose of furnishing the poor with blankets ; but as they proceeded they had the pleasure to find they should be **enabled to** enlarge their intended **bounty,** and came to a resolution to **give a** supply of linen in addition, to most of the poor families in the **parish.**

PALGRAVE.—Upwards **of 300** persons, men, women, and children, **sat** down to dinner **at one** o'clock, on the Bowling Green, **at** the Swan Inn, which **was** provided for them by Charles Harrison, Esq., and the principal inhabitants of the parish.

RENDLESHAM.—Lady Rendlesham gave a donation of £20 for the purchase of **coals,** for the relief of the poor of the parish of Rendlesham.

SAXMUNDHAM.—**A** liberal subscription took place, and **bread,** meat, and beer, **were** distributed to the poor.

STOKE.—The poor residing in the parish of Stoke, by Nayland, were liberally supplied with meat, bread, and beer : 17 sheep, 3 hogsheads of beer, and 731 loaves, **were** distributed amongst them.

SUDBURY.—The principal inhabitants **of** Sudbury subscribed upwards of £200 towards enabling their indigent townsmen to enjoy the **day, to** which Sir J. C. Hippesley, M.P., for the Borough, added £100 **and 2s.** were allowed for each person.

THORNHAM.—The Duchess Dowager of Chandos gave to the inhabitants of Thornham, a fat ox **and** £20 in money, to be distributed **to** that and two adjoining parishes. The Hartesmere Rangers, under the command of Major Frere, fired an excellent *feu de joie* in the Park, after which three barrels of beer, **with** bread and cheese, were given to the corps, and the Officers adjourned **to** Major House (the seat of her Grace), where **they** were hospitably regaled.

THORPE.—The **Rev. Mr.** Carlos, Rector of Thorpe, by Haddiscoe, after delivering **an excellent** sermon to his parishoners, retired with them to Haddiscoe Crown, where a good dinner of pudding **and** beef was provided by **him** for all the poor ; **after** which **he gave** them plenty of strong **ale.**

WOODBRIDGE.—The **day** was ushered **in** by the ringing of bells. In the forenoon, the Regiments in Garrison there, consisting of the Royal Horse Artillery, the 2nd Light Dragoons of the King's German Legion, the 92d Highlanders, and the Berwickshire Militia, attended by the Woodbridge Volunteers, with their bands, paraded in the Market Place, and from thence marched to hear divine service at the parish Church, where a most excellent discourse was delivered by the Rev. **T.** Carthew, from 1st Peter, 2nd chap., part of the 14th verse. After divine service the respective Regiments, with the Volunteer corps, fired a *feu de joie* at the Garrison, in honour of the day. About 60 of the Officers afterwards partook of **an** excellent dinner at the

Crown Inn. In the evening the young Gentlemen of the Grammar School exhibited a large collection of fire-works on the joyful occasion. Previous to the celebration of the day, £230. was raised by subscription from the inhabitants, as a fund for relieving the poor with useful necessaries, as occasion might occur during the ensuing winter.

―――――o―――――

SURREY.
(SOUTHWARK.—SEE LONDON.)

ASH-HENLEY PARK.—Mrs. Halsea, after very large donations to the amount of £150 to her labourers, made glad the hearts of 70 families, with beef, pudding, and strong beer. The Rector contributed by his liberal example to make the whole parish happy. Bells ringing, and music playing "God save the King," &c., was continued through the evening. The whole concluded with a very grand illumination of the Rector's house, a thing never seen in that place before; and all the country people who came to enjoy the sight, were treated with wine and cake by the Rector and his amiable wife.

BANSTEAD.—Extract of a letter,—" We spent our own day in a very satisfactory manner, the small circle of neighbours attended on the Sunday School after divine service, and with pleasure assisted in waiting upon 70 children, who with smiling countenances were enjoying a hearty meal of roast beef and plum-pudding: the girls were each presented with red cloaks, by the Ladies who patronised the School, and the boys were all clad in brown jackets and trowsers, by Mr. Parry. The rest of the poor partook of the festivity of the day; the men had their dinners together, those of the women and children were sent to their respective homes, but all joined in the general joy. The same circumstances, with little variation, took place in most of the adjacent villages, and in almost all parts of the kingdom. Benevolence to our fellow creatures, I have ever regarded as the best manner of showing our gratitude to our Creator, and in the present instance, this seems to have been the universal opinion. Our parish is very extensive, and in that part of it where Lord Arden lives, the poor were entertained by his Lordship, and every person received a shilling. Lady Arden sent to each child of the Sunday School a white metal medal, in commemoration of the day."

DORKING.—The inhabitants, led by Lord Leslie, Sir Charles Talbot, Mr. Hope, Mr. Barclay, &c., entered into a spirited subscription, for the purpose of enabling the indigent poor in the town and neighbourhood, to partake of the festivities of the day, and from which subscription 1800 persons were provided each with 1 lb. of beef and a quartern loaf of bread. The morning was ushered in by the bells ringing, and every other demonstration of joy and enthusiastic loyalty. The first troop of Surrey Yeomanry Cavalry, the Rifle Company attached to the regiment, and the Right Hon. Lord Leslie, their

Colonel, with the regimental band, paraded, and marched to Church, attended by a great concourse of the inhabitants, where a very excellent and appropriate discourse was delivered by the Rev. John Warneford. After divine service, the military again paraded, and marched to the Commandeau, where they fired several volleys, and, joined by a great body of the inhabitants, gave three cheers in honour of their beloved Monarch having entered the 50th year of his beneficent reign. At five o'clock, most of the neighbouring gentlemen, the troop of Cavalry, and a great many of the inhabitants, sat down to an excellent dinner at the Red Lion Inn, Lord Leslie in the chair; where harmony and convivial mirth prevailed throughout the evening. The poorer class of persons had a bonfire and fire-works provided for their amusement, and were regaled with three barrels of ale.

DURDENS.—At Durdens near Epsom, the poor were made happy by the liberality of the neighbourhood.—George Blackman, Esq. presented to the parish of Epsom, a round Salver of about 22 inches diameter, extremely plain in its decorations, but well-finished in point of workmanship. The centre of the Salver exhibits the Attributes of the Trinity, encompassed with a Glory. Above the centre is inscribed in capitals,—" *Fear God*,"—beneath it—" *Honour the King*,"—and towards the bottom in a scroll,—" *This Salver was presented to the parish of Epsom, in commemoration of the 50th Anniversary of the Reign of his Gracious Majesty, George the Third; by George Blackman, (of Durdens) Esq.*"

FARNHAM.—The inhabitants zealously expressed their loyalty to our excellent and venerable King, by a large collection and distribution of charity amongst the poor, of whom also a considerable number were hospitably and bountifully entertained at dinner, in the Great Hall at Farnham Castle.

FRIMLEY HOUSE.—John Tekell, Esq., of Frimley House, by Bagshot, and his Lady, the Right Hon. Lady Griselda Tekell, most hospitably entertained the poor of the parish of Frimley, and their neighbours, tenantry and tradesmen; for the former of whom, who composed a body of about 400 persons, an ox was roasted whole, and distributed in the most judicious manner, to the satisfaction of every person, with a liberal allowance of bread, potatoes, plum-pudding, and beer; while for the latter, an elegant ball and supper were given in his Mansion, in which the dancing was kept up till a very late hour.

KEW.—The morning was ushered in by the firing of cannon, and the ringing of bells. The board of Artificers walked in procession to Church at ten o'clock. After divine service, Messrs. George and Henry Warren entertained 100 persons with roast beef, plum-pudding, &c., in a spacious marquee, erected for the purpose, upon Kew Green. Porter, ale, and punch, were likewise plentifully distributed. On his Majesty's health being drank, 50 pieces of cannon were discharged. In the evening, the whole town was illuminated. A grand gothic arch was erected, from the centre of which the British Star was suspended, and underneath a striking likeness of his Majesty, with the motto of " *Virtue, Honour, and Glory.*" The whole of the trees around the green were illuminated by variegated lamps, in radiant arches, wreaths, and columns, and the evening concluded with a rustic dance, and fire-works.

KINGSTON-UPON-THAMES.—A numerous company assembled at the Town Hall, to celebrate the Jubilee at Kingston-upon-Thames. After a very plentiful dinner, the Recorder, Mr. Evance, addressed them in the following words :—" Gentlemen, It is with infinite pleasure I rise to give the health of our gracious Sovereign, who this day enters on the 50th Anniversary of his Accession to the Throne, and on this happy event I feel highly gratified in giving the health of the King in this place, because the town of Kingston has always been, and, I trust, ever will be, distinguished for its loyalty. In his private life, Gentlemen, you will accord with me, the King has shown himself a man of exemplary piety, a pattern of conjugal fidelity, and parental tenderness, humane and charitable to the poor, and a kind and indulgent master to those who serve him. In his public character, the King has been always a firm supporter of the Established Religion of the Country—a liberal patron of the Arts and Sciences—a promoter and encourager of Agriculture. Manufactures and Commerce—at all times anxious for the welfare of his People, and the independence of the Nation.—May it please Heaven to preserve a life so truly valuable to us for many years, and may those years be crowned with unanimity at home, and peace with all the world." The King's health was then drank with three times three, under a discharge of cannon, and the loud acclamations of the populace below, who were regaling themselves with three barrels of strong ale round a bonfire.

PETERSHAM.—A liberal subscription had been made by the inhabitants of this little parish; and that friend of humanity and religion, the Earl Kerry, ever foremost in active benevolence, and in promoting the comforts of the poor, had kindly consented to undertake the direction and management of this Parochial Jubilee, and had determined to defray, from his private purse, whatever expense might remain after the application of the money collected. In consequence of this regulation, all the children in the parish, amounting to about seventy, where completely clothed in such colours as their parents desired. To every poor family was distributed a quarter of a chaldron of coals, and the whole population feasted at one immense table. In the morning, at half past ten o'clock, the whole parish, by appointment of the Churchwarden, having assembled in the avenue leading to Lord Dysart's house, and in front of Lord Kerry's, with their children, boys and girls, thus newly clothed, thence went in procession to Church, preceded by the Churchwarden, Overseers, and Beadle, with a band of music. Arrived at the Church, the pews and aisles were completely filled; and to the honour of the audience be it said, that more decency, more regularity, or more respect for the Sacred Place where they were assembled, could not possibly be observed. Every heart exulted with holy joy at the animating sight. The prayers were read in a very impressive manner, an appropriate sermon delivered, and the whole closed with "God save the King." All then returned to the avenue to wait the hour of dinner, when the spacious walk was quickly crowded. A table was raised in the avenue exactly facing Lord Kerry's gate; it was 90 feet long, under a covering very elegantly festooned all round within and without with laurel; the pillars which supported it were covered in a similar manner, so that the whole had the appearance of being in a laurel bower; and to diffuse as widely as possible the joy resulting from this happy occasion, his Lordship had invited to his house, the better to see and witness the entertainment, not only all that resided in the village, but whoever were in a remote degree connected with the parish. At two o'clock precisely, dinner was served, the worthy Churchwarden taking his place at the head of the table, the Overseer at the bottom, the Constable and Deputy at each side of the middle; and the Marquis of Bute's, the Earl of Kerry's, Lord Stopford's, and Lady Beverley's house-stewards seated themselves at proper distances for the purpose of helping the happy guests. Then the Curate from the head of the table said grace, which he did also at the end of dinner, all standing up and uncovering. There was then prepared for the whole company a vast quantity of punch, sufficient to give to every person at table (about 140) to drink two loyal toasts,—1. "May God long preserve our best of Kings to his grateful people."—2. "May the successors of our beloved King ever imitate his virtues both public and private, that all future generations may be as happy as we are." With the first were given three cheers, and "God save the King," and during all the time of dinner the band of music had been playing. When the whole company had thus completely satisfied themselves, and had nearly emptied their hogshead of ale, another party sat down to consume the remainder of the feast. This was soon done, and then the first company, the inhabitants of Petersham, began dancing in three sets, which was continued with the greatest gaiety, good humour, and decorum, till nine o'clock, when all retired content and happy.

STOKE D'ALBORNE.—In the morning a very appropriate and excellent discourse was delivered by the Rector, the Rev. Mr. Vaillant, after which he entertained the farmers with a dinner, and in the evening presided at a supper, given by a subscription of the inhabitants to the poor of the parish, who with one heart and voice drank the King's health, and sang "God save the King," till a late hour.

WORNERSH.—Lord Grantley entertained the Mayor and Corporation of Guildford, at his house at Wornersh, and ordered wine and punch to be given to all the inhabitants of the place, to drink the health of the King and the Royal Family.

SUSSEX.

CHICHESTER.—The Jubilee commenced by the ringing of bells, hoisting flags, &c., on the ancient tower in the Cathedral Churchyard. At one o'clock the troops in the barracks and adjacencies, commanded by his Grace the Duke of Norfolk, fired a *feu de joie*. In the evening, the ball at the Assembly Room was attended by upwards of 400 fashionables. A Jubilee ball, at the Dolphin, had many visitors. The room was tastefully decorated. The Swan Inn had the honour to entertain the Corporate Body of this city. The beam of hilarity and content prevaded all ranks, and the emulation to evince true loyalty, was not exemplified in a greater degree in any city in the United Kingdom. The illumination at the Cross, in the evening, was the most brilliant spectacle that can be imagined.

BRIGHTHELMSTON.—The Jubilee rejoicings commenced with ringing of bells, display of flags, and religious duties at the different places of divine worship. At a little before ten in the morning, the Royal Clarence Lodge of Freemasons was assembled by the Master, Wardens, and Brethren, who soon after, in full regalia, and the symbols of the order, attended by the Lewes and Shoreham Lodges, moved in procession to the church, preceded by the band of the Royal South Glocester, playing "God save the King." The church, as was expected on the occasion, was crowded to an excess, by a congregation that seemed fully to feel the solemnity of the occasion, and justly appreciated the merits of a most appropriate, animated, and eloquent discourse, by the Vicar, the Rev. R. Carr; wherein the blessings enjoyed under the reign of our august Sovereign were plainly and impressively delivered. At the close of the service, the Freemasons returned through the principal streets to their Lodge, the Old Ship Tavern, preceded by the Pandean Band of his Royal Highness the Prince of Wales, attended by a large concourse of spectators. Some excellent *feux de joie* were fired. At half-past one the doors of the Royal Riding-House were thrown open, for the reception of P. Mighell, Esq., and his party of 2000 poor inhabitants, for whom, at his individual expense, a good and plentiful repast had been prepared, of bread, beef, mutton, and strong beer, all of which would not, in point of excellence, have disgraced the tables of the first quality. One hundred of the principal inhabitants, decorated with a white ribbon, on which the words 'God save the King,' were imprinted, came, each provided with a carving knife and fork, and officiated as stewards on the occasion, by cutting up and distributing the viands to the grateful and delighted guests, who fed with rapture, and poured unmingled blessings on their Sovereign and the generous founder of the feast. The tables were so conveniently disposed, the whole length of the Riding-House, that 300 more than the originally intended number were entertained, each steward accommodating 20 persons, while the beer was taken from well scoured pails, placed at proper distances in the centre of the tables, which were kept constantly full by well arranged hogsheads, and persons employed to attend them. In two elevated seats, in the upper and lower end of the hall, sat Mr. Mighell as the donor, and Mr. Phillips as the provider of the feast. By the sound of a bell, silence was instantly obtained for the delivery of grace, and for the complimentary ecomiums with which Mr. Mighell preluded the health of the king, which all the multitude rose up to, composed of the women and children, all breathing one united sentiment of loyal gratitude and joy, presenting one of the grandest and most interesting sights that ever human eye delighted in, while the hats were waved, and nine hearty cheers, which succeeded the communication of the health, produced a spontaneous gust of joyful tears of all that either partook or witnessed the rapturous enjoyment. Plenty presided over the hospitable board in large abundance; and after all were sufficed, the fragments, which were great, were borne away by the elderly branches of large families. The rejoicings of this multitude, great as it was, and increased by the presence of some of the first families and inhabitants, drawn by curiosity to the spot, passed off without the slightest interruption or accident whatever. A party of 1500 were in a similar way entertained in the farm-yard of Mr. Scrace, by a private subscription of a few inhabitants. A handsome collection was made in the Chapel Royal, where a suitable discourse was delivered by the Rev. Mr. Portis, and the Coronation Anthem excellently sung, assisted by the Prince's Band, who appeared in full uniform. The amount of collection was delivered to the poor, in bread, beer, coal, and candle. At five o'clock a large assemblage of Freemasons sat down to an excellent dinner at the Old Ship, where, amidst hilarity and good humour, many excellent songs and toasts were given. After the dinner, a ball and supper closed the day of rejoicing, at which 300 persons were present, some of whom kept up the dancing till nearly six in the morning. Thx Castle ball and supper were on the most splendid scale of elegance and excellence, with a beautiful transparency of Time and Britannia placing a wreath on the head of his Majesty, surmounted by Fame.—The inhabitants of the town of Brighthelmston, being desirous of perpetuating by some public testimony, their cordial attachment to the person, and unfeigned respect for the character of his Majesty, conceived that no act would be more grateful to his royal heart, or more expressive of their loyalty than to signalise the Jubilee day by establishing a charaitable accumulating fund, for the benefit of such persons, resident in Brighton, that might be sufferers from casualities, either by sea or land. This Institution consists of a Patron, (His Royal Highness the Prince of Wales), President, six Vice-Presidents, and 32 Trustees. The Society is so constituted that it has every prospect of going on, and increasing in magnitude and consequence; and it is hoped, at no very distant period, may afford such relief to all those in the parish, who may be sufferers, as may enable them to support the difficulties of their situation, without that degradation which attends parochial assistance.

BOGNOR.—A Sunday School was instituted, under the patronage of her Royal Highness the Princess Charlotte of Wales, in honour of this auspicious day, which it is hoped will prove useful to future generations. The work, carried on here by Colonel Scott, for the prevention of future encroachments of the sea, exhibit a fair prospect of success, and were solemnly dedicated to his Sacred Majesty, on the Grine called the Duke of Kent's Bulwark.

Duke of Kent's Bulwark, October 25*th*, 1809.

" This day having been marked as a day of rejoicing, on account of his Majesty's entrance into the 50th Year of his Reign, We, the Bognor Griners, do humbly dedicate this specimen of our new art to His Majesty ; in the humble hope, that our exertions will be crowned with success ; and that it will prove the means of saving many thousand Acres of his Majesty's Dominions from the raging of the tempestuous Ocean. We have had the satisfaction of seeing, that the last Spring Tides have not been able to affect the bank of this beautiful Field : Whereas, it is well known that if it were not for the works lately erected, the present Spring Tides would have burrowed into it like a rabbit warren; and when our works are completed, we look with confidence to their withstanding their utmost rage of winds and waves."

"God save the King," was then cheered with three times three, after which the Griners regaled on a roasted sheep, and a plentiful sufficiency of Turner and Hardwick's excellent ale, provided for the occasion by Colonel Scott, to which an additional barrel was presented by those honest and patriotic Brewers.—About seven o'clock, the Griners' feast was concluded, with that decent hilarity which characterises the labouring order of men at Bognor. The King, (with many other loyal toasts), and long may he live to reign over us, was enthusiastically cheered by the Griners, and a numerous and grateful populace ; but more especially that of their Royal Benefactress, the Princess Charlotte of Wales, and the worthy founders of the Jubilee Institution. The Southern Coasts of Britain have been preyed upon for ages by the insatiate Ocean, which is supposed to have swallowed up millions of acres from Selsea Point to Beachy Head, all of which might have been saved, provided this mode of Grining had been known, in the efficacy of which, Colonel Scott puts every confidence, having found his hypothesis to be well founded, in every trial he has hitherto made ; and also well knowing that, if it should prove defective in any respect, he has a Corps de Reserve, equal to all emergencies. The field thus saved, has a sea front of 1200 feet, commanding the most beautiful sea views and landscapes, which will be laid out for building ground, upon a plan perfectly unique and picturesque.

BRIGHTLING.—The poor were liberally regaled with a Jubilee dinner, by subscription, at the head of which was John Fuller, Esq., who gave ten guineas. The Rev. Mr. Haley, and a number of farmers and tradesmen, also subscribed very handsomely, and a great plenty of beef, bread, and strong beer, was distributed to gladden the hearts of the indigent.

BLETCHINGTON.—The Officers of the Nottingham Militia celebrated the 25th, at Bletchington, by a sumptuous dinner to the neighbouring Gentlemen, and the Squadron of the 3d Dragoon Guards, and of the 81st Regiment quartered there. The Serjeants and their wives had a most excellent dinner, and a bottle of wine each. The rest of the regiment with their wives and children, were entertained with roast beef and pudding, and as much ale as they could drink, all at the expense of the Officers.

CHIL-GROVE.—Mr. Woods, of Chil-Grove, near Chichester, gave two sheep, which were killed, and distributed in joints proportionable to the size of each labourer's family in the parish, to the number of 22, containing about 105 persons.

COMBE.—Mr. Shiffner gave a fat bullock and plenty of beer to the poor of Hamsey, and in the evening, his summer house, in an elevated situation, was handsomely illuminated.

CUCKFIELD PLACE.—The seat of Warden Sergison, Esq., was a scene of great festivity and joy. At an early hour in the evening, the avenue of venerable limes, and ancient turret, leading to the hospitable mansion, were brilliantly illuminated with variegated lamps, and thronged with multitudes of spectators from the neighbouring towns and villages. The company invited, consisting of the Nobility and Gentry in the neighbourhood, and a number of the fashionable visitors from Brighton, were ushered into the hall, where some happily designed transparencies engaged the admiration and attention of every one present. An excellent likeness of his Majesty, the Crown, and the number 50, decorated with wreaths of roses, &c., were the principal devices. About ten o'clock the Prince of Wales's band struck up "God save the King," when a grand display of fire-works was seen from the turret, and a large bonfire was lighted at the extremity of the avenue, which had together, a very fine effect. Soon after the fire-works, a ball was apened, and the company, about 70 in number, continued the cheerful dance till two in the morning, when they sat down to a supper composed of all the delicacies of the season; after the repast, his Majesty's health was drank with enthusiasm, and "God save the King," was sung in full chorus. The elegant party immediately afterwards resumed the ball, and about seven in the morning departed, highly gratified at the splendid exhibition of loyalty with which they had been so liberally entertained. Plenty of strong beer was distributed to the populace in the Park.

EASTBOURNE.—The visitors and inhabitants of this fashionable watering place, anxious to show their loyalty and attachment to our most gracious and beloved Sovereign, celebrated his Accession to the Throne in a most distinguished and spirited manner. The Royal Artillery, and Royal Surrey and Shropshire regiments mustered at one o'clock, in the field near the Sea Houses, and fired a *feu de joie*, which was answered by the Martello Towers along the Coast, beginning at Beachy Head, and ending at Hastings. Two hundred and seventy women and children belonging to the Shropshire, were feasted in the Barrack square with roast beef and plum-pudding, the band of the Shropshire playing "God save the King." The Lodge of Druids assembled together to dine at the King's Arms; and in the evening the Shropshire and Surrey Officers, and a numerous party, dined, and concluded the day with a ball.

EAST HOATHLY.—To each poor person, whether man, woman, or child, were distributed 2 lbs. of beef, a sixpenny loaf, and a pint of strong beer, the comforts of which were extended to 230. In addition to the above, the peasantry had a good supply of strong beer, to drink his Majesty's health.

FLETCHING.—The Jubilee was observed with due attention. After divine service, which was numerously attended, all the workmen employed by Lord Sheffield, with their wives and families, upwards of 130 in number, assembled at Sheffield Place. When they had plentifully feasted on roast beef, plum-pudding, and other viands, Lord and Lady Sheffield entered the festive hall, and his Majesty's health was drank with three times three, accompanied by a royal salute from the cannon in the Park. His Lordship then took the opportunity of observing that, "under the government of our excellent King, this country continues to flourish and grow rich, while all the other nations of Europe are sunk in the most abject state of slavery and misery; and their young men dragged from their homes to fight the battles of their enemy and tyrant in foreign and distant countries, where they perish by hundreds of thousands; that, in consequence of the prosperity of this country, we are enabled to pay taxes to an amount never experienced before; but that the Legislature had taken care that no taxes should fall on the absolute necessaries of life, such as corn, bread, meat, fish, and other articles, which are most severely taxed in other States; that, the great mass of taxes is imposed on the rich, and on those who can best afford to pay them; that the taxes they pay are very heavy indeed, to which, however, they cheerfully submit, knowing that their property, their families, their freedom, and their religion, cannot be preserved by any other means; that, amidst all the calamities of the rest of the world, we have lost neither territory nor credit; we have expended large sums, it is true, in defence of our Allies, and of the liberties of mankind; we have sent forth great armies, who have raised the character of British valour to a height even beyond what it had reached before; and, at no period has the name of Britain ever attained greater honour and renown, and the manufactures, the commerce, and the revenue of the country, have never been in so prosperous a state as under the beneficent reign of the Sovereign, whom it has pleased God to spare so long to us." The healths of Lord and Lady Sheffield were cordially drank, amidst repeated cheers; and an excellent song written by the Steward on the occasion of the day, was then sung by him, and received with the greatest applause. The principal farmers, also, entertained their workmen and families, and the poor widows, and other persons residing in that extensive parish, who did not come with the description of those invited, received three shillings each, from a fund which had been raised by subscription for that purpose.

HASTINGS.—The dawning of the finest day that ever appeared in October, was ushered in by ringing of bells, firing of cannon, and music playing. A great many houses were decorated with flags, and proper mottoes for the day. Large branches of oak, boughs of laurel, and evergreens of all sorts, ornamented the fronts of several houses, others had devices suited to the occasion. Flags were hoisted upon the Church steeples. At the Custom House was a Crown in Glory, surrounded by a grove of laurel, surmounted by a large St. George's Ensign, and under the Crown this inscription :—" *God bless the King! Preserve him long to reign, and grant Him after death, a Crown of Glory!*" The service at Church was properly attended, and an excellent sermon preached by the Rev. Mr. Whester, the Rector. The Royal East Middlesex Regiment attended at All Saints' Church. After service they proceeded to East Hill, where, extending their files along the irregular summit, for about a quarter of a mile, they fired a *feu de joie*, whilst the band at intervals played "God save the King." About the same time, the Sea Fencibles fired a royal salute from the battery, and the Martello Towers continued a distant thunder from a line of twenty miles in Pevensey Bay. The appearance of the Military, with the echo of the firings across the valley, had a grand and pleasing effect. Having finished three loud huzzas, which were answered by the spectators on the Castle Hills, the Regiment paraded the streets, with the band playing, colours flying, people huzzaing, &c. Colonel Wood then marched them to the Barracks, where upwards of 1000 men, and the Officers, sat down to dinner in the Barrack-yard, on roast beef and plum-pudding. In the mean time, the Mayor, J. G. Shorter, Esq., (who had exerted himself, with great loyalty and spirit, in making arrangements for the day), and the principal inhabitants, assembled at dinner in the Town Hall, and spent the afternoon with the greatest joy and festivity. There was a bonfire on the hill, composed of ten waggon loads of faggots and combustibles, and a tar-barrel on a mast, 50 feet high. Fifty rockets were discharged, and many fire-works exhibited. A ball at the Swan Inn was attended by about 250 persons, and in the room was a transparency of Neptune, yielding the Empire of the Seas to Britannia, in the Reign of George Third ! The poor in the different Workhouses feasted on roast beef, plum-pudding, and strong beer. Every one had a holiday, the men and women a shilling apiece to spend, and the children six-pence. A subscription was raised, amounting to £400 1s. 6d. from which 1850 persons were supplied with 2880 lbs. of beef, 1850 six-penny loaves, 2880 pints of porter, 2872 gallons of potatoes, and a balance of £188 left to be distributed among 36 prisoners of war in France.

HORSHAM.—The Jubilee was celebrated in the most joyous, loyal, and benevolent manner; the day was ushered in by the ringing of bells, which continued till noon, when the garrison, consisting of the 51st Regiment, with part of the 23rd, and 32nd, fired a *feu de joie* on Den hill, which was returned by the Volunteers in the town; after which the regiments of the Garrison marched to the Market-square, and gave three hearty cheers, in which they were joined by the inhabitants with the greatest enthusiasm; at three o'clock a large party dined at the King's Head. A subscription was raised for the poor, from which nearly 1900 received 1 lb. of bread, 1 lb. of meat each, and money in proportion to the number in family.

LEWES.—In the morning, the bells of the several parish Churches and the great town bell, announced the third occurrence of the 50th Anniversary of a British Monarch's Reign; about eleven o'clock, the inhabitants assembled at their several places of religious worship, to return thanks to the Almighty, for the happiness bestowed on this favoured land, by the long continued life of their mild and virtuous King, under whose benignant government they have enjoyed so many blessings. Soon after one, the brave 82nd Regiment, dressed in new clothes, were drawn up on Cliff Hill, where they fired three excellent *feux de joie*, and gave three hearty cheers, their band playing "God save the King," after which they marched back to their Barracks, where the men were plentifully regaled with roast beef, plum-pudding, and strong beer, by their Officers.—The Yeomanry Corps of Captain Shiffner and Captain Reed Kemp, after attending divine service, also fired in honour of the occasion. The Union Flag was hoisted at the New Shire Hall, and the town's people assembled with their worthy Representatives, at an excellent dinner provided at the Star. While these proofs of loyalty were celebrated by the higher and middling ranks of society, the poor were partaking of plentiful dinners of beef, and plum-pudding, provided by the kindness of their wealthier neighbours, and the whole day was spent by all ranks with the greatest thankfulness, mirth, and hilarity. In the Cliff, upwards of 400 were plentifully regaled at dinner, in a large room fitted up for the occasion. In Southover, the poor were also liberally supplied with bread and meat by the wealthy. In the evening, the Barracks were tastefully illuminated by the Officers, and a grand display of fire-works was exhibited both there and in the town.

NEWHAVEN.—The 50th year of his Majesty's reign was celebrated with the utmost loyalty and patriotism; the whole of the inhabitants who chose to partake thereof, were regaled with beef and beer, at the expense of the principal inhabitants of the place; the parties were entertained at three houses, and in the whole, nearly 150 met on the occasion; the utmost harmony and good humour prevailed, and every person seemed to hail the day with the greatest pleasure imaginable; the Volunteers attended divine service, and afterwards gave in the ranks, "Long live the King," with three times three. About 20 of the principal inhabitants dined together at the White

Hart Inn, where the greatest joy abounded until about ten o'clock, when they departed, highly gratified, to their respective homes.

STANMER.—Earl of Chichester's seat. Among other festivals which marked the joyful commemoration of our beloved Monarch's 50th year of his reign, the liberal and generally diffused merriment and charity of the Earl of Chichester among the poor of his estate at Stanmer, deserve to be noticed. About 100 of his labourers, with their wives and children, sat down to old English roast beef and plum-pudding, with plenty of strong beer. To the head of each family a new guinea was given, to the wives and children each a new dollar, and a Jubilee medal. Fire-works were let off in the Park, and other demonstrations of joy noted the memorable day. The happy peasantry closed the day's regalement by loudly and heartily uniting in the truly national anthem of "God save the King." Similar acts of munificence were giving by his Lordship to the several parishes of Falmer, Plumpton, and Hoadley, in this county.

WISTON PARK.—The seat of Charles Goring, Esq., was the scene of unbounded festivity. Its generous owner, with a degree of loyalty and liberality worthy a true English Gentleman, entertained all his tenantry and inhabitants of the parish in which he resides, from the most aged to the child in arms, amounting to 400, in the fine Gothic Hall of his ancient and venerable Mansion. In the course of the evening, there was a display of fire-works, and the night closed with a dance, in which all ranks joined with the greatest cheerfulness.

WORTHING.—About 2000 of the poor inhabitants sat down on the Steyne, to the following repast :—1000 loaves of bread, 1 fat ox, 10 sheep, 5 bushels of potatoes, 200 cabbages, 3 bushels of turnips, 1 bushel of carrots, 150 rich plum-puddings, a large quantity of cheese, and 9 hogsheads of strong beer. Fifty Gentlemen of the town attended to carve and wait on the happy party, a band playing in the centre, the flags flying at the angles, and the Nobility and Gentry parading. The old men were provided with tobacco and pipes, and the pipe and tabor were not forgotten for the younger part.

At Rye, Battle, and other places in this county, great rejoicings prevailed among every description of his Majesty's subjects; and loyalty and jollity were everywhere conspicuous, from the gilded mansion to the lowly cottage ! The opulent farmers also gave very liberally to their work people and others, and they were very few, within a number of miles, who had not the means as well as the will, to render the 25th a real day of Jubilee

---

WARWICKSHIRE.

WARWICK.—The auspicious morn was ushered in with ringing of bells ; public worship was performed at both the churches, chapels, &c. The Mayor and Corporation attended at church, and most of the shops were shut up. A very liberal subscription was made, amounting to about £360, which was most judiciously applied to the relief of the poor; not less than 3780 persons received each 2 lbs. of meat and 1 lb. of bread; ale was not given, in consequence of the large proportion of meat. The total quantity of meat given amounted to 7800 lbs., and bread 3780 lbs. Ten guineas were voted to the Commanding Officer of the 103rd regiment, to be applied in purchasing ale for the soldiers to drink his Majesty's health. A liberal supply of bread and meat was also given to the prisoners in the town and county gaols. Neither fire-works nor illuminations were permitted. Every description of people united as with one heart, in celebrating the day.

ALLESLEY.—A very handsome subscription was set on foot by the Earl of Clonmell, the Rev. Mr. Bree, and other Gentlemen, to which the rest of the inhabitants subscribed in a generous manner, and upwards of 400 persons were very liberally supplied with meat, bread, and beer, to celebrate the joyful day.

BADDESLEY. In the small parish of Baddesley every poor person received money according to the number of their family, but none had less than five shillings.

BIRMINGHAM.—The morning was ushered in with the ringing of bells, and the shops were mostly shut throughout the town. A very general attendance took place at the different churches and chapels, and other places of worship, at the doors of which the sum of £310 3s. 7d. was collected for the benefit of the poor; in addition to which the Right Hon. Lord Dudley and Ward, with his usual liberality, presented £25 and Heneage Legge, Esq., £10. After service the 4th Dragoon Guards fired three volleys in honour of the day, as did also the Handsworth Volunteer Cavalry, drawn up in the Market Place.—At three o'clock commenced the Druids' Procession, consisting of nearly 1,400 members, from Lodges 17, 31, and 32. of the town, and No. 40 from Walsall, which was attended by a vast concourse of people. After proceeding round the Statue of Nelson, they attended divine service at St. Philip s Church, where an excellent and appropriate sermon was delivered by Dr. L. Booker, from the following text, 1 Pet. 2 c. 9th and 17th v. The festival was commemorated in the evening, by different dinner parties at most of the inns and public places in the town. Edward Cairns, Esq., the Low Bailiff, gave a sumptuous entertainment at the Shakspeare Tavern; amongst whom were the Members for the County, the Magistrates, Clergy, &c., &c. It is unnecessary to add that the evening was spent in the greatest loyalty and good humour.—A circumstance which added not a little to the pleasure of the day, and the beauty of the scene, was the opening to public view the celebrated Bronze Statue of the ever to be lamented hero, Viscount Nelson. Every thing was ready for submitting this statue to public inspection on the 21st, the anniversary of the glorious victory of Trafalgar, but the Committee properly conceived that it would be better to defer the ceremony till the anniversary of his Majesty's accession, in order to heighten the joy of the public, on an event so interesting to the nation. At twelve o'clock at night, on the 24th, the signal for opening the statue **was** given, to usher in the morning of our good King's fiftieth anniversary, and such **a** scene of popular eagerness was hardly ever witnessed **before.** Peace officers were stationed to protect the workmen, until **the awnings of** the scaffold immediately connected with the monument were removed, but **this business was** hardly a moment over, **when the** populace broke down every impediment, and not fewer **than** 5,000 people present immediately gave three cheers for Nelson, and joining a fine band **of** music **who** attended on the occasion, sung "God save the King." **The** loyal enthusiasm of the people was not surpassed in any part **of the** Empire. The Local Militia, in the course of the day, formed round the statue, and fired a *feu de joie*. The whole of the day **was marked** by patriotic festivity.—The following illustration of the **statue was** given to the public, and it is admitted that the **artist,** Mr. Westmacott, has fully supported his high reputation by this **work, and** that it is in all respects worthy of the dignified and impressive **subject.**

"In this work, **intended to** perpetuate the greatest example **of** Naval Genius, simplicity has been the chief object in the arrangement. The Hero is represented in **a** reclined and dignified attitude, his left arm reposed upon an anchor: he appears in the costume of his country, invested with the insignia of those honours by which his Sovereign and distant Princes distinguished him. To the right of the statue is introduced the grand symbol of the Naval profession ; Victory, the constant leader of her favourite Hero, embellishes the prow. To the left is disposed a sail, which passing behind the statue, gives breadth to that view of the composition.—This group is surmounted upon a pedestal of statuary marble. A circular form has been selected as best adapted **to** the situation.

"To personify **that** affectionate regard which caused the present patriotic tribute to be raised, the Town of Birmingham, murally crowned, in a dejected attitude, is represented mourning her loss ; she is accompanied by groups of Genii, or children, in allusion to the rising race, who offer her consolation by bringing her the trident and rudder.—To the front of the pedestal is the following inscription.—

"THIS STATUE, IN HONOR OF ADMIRAL LORD NELSON, WAS ERECTED BY THE INHABITANTS OF BIRMINGHAM, **A.D.** 1809."

CASTLE BROMWICH.—By a very liberal subscription at this place, sufficient money was collected to distribute coals, blankets, and various articles of **wearing** apparel, amongst the labouring poor of the village.

COMPTON.—The Right Hon. Lord Willoughby de Broke caused an excellent sermon to be preached at his own chapel, by the Rev. Dr. Meade, to his labourers, and a numerous congregation; after which they were all directed to the front of the house, and being led by his Lordship's son, the Hon. Major Vernon, they sung "God save the King," with three times three, concluding with "Long live the King." They afterwards partook of a sumptuous dinner, in his Lordship's hall, and the remainder of the day was spent in festivity and singing, with plenty of good old English ale.

COVENTRY.—At half past five o'clock in the morning the propitious epoch was ushered in by the military band belonging to the 14th Regiment of Light Dragoons playing "God save the King." At six, the bells at the different churches commenced their melodious peals. The Mayor and Corporation attended at St. Michael's Church, where a most excellent and impressive discourse was preached by the Rev. R. Simpson, from Psalm 22nd, verse 28th. During divine service, the "Coronation Anthem," and the "Hallelujah Chorus," were performed in a very superior style, by a numerous and able choir. At the end of the service the organist played "God save the King." At the other churches and chapels suitable discourses were delivered to numerous auditors: indeed, they were never remembered to have been so crowded as upon this occasion. The liberal subscription of the inhabitants amounted to £756 5s., by which upwards of 11,000 individuals were supplied with meat, bread, and ale. All the debtors in the gaol were released from confinement; and the criminal prisoners were, both in gaol and bridewell, provided with an ample supply of roast beef, and five shillings given to each person. The boys belonging to Bablake had sixpence each, and plenty of roast beef and plum pudding. The women at Ford's Hospital, and the old men at Bablake Hospital received two shillings each. The 40 girls belonging to the Blue Coat Charity School received two shillings each, which were gratuitously given by the Trustees of that charity. The poor of the House of Industry were most munificently regaled with roast beef, plum puddings, and ale, being the liberal donation of Lord Grey, and the officers of the 4th Warwickshire Regiment of Local Militia. An excellent supper of old English cheer, roast beef, plum pudding and ale, was given at the Barracks, by the Officers of the 14th Dragoons, to the men; they had also a capital display of fireworks, which proved highly gratifying to numerous spectators. A numerous and respectable company dined together at St. Mary's Hall, B. Goode, Esq., Mayor, in the chair. At the upper part of the Hall a full-length portrait of our revered Sovereign, in the possession of the Corporation, was placed between two Corinthian columns, and on the top of the painting were the letters G. R. supporting a crown; the whole of which was beautifully illuminated with variegated lamps, which produced a grand and magnificent effect, and underneath the portrait the following motto:—"*We ne'er shall look upon his like again.*" Many loyal and constitutional toasts were drank. Many other dinners were provided for select parties, at the different inns in the city. A grand display of fire-works was exhibited in Cross Cheaping, and in every part of the city were bonfires and sheep roasting; in short, the whole day was celebrated with that harmony, satisfaction, and loyalty, which clearly evinced that the " Men of Coventry" were alive to the private virtues of their beloved Sovereign; and were disposed, in the greatest possible manner, to testify their regard for his august person and family.

DUNCHURCH.—The inhabitants of Dunchurch, Atherstone, Coleshill, and Kenilworth, testified their loyalty and attachment to the venerable and beloved Monarch, by celebrating the day with every possible demonstration of joy.

HENLEY.—The day was ushered in by ringing of bells, and after divine service, a numerous company of the inhabitants, and neighbouring gentlemen, dined at the Swan Inn, where the afternoon was spent with the greatest conviviality; and every poor inhabitant was liberally supplied with bread and money.

KINGTON.—The whole of the female poor were entertained with a plentiful dinner, by the Lady of the Manor, at her own house, and from a benevolent subscription of the parish at large, (to which her Ladyship also contributed), every family was served with a sufficient quantity of meat, bread, and, ale. The day was ushered in by the ringing of bells—observed by a decent and full attendance on divine service, (where an admirable and appropriate discourse was delivered by their minister), and concluded by orderly demonstrations of joy.

KNOWLE.—In the village of Knowle, the subscriptions allowed of three shillings being given to every poor parishioner.

LAPWORTH.—The liberal contributions of the Rev. H. A. Pye, and the Rev. J. Way, together with those of the principal farmers, allowed of seven shillings being given to every poor person throughout the parish.

LEEK WOOTTON.—Each poor man and poor woman received, after divine service, half a crown, and an additional shilling for every child. A subscription was raised by the parishioners for this purpose, assisted most liberally by Mr. Leigh. Between two and three hundred persons partook of his bounty.

NUNEATON.—The subscription for the relief of the poor, amounted to £87, which was distributed to every poor individual, the same morning:—the day was spent with the greatest loyalty, festivity and decorum.

PACKINGTON.—The Right Hon. the Earl of Aylesford distributed amongst the poor of the four following parishes, Great and Little Packington, Meriden, and Bickenhill, 3000 lbs. of fat ox beef; one loaf of bread, and one pint of strong ale, (brewed 24 years ago) to every man, woman, and child. His Lordship likewise killed thirty brace of hares for his tenants who did not want relief.

RUGBY.—Bread, meat, and coals, were distributed in a plentiful degree to 700 individuals. The School, consisting of more than 230 boys, followed their Master in public procession to Church, the six senior scholars having before assisted in delivering the charitable donations to the poor. A flag was hoisted on the tower of the Church, and the bells rang merrily through the day.

SOWE.—The inhabitants of the villages of Sowe and Woken manifested their loyalty towards his Majesty, on the day, by raising such a subscription, (assisted by the liberality of the Earl of Craven, who gave them £20) as enabled them to distribute to 850 poor persons, 1 lb. of meat, and one six-penny loaf each.

SOLIHULL.—No place in the vicinity of Birmingham was more conspicuously loyal than Solihull, and its neighbourhood, on the Accession day of his Sacred Majesty King George the Third. A very full congregation attended the Church Service, with the music appropriate to the day, after which a distribution of bread and money, the produce of a subscription of the inhabitants, to the amount of £40 took place. A dole, the surplus of the charity estate, was likewise given away to the poor of the parish. In the morning a fat cow, and a proportionate quantity of shilling and six-penny loaves, were delivered at Malvern Hall, the seat of H. G. Lewis, Esq., to upwards of 140 people. At night, the neighbouring tenants and tradesmen supped at the Hall, and drank the King's health with great spirit and conviviality. The front of the house had an illumination of coloured lamps, of "God save the King," surmounted by a brilliant star, and the day was spent with great loyalty and festivity.

STIVICHALL.—The poor of Stivichall, Anstey, Willenhall, Coundon, Coleshill, Hasely, Wroxall, Honiley, &c., were liberally supplied with meat, bread, and beer.

STONELEIGH.—The morning was ushered in by the ringing of bells, and every family in the parish was most handsomely treated with a plentiful supper of bread and beef, and money in proportion to the number of their families, by the kindness and benevolence of the Rev. Mr. Leigh, of Stoneleigh Abbey. A handsome subscription was also raised by the Rev. Mr. Roberts and the inhabitants of the parish, and three fat sheep were roasted, and a hogshead of ale given away to the poor; all of whom, after attending divine service, sat down to dinner in the street of the village, and made a most hearty and comfortable meal. In the evening, a ball was also given to the parishioners, from the subscription, and the merry dance was kept up till six o'clock the next morning. Mr. Thomas Judd, the butcher of the village, gave a sheep to roast, and also the coals to roast it.

STRATFORD-ON-AVON.—A subscription was opened for the purpose of providing the poor of that town, the comforts of a good meal, and to cheer their hearts on the 50th Anniversary of a good Monarch's Accession to the Throne ; the Corporation attended divine service, and afterwards dined together.

SUTTON COLDFIELD.—The Warden and Corporation, and many **of the** neighbouring Gentlemen, dined together at the Town Hall, and celebrated the day with much festivity. At the Church doors, after service, the sum of £25 was collected, which was distributed to **the poor.**

WESTMORELAND.

BRAMPTON.—At this place, the day **was** kept with the greatest joy and festivity. After attending divine worship, and hearing an excellent and appropriate discourse by the Vicar to a numerous congregation ; a division of the Cumberland Rangers fired several rounds at the Cross, after which three barrels of ale were given to the populace. Many of the principal inhabitants adjourned to the Howard's Arms. Bonfires, and other demonstrations of joy, concluded the day.

BROUGH.—The morning was ushered in by hoisting a large British union flag, under the discharge of eight pieces of cannon, ringing of bells, &c. Divine service was well attended at Church in the forenoon, where a most excellent and appropriate discourse was delivered by the Rev. L. Bellas, Vicar. At one o'clock, **a** royal salute of 21 guns,—in the afternoon, divine service was performed at **the** Methodist Chapel, where an excellent discourse was given by the **Rev.** Mr. Poole, the resident Minister. In the evening a beautiful transparency, painted by Mr. Horsley, of Sunderland, representing the Eye of Providence looking on the British Crown, with G. III. R. and "God save the King," was exhibited on the front of the house of Mr. Rumney, Surgeon.—A brilliant display of fire-works, prepared by Mr. Todd, **of** Mr. Bailey's Academy, and another royal salute of cannon, and three cheers, closed **the scene.** The principal part of the rejoicings was under the direction of Major Bland ; whose Lady, in commemoration of the event, distributed to the poor of the place 50 loaves of bread.

KENDAL.—The National Jubilee was observed **with a spirit that** manifested the attachment of the people to their gracious Sovereign. The Local Militia attended divine service ; after which they fired several volleys. The Corporation and principal Gentlemen of the place, dined together at the Crown Inn, and spent the evening in a truly social and harmonious manner. In the evening, a ball at the Assembly Room was very numerously attended. The Churches were well filled, and excellent discourses delivered by the respective Clergy.

TEMPLE SOWERBY.—The Jubilee was celebrated at this place in a loyal and spirited manner. The Gentlemen partook of an excellent dinner prepared at the New Inn, and drank the usual loyal toasts upon the happy occasion. They provided an equally good supply, with plenty of ale, for the villagers. The evening's amusements concluded by a pleasant assembly.

———o———

WILTSHIRE.

SALISBURY.—The inhabitants were most liberal in their subscriptions, by which means the poor amply partook of the festivities of the day; there remained a large overplus, which was to be expended for their more permanent comfort. A Gentleman of this place gave to every father of a family among a certain class of the poor of that city, "a Jubilee pipe of tobacco," or rather a paper of tobacco, with a tobacco stopper, exhibiting in profile a likeness of the King.

BOCKHAMPTON.—M. Pitt, regaled 300 poor of Bockhampton, with a good dinner.

BRADFORD.—Among the festivities to commemorate the 50th Anniversary of his Majesty's Reign, must be noticed the very hospitable way in which the Firm of Divett, Price, Jackson and Co., regaled a numerous body of poor people, employed in their Manufactory at Bradford, consisting of nearly 500 persons, by giving them three fine fat sheep, roasted whole, plenty of bread, and a large portion of Wiltshire strong beer.

DEVIZES.—A considerable time previous to the appointed day, a Meeting was convened and attended by all the respectable inhabitants of the town, who came to the unanimous resolution, that all classes should partake of the general festivity. A subscription was immediately set on foot, to which every one liberally contributed. The usual demonstrations of joy were manifested early in the morning, by the ringing of bells, display of flags, &c. The Mayor and Corporation, part of the Local Militia, the Cavalry, the different Clubs, and the Schools of the Charity Children, walked in procession to the Church; on their return, a *feu de joie* was fired in the Market Place, after which the poor were plentifully and judiciously regaled at their own houses, with beef, potatoes, bread, and beer. Miss Beffin, the celebrated Lady without arms and legs (who on that day attained her 25th year), with a magnanimity that does her credit, gave an ox to be roasted whole on the green. Many private dinner parties were made, and the evening concluded with a grand ball and supper, at the new Town Hall (which was appropriately illuminated), given by the Mayor and Corporation.

DONHEAD LODGE.—Mrs. Cook (widow of Captain Cook, who fell in the Battle of Trafalgar), entertained 500 people on the lawn before the Mansion, with an excellent collation, and a profusion of beer.

LONGLEAT.—Marquis of ~~Salisbury's~~ Bath's fete. The Jubilee day was announced by the ringing of bells at the adjoining parish Churches, and his Lordship, with his usual liberality, gave away to the poor four **oxen, with** bread in proportion. About 40 Charity Children, **which are** under the patronage of Lady Bath, **after** divine service, **walked in** procession from the parish church to his Lordship's most **noble** mansion, **where a** dinner was provided for **them** in the grand **hall, of** plenty of roast beef, plum-pudding, &c., **headed** by the Clergyman **of** the parish church ; **when the** cloth **was removed,** the children each had strong **beer** set before them, **and his** Majesty's health was drank with three times three, to the gratification of Lord and Lady Bath and company The domestics were equally entertained, and his Majesty's health was drank with enthusiasm. Two Society Clubs were regaled **with** English hospitality at the Parish Inn, and plenty of strong beer **was** given them, at his Lordship's expense. His Lordship further extended his liberality by giving to upwards of 100 **workmen, who were employed** in beautifying that ancient building, **as well as to the workmen** employed about his Lordship's garden, **pleasure-grounds, park,** farm, &c., **each of them a holiday,** with their day's pay.

MARLBOROUGH.—Besides the usual demonstrations of **joy,** by bell-ringing, firing, display of colours, &c., liberal donations **to** the poor, in proportion to their families, were distributed. The **Mayor and** Corporation, the Marlborough troop of Cavalry, and four **companies of Loyal** Volunteers, placed under the command of Col. **Lord Bruce, with all the** principal inhabitants, walked in procession to Church, after which, the several corps **of** military fired a *feu de joie* in honour of the day, **which was** concluded in the greatest harmony **and loyalty by** public dinners at the Town Hall and principal Inns, **and the festivity was continued the** following evening by a ball at the Town Hall.

ST. GILES'S.—The **Earl** and Countess **of** Shaftesbury furnished upwards **of 2000** persons (including all the poor in eleven parishes in the neighbourhood of his Lordship's seat at St. Giles's), with beef and bread, in the proportion **of** 2 lbs. of beef, and 1½ **lbs.** of bread to each individual. His Lordship likewise sent liberal **dona**tions of money to several other parishes, in aid of subscriptions, **to be** employed for **the same purpose.**

STANTON PRIOR.—Divine **service was attended** in the morning ; after **which, the** parisioners repaired **to their** neighbouring lofty hill, **the** Barrow, to partake of a plentiful dinner, supplied by the families **of the** Clergyman, and respectable Farmers resident in that parish. **Two fat** Leicester sheep were roasted whole for the entertainment, **and** good **ale,** bread, and potatoes, bountifully supplied. The villagers, to the number of about 120, like one large and united family, attended by the donors of their feast, evinced a lively interest in the cause of their happy **assem**blage, by drinking to his Majesty's health, with **loud and** enthusiastic acclamations.

SYRENCOT.—W. Dyke, Esq., entertained 300 poor people with beef, bread, and beer; and all his labourers received full pay for the day, although no work was done after the hour of morning service. It was highly gratifying to see Mr. Dyke proceeding immediately from the Church to visit the different cottages at Figheldean, in order to satisfy himself that his bounty was regularly bestowed, and that every poor man in the parish possessed on that day those comforts which could not fail to incline his heart to participate in the general joy which the occasion inspired.

THATCHAM.—The day was ushered in by the ringing of bells, and firing of cannon, the troop of Cavalry attended divine service at Church, and afterwards partook of a sumptuous dinner at the White Hart Inn. After an excellent sermon preached at the Meeting by the Rev. Mr. Isaacs, from Psalm 21, verse 7. 150 poor families were [relieved by the hands of John Barfield, Esq., who gave to each family half a gallon loaf and a shilling.

TOTTENHAM PARK.—The Earl of Aylesbury displayed the purest feelings of genuine loyalty, by his liberal donations to his Majesty's least opulent subjects through his Lordship's extensive manors. Upwards of 5,300 persons were sharers of his munificence. The numerous peasantry in his more immediate neighbourhood were feasted on the lawn, with a plentiful supply of roast beef, plum-pudding, and strong beer. The Marlborough troop of Wiltshire Yeomanry Cavalry, commanded by Lord Bruce, fired a *feu de joie* on the occasion, and were afterwards regaled with a sumptuous dinner, and enjoyed themselves with their Noble Commander to a late hour.

WARMINSTER.—Six fat bullocks, six sheep, and 700 loaves of bread, were distributed to the poor by a general subscription. A dinner was given in the Town Hall, for 128 Children of the Sunday Schools, by Mr. and Mrs. Brooks, of the Angel Inn. The 5th Local Wilts Militia, and other military parties, assembled from the surrounding parishes, and were attended to the church by the Friendly Societies.

WOOLLEY.—John Jones, Esq., gave to 800 poor persons of that neighbourhood, a quantity of bread, strong beer, and mutton, in the presence of a large concourse of loyal subjects.

———o———

WORCESTERSHIRE.

WORCESTER.—A Chamber Meeting of the Mayor and Corporation was held for the purpose of voting an Address to his Majesty. They then proceeded to the Cathedral, as did the Worcester Local Militia, the second battalion of the 36th regiment, and the several recruiting parties stationed in the city. The sermon was preached by the Dean of Worcester, in a very impressive and persuasive manner, and was admirably adapted to the occasion. A numerous meeting of the nobility, clergy, and gentlemen, took place at the Town Hall, who voted an address, which having been agreed to, the High Sheriff proposed a subscription for releasing the debtors in the county gaol, which was immediately entered into. At three o'clock 232 persons partook of a dinner in the Long Room, at the Guildhall, on the occasion. On the removal of the cloth, "*Non nobis Domine,*" was sung, and immediately afterwards the King was given by the Earl of Coventry, with an appropriate speech, which was received with enthusiastic applause. Sumptuous dinners were prepared at the Crown, Star and Garter, Unicorn, Bell, Hop Market, and other Inns; and the Masonic Lodge, at the Rein Deer, was fully attended.—Balls, parties, &c., were held in commemoration of the day, and universal harmony pervaded every part of that loyal and populous city. Between £400 and £500 were distributed among the poor, and many of the inhabitants were conspicuous in their particular donations. Lord Dudley and Ward presented £25 to the subscription for the poor.

BEWDLEY.—£152 were collected to enable the poor to celebrate the day. Early in the morning, meat and bread were given to about 2,000 poor persons.

BROMSGROVE.—In honour of the day, the Bromsgrove Union Society rung a complete peal of trebles, containing 1809 changes, being the date of the year in which his Majesty entered the 50th year of his reign. The intricate composition was composed by one of the Members of the Society. The day was spent in harmony by the whole town.

DUDLEY.—The morning was ushered in by the ringing of bells, the shops were shut, and sermons were preached in St. Thomas's Church and the Meeting Houses. The volunteer infantry after divine service fired a *feu de joie*, and were regaled with plenty of ale and an allowance of money to each man. A subscription having been previously entered into by the principal inhabitants, a liberal distribution of bread and money was made amongst more than 1,400 families. Another subscription was afterwards entered into by a few spirited persons for the purpose of purchasing an ox and five sheep, and the ox and two of the sheep were roasted whole, and distributed, with three hogsheads of strong ale, amongst the surrounding populace. This distribution was conducted with great order and regularity, and received gratefully by the poor, who retired peaceably from the ground before three o'clock. The remaining part of the latter subscription was expended in providing two dinners and ale for 129 old men and women, whose united ages amounted to 9,050 years. Eight sheep were roasted whole in and near the town, and distributed among the workmen of several opulent manufacturers. Large parties dined at the principal inns, and every demonstration of loyalty and festivity was displayed on this happy occasion.

EVESHAM.—The Mayor and Corporation of the Borough of Evesham attended divine service, and **voted** an Address to his Majesty. From the liberal subscriptions of the Right Hon. Lord Northwick, the Earl of Coventry, Wm. Manning, Esq., M.P. (who gave £50) the Corporation, &c., &c., together with the money collected in church, and a donation of a fat ox by the Earl of Coventry, the Committee appointed for the purpose of distributing amongst the poor **were** enabled to give four pounds of beef, and one shilling and sixpence in money, to every widow, and two pounds of beef and one shilling in money **to** every individual of each poor **family** throughout the parish.

FLADBURY.—The Rector, the Rev. Stafford Smith, **and J. W.** Hicks, Esq., with the principal inhabitants of the village, made such a liberal subscription that upwards of 260 poor persons received **meat** and bread in the following proportions: to a grown **person, two** pounds of meat, and a due proportion of bread and **ale**; to the younger branches, one pound of meat, with a proper proportion **of** bread.

HINDLEAP.—The young ladies of Miss Martin's School having obtained a holiday, proposed treating the poor of the parish with roast beef, etc. Their intentions having been announced on the Sunday preceding by the Rev. Mr. Williams, (who likewise contributed towards the expenses of the entertainment), 101 poor persons, after attending divine service, assembled in the Green Court at Hindleap, where tables were laid for them; after dinner the King's health, the donors of the feast, &c., were drank with sincere enthusiasm; and a band of **music** being in attendance, all present concluded the evening **with a** merry dance. What remained of the feast was distributed amongst those whose infirmities prevented their attendance.

SHIPSTON-UPON-STOUR.— A liberal subscription **of** some gentlemen enabled a Committee to distribute to every poor man, woman, and child, a pound and a half of meat, and threepence in money to buy bread, which were gratefully received. The Rev. Dr. Jones preceded the Members of the Club and the children of the Sunday Schools to church, where **an** excellent sermon was preached by **the** Rev. Mr. Evans. The Rev. Mr. Buck preached at the Baptist Meeting; and the day was afterwards spent with great cheerfulness and conviviality by the inhabitants in general.

YORKSHIRE.

YORK.—The morning was ushered in by the ringing of bells, firing of guns, and the display of flags from the different churches. At nine o'clock the Corporation assembled at the Mansion House, and partook of an elegant breakfast with the Lord Mayor; after which they accompanied his Lordship in procession to the Cathedral, and were joined by upwards of 50 gentlemen from the York Tavern, where an excellent public breakfast had been provided. His Grace the Lord Archbishop delivered a most appropriate and impressive sermon, from Psalm 128, v. 1. After service, pursuant to a requisition signed by the Archbishop, and several respectable gentry, a general meeting of the inhabitants was held in the Guildhall, when an Address to his Majesty was unanimously agreed to. Several parties were held in the city, to celebrate the occasion; the poor shared in the general festivity, and 9000 persons were regaled with meat, bread, and ale, from the fund subscribed for that purpose. Upwards of one hundred gentlemen dined together at Clark's Hotel, Sir M. M. Sykes, Bart., in the chair. The tables were covered with every delicacy of the season, displayed with unusual taste and elegance. Sir W. Milner and Sir M. Sykes each contributed £20 to the subscription for the relief of the poor. Sir M. Sykes also sent a handsome sum of money to each of the benefit societies. The Archbishop very munificently directed a liberal distribution of beef, bread, and ale, to be made among the debtors in the Castle, (64 in number); also the sum of five guineas to be laid out in coals. The prisoners on the crown side, (53 in number), also received a liberal distribution of beef and ale, given to them by the Rev. G. Brown, the Ordinary, and Mr. Staveley, the Governor. The Brotherly Society, and the Farmer's Union Society, assembled at their respective club rooms, and spent the evening in the true spirit of friendship and mutual kindness. Ten poor women and three blind men belonging to Fossbridge Hospital, 20 boys clothed and educated in the Free School there, and 6 girls, educated by the said Charity, attended divine service, along with the Steward, Master, and Mistress, and were afterwards, with the tradesmen who work for the boys, regaled with roast beef, plum-pudding, and malt liquor, by order of the Governors.—A donation of £400 was subscribed by the Officers of the Carbineer Regiment of Dragoons, which was distributed amongst the women and children. The men had what money they chose to draw. After dinner, all went to enjoy themselves, as each thought proper. The necessary preparation having been previously made, a signal was given by a bugle-horn at eight o'clock in the evening, when, instantaneously, the whole Barracks became brilliantly illuminated, and appeared as if on fire. The arms of his Majesty, in front of the Officers' building, was grandly displayed by the reflection of the lights placed round them. The motto " *Vive le* (G. III. R.) *Roi* " adorned the top of the Hall. The evening was spent with the utmost conviviality, and no jarring string was heard to confound the general harmony.

ARMELEY.—In the morning the Sunday Scholars of the Established Church, to the number of 210 boys and girls, went in procession from the school to the chapel, and after divine service, were regaled with cakes, &c.: 174 poor men and women partook of a good dinner of roast beef, provided for them at the school, after which the principal inhabitants dined together, and the day was spent in loyalty, mirth, and good humour.

BAWTRY.—Upwards of 500 persons were plentifully regaled with roast beef and plum-pudding, by the Rev. Mr. Armitstead.

BEVERLEY.—The Corporation went in a body to Church, preceded by Lieut. Gen. Vyse, his Staff, and the Troops quartered in the town, followed by the Freemasons, Benefit Societies, and townspeople.—After divine service, the troops were drawn up in the Market Place, and fired three volleys in honour of the day.

BRIDLINGTON.—A liberal subscription was made, and a quantity of beef, bread, &c., distributed among the poor. An elegant dinner was provided at the Britannia Inn, Bridlington Quay, Col. Creyke in the chair, and a number of loyal toasts given. The evening was spent with the utmost conviviality.

CASTLE HOWARD.—The Earl of Carlisle displayed his usual goodness, in commemoration of the joyful day, by giving large sums of money to the poor, and liberal entertainments, accompanied with bountiful supplies of venison and hares, to the tenantry, work-people, servants, labourers, &c., in the respective townships of his Lordship's estates in the neighbourhood of Castle Howard.

CATTERICK.—After divine service, the Rev. George Chamberlaine, Rector of Wyke, and formerly Vicar of Catterick, give 100 bushels of coals, and a quantity of potatoes, amongst his late poor parishioners, as a mark of affection for them, in honour of the day.

COXWOLD.—The morning was ushered in by the display of flags and ringing of bells: never was a parish more united in showing their loyalty to their good old King: the troop of Newburgh Rangers assembled at half past ten in the morning, and went in orderly procession to Church, attended by their Captain, (Thomas Wynn Belasyse, Esq.) when an appropriate sermon was preached on the occasion by the Rev. Thomas Newton, from 12th chap. 1st Samuel, 14th verse. After divine service, the troops fired three excellent volleys in the street. Amongst a vast concourse of spectators, were Lady Charlotte Wynn Belasyse, Lady Newborough, and Lady Frankland. At two o'clock the troop had a dinner at the Inns in the usual style of English hospitality, given by their Captain, when many loyal and patriotic toasts were drank. At eight o'clock they attended a ball, given by Lady Charlotte Wynn Belasyse; when her Ladyship with her party, the Captain and the rest of the Officers, entered the room, the band played "God save the King," after which dancing commenced, and was kept up with great spirit until an early hour. On this Jubilee day every countenance smiled, every heart rejoiced; the cottage was as happy as the palace. To every one that could not afford to make merry, money was given to rejoice.

CONISBROUGH.—A venerable party dined with the Rev. H. Watkins, comprising 16 old men of that place, whose ages amounted to 60 each and upwards. They were treated with roast beef and plum-pudding, with good old English beverage, strong ale; after drinking the King's health, pipes and tobacco were introduced, and the afternoon was spent in joyous comfort.

CRAVEN.—The morning, ushered in by the usual demonstrations, was succeeded by a general attendance at the parish Church, and afterwards by a most liberal distribution, enabling the lower ranks to join in the festivities of the day. The ball was of the most splendid and animating description.—The old Castle, by the polite indulgence of Lord Thanet, was fitted up in a very handsome manner. —The approach to the ancient pile was judiciously decorated with lamps, and guarded by a party of the Craven Legion, whose celebrated bands contributed their cheering sounds to the universal harmony and rejoicing of the evening. The Assembly room was most judiciously, indeed magnificently arranged.—By favour of Lord Ribblesdale, the five sets of military banners, of which his Lordship is possessed, from a long and truly patriotic defence in the cause of his King and Country, were at a general request on this occasion displayed, (and with great taste) within the compartments of this lofty and spacious saloon, which afforded ample accommodation for two sets of dancers, of upwards of 25 couple each.

EASINGWOLD.—The day was ushered in by the ringing of bells, and other demonstrations of joy. At ten o'clock the inhabitants proceeded to Church, where, after divine service, a distribution was made of two shillings each to upwards of 150 poor persons, to enable them to join in the festivities of the day. The gentlemen of the town sat down to dinner, at four o'clock, at the Crown Inn, Capt. Goulton in the chair, where many appropriate toasts and sentiments were given.

FARNLEY.—The Anniversary after his Majesty's entrance on the 50th year of his Reign was celebrated in a manner highly creditable to Edward Armitage, Esq., and the respectable inhabitants of that place, who, by a subscription raised for that purpose, distributed to every poor family in the township, a quantity of butcher's meat, ale, potatoes and bread. At eleven o'clock the family, tenants, and children educated at the Sunday School, assembled in front of the house, and went in procession to the Chapel; after divine service, the Sunday Scholars were regaled with wine and cake, and had each one shilling given them by Mrs. Armitage; and the tenants drank his Majesty's health with Mr. Armitage.— Every person seemed highly gratified with the kind and hospitable manner in which they were entertained; a number of the principal inhabitants afterwards dined together at the Inn, and through the whole of the day, loyalty and harmony prevailed.

HALIFAX,—Always conspicuous for its loyalty, and acts of public charity, was particularly so on the present occasion. Articles of clothing were distributed to 950 females, and suppers were provided for 780 men, at the different Inns. There were great public rejoicings, and festive harmony every where prevailed. The West Halifax Volunteers, after firing a *feu de joie*, were regaled by Col. Moore, at Brockwell, and the Officers of the corps afterwards dined at the Triangle Inn. The non-commissioned Officers of the Halifax Local Militia also fired a *feu de joie*.

HAREWOOD.—Flags were hoisted on the Church and at the Great Lodge at the entrance of the Park; and the day was ushered in by the ringing of bells. The tenantry of Lord Harewood, about 500 in number, assembled at the Church, and after divine service, marched in procession, attended by a band of music, to the hospitable mansion of his Lordship, and sung "God save the King," on the lawn. As many as could conveniently dine in the house, remained; and such as could not, went to the Inns at Harewood, which were thrown open for the day, to all the inhabitants of the neighbourhood. At two o'clock dinner was announced, when Lord Harewood took the head of the table in the great room, which formed three sides of a square, and at which sat 190 guests. Different tenants presided at the other tables. During the whole of dinner a full band of music performed select airs. The toasts were appropriate for the occasion. At intervals the company was charmed by the vocal powers of Mr. Bradbury, &c., and hilarity prevailed at the festive board till nearly eight o'clock. A little before this time, Lord Harewood retired, when the health of his Lordship was given by the Earl of Tyrconnel, and drank amidst thunders of applause. Mr. Lascelles returned thanks, in his Lordship's name, and drank the health of the company, and of their families at home. He then gave "The immortal memory of Lord Nelson." Mr. Henry Lascelles also addressed the company in a short speech, and gave "The land we live in; and may those that don't like it, quit it." While these festivities were given to the wealthier part, the poor were all regaled at the Inns: money and clothing were given to them; and the country people who were attracted to the spot, were regaled with strong beer. At eight o'clock, there was a large bonfire, and a beautiful display of fireworks. At nine, two rooms were thrown open for dancing, which was continued with great spirit till one. Supper was then served up in the gallery, the decorations of the rooms and the tables did infinite credit to the manager; transparencies (one of them an excellent likeness of the King), and devices of flowers in different compartments, had a most beautiful effect. At three, dancing was resumed, and continued with great spirit till six, and about eight, all the guests had taken their departure, deeply impressed with the splendid hospitality, the amiable condescension, and the disinterested patriotism, of the noble house of Harewood. It must not be omitted that the Lady of Mr. H. Lascelles distributed to all the poor boys and girls of the neighbourhood, a pair of stockings and half a crown each; and Lord Harewood gave to each of the poor widows half a guinea.

HEDON.—The morning was ushered in by the ringing of bells, and a display of flags. At half past ten, the Mayor, Aldermen, and

Bailiffs, with regalia—the Volunteers in full uniform—the Members of the Union Society with their flags—the Apprentices—and the principal inhabitants, formed a grand procession; and, preceded by a band of music, paraded the principal streets, and thence to Church. The ancient fabric of St. Augustine exibited a grand and interesting spectacle; it was crowded to excess; and the beauty and fashion which in the windows had graced the procession, now adorned the congregation. Divine service, with prayers suited to the purpose, was performed, and a most excellent and appropriate sermon delivered by the reverend Pastor. The Volunteers marched to the Champ-de-Mars, where they fired several volleys, and a *feu de joie*. An elegant dinner was given by the Mayor, to the Corporation and principal inhabitants. The Members of the Union Club dined together. Dinners were provided for the Burgesses: for the class of aged and infirm; for the Apprentices; and for such of the Volunteers as were not included in the other Societies; and distributions were made to the poor. In the afternoon, ale was liberally distributed to the populace in the Market Place, and all the women were regaled with tea. In the evening a display of fireworks was exhibited; and a ball concluded the festivities of this memorable day.

HESLINGTON.—In the evening there was bonfire on the highest part of the hill in the town field, consisting of several loads of whins, &c., which illuminated the whole country for many miles round. The villagers were regaled with several hogsheads of ale, an abundance of fine Cheshire cheese, and loads of bread, and with favours in their hats followed an excellent band of music, playing "God save the King," "Rule Britannia," &c., through the whole village, not forgetting to cheer their donor, Henry Yarburgh, Esq., every time they passed the Hall.

HUDDERSFIELD.—After the bells had been long ringing, divine service began at the parish Church, and concluded with "God save the King." The congregation being dismissed, the Gentlemen engaged to distribute the charity, retired to their delightful work. The public fund enabled them to relieve between six and seven hundred distressed objects. The girls of the School of Industry, also, and the children of the several Sunday Schools, along with their respective teachers, the same day gratuitously dined together. After service was ended, the bells continued ringing for the remainder of the day. Between four and five in the afternoon, dinner was on the table, and the company assembled at the George.—Sir George Armytage presided. After dinner, several loyal and patriotic toasts were drank with enthusiasm.—The address to his Majesty was then read from the chair, and unanimously passed. The whole evening was spent in hilarity and good humour.

HULL.—At day break, the Union flag was hoisted at the Garrison, and a royal salute of 21 guns was fired. The colours were also hoisted at the Churches, and other public buildings; and by all the vessels in the Docks and **Harbour**. **At** the same time, the bells of the Churches began to ring a merry peal. At eight o'clock, a royal salute of 50 guns was fired at the Citadel. The Royal Cumberland Militia also fired three volleys, in **honour** of the day. Several public breakfasts were given in the town and neighbourhood. J. K. Picard, Esq., entertained a party of about 60 Gentlemen, at his house at Summergangs, in a style of elegance and hospitality which drew forth the highest encomiums from all who partook of it. In the **centre** of the entrance hall, was placed a bronzed statue **of his Majesty, six** feet three inches high. The company set out **about ten o'clock, in** order to join the procession at Guildhall. The house **was then thrown open** for the populace to view the Statue, which **was visited by** great numbers during the day. At nine o'clock, Quatton Levitt, **Esq., the** Master of the Rodney Lodge of Free Masons, gave an elegant **breakfast to** a numerous company of the brethren of that Lodge, **and the** visiting brethren from the neighbouring Lodges. At ten o'clock, **the** party was joined **by** the Master and **brethren** of the Minerva Lodge; and the whole forming with their appropriate banners and insignia in Masonic order, **proceeded to the** Guildhall **to** join the Corporation. Between nine and ten o'clock, the **inhabitants, and** the members of the different Benefit Societies, began **to assemble in front** of the Mansion house. The corps of Royal Artillery, **commanded by** Colonel Sproule, was previously formed in Salthouse-lane; **and the** non-commissioned Officers of **the 4th East** Local **Militia, and the** regiment of Royal Cumberland Militia, **assembled on the south side of** the Dock towards High-street, **in readiness to join the procession.** At eleven o'clock, the company **moved from the Mansion house in** grand **order**. The first part of it **reached the Church about twenty** minutes before twelve o'clock, just one **hour after setting out. Some idea** may be formed of the **numbers** who joined it, **from this circumstance** —that, independent of **the** multitude of **spectators, the procession** reached the whole length of Charlotte-street, **George-street, and Saville** street. An excellent sermon was preached by the **Rev. J. H. Bromby** from 2 Kings, chap. **18, verse** 5th. **A** collection was made **after the** sermon. Appropriate sermons and similar collections were made **at** the other Churches and Chapels throughout the town, **for the** relief of our fellow subjects in France. Near five o'clock, a company **of 169** persons sat down to dinner at **the** Assembly Room. **An** elegant transparency of a Crown beneath the **letters G. HI. R.** and the figures (50) underneath the Crown, was displayed over the door **into** the Card Room, just behind the Mayor; and **opposite to** him **a** baron of **beef was** placed, over which a blue flag **was** suspended with **the words** "God save the King," and the Sword **Bearer** was stationed there in his beef-eater's robes, as Grand Carver. **The cloth** being removed, all present stood up while a grace and amen were sung, the company joining in chorus. The Worshipful the **May**or then **gave** "The King," —which was drank with three times three cheers, **and a** burst of approbation from the whole company. At this moment **a** detachment of the Royal Artillery, stationed on **the** Myton Walls, **fired** a royal salute of 50 guns, answering to the 50th Anniversary which the company was then assembled to celebrate. The national song of "God save the King," was then sung, the whole company joining in chorus. The toasts were appropriate, the speeches loyal and patriotic, and the vocal part of the entertainment well selected. The company did not separate till a late hour, and it was observed that a greater degree of cordiality and unanimity never prevailed in any public meeting more than on this auspicious occasion. The Warden and Brethren of the Trinity House attended divine service at the Holy Trinity Church, and afterwards gave a dinner, of which about 40 Gentlemen partook. Every person receiving relief from that Corporation had two shillings given to them, and each of the Marine boys educated through the benevolence of that Institution, received one shilling. The Members of the Minerva Lodge, after joining the procession to and from the Holy Trinity Church, retired to their Hall in Princess-street, where they, together with a multitude of visitors, partook of an excellent dinner. Afterwards a subscription was made for the relief of the poor, which was paid to the Committee appointed for the receipt and application of the subscription for that purpose. The Lodge of Ancient Masons, which is held at the Fleece, did not join the procession, but dined at their Lodge Room. The Mayor and Corporation very liberally gave £50 for fire-works, in order to avoid the disagreeable consequences of illuminations. On the evening of Thursday, the day after the Jubilee, there was a ball and supper at the Assembly Rooms, which was brilliantly attended by 170 Ladies and Gentlemen, amongst whom were many Military and Naval Officers. The benevolence of a nreat number of the inhabitants of this town and neighbourhood, it is but justice to say, have not been confined to the public subscriptions. Many of them treated their different workmen with a dinner and liquor: and many displayed a still more extended benevolence. J. K. Picard, Esq., in addition to other relief given to a number of families in Drypool and Witham, distributed 700 sacks of coals among them, according to their respective wants. Most of the Gentlemen possessing estates in this neighbourhood, gave money to the families of their poorer tenants and labourers; and beef, bread, and ale, to the men more immediately in their employ; the inhabitants of every village and hamlet were actuated by the same loyal ardour; and dinners, suppers, &c., were given by the generality of the farmers to their servants and labourers. The amount of the subscriptions for the relief of the poor amounted to about £800.

HUNMANBY.—After a very full attendance on divine service, a Jubilee salute of 49 was fired in a field near the village, from three pieces of cannon. Two barrels of ale, given by H. Osbaldeston, Esq., were drank upon the field by the crowd who attended, and after several pieces of music, the whole concluded with "God save the King," and an unanimous and hearty three times three. Mr. O. likewise gave an excellent dinner of roast beef and plum pudding to 60 children belonging to the Lancaster School, and ordered a shilling a piece to be distributed to as many of the poorer inhabitants as attended divine worship, besides additional supplies of ale in the evening.

KNARESBOROUGH.—The morning was ushered in by the ringing of bells, firing of cannon, and other joyful demonstrations. A liberal subscription was made by the town, that every description of the inhabitants might participate in the general joy. A large quantity of meat, bread, &c., early in the morning, was given to those who chose to apply. After attending divine service, a part of the 15th. regt. stationed there, were drawn up in the castle yard, and fired three excellent volleys, and gave three cheers, in which they were enthusiastically joined by a vast number of the inhabitants assembled on the occasion. Fifty rounds were then fired from a party of artillery, placed under the directions of Captains Nursaw and Robinson, of the Local Militia; this had a grand effect, it being on an eminence 200 feet perpendicular from a large river. At three o'clock, a number of gentlemen of the town and neighbourhood sat down to elegant dinners, provided at two of the principal inns (one not being large enough to accommodate them). This separation of the company was not the least drawback on the hilarity of the day, as each individual was only anxious how he could best testify his attachment to his King: communications, therefore, betwixt the two houses took place during the afternoon. Songs and toasts applicable to the day, with the best sentiments the heart could dictate or the tongue express, were given; good humour and conviviality continued until eight o'clock, when the Gentlemen adjourned to the ball room, to enjoy the society of a genteel assemblage of Ladies, most of whom were decorated with some emblem of loyalty. Dancing immediately commenced, and was continued with great spirit to a late hour in the morning. A second subscription having been made for the purpose of general amusement, the afternoon of the following day was appointed, when various articles of wearing apparel were given to those whose superior strength, art, or agility, were judged to entitle them to. The day concluded with a display of the most brilliant fire works ever seen in that part of the country. A very handsome collection was made at the Church, which was left in the hands of the Ministers, to purchase warm clothing for the poor, and to be distributed at their discretion.

LEEDS.—The day was ushered in by a display of flags, ringing of bells, firing of guns, &c. About ten o'clock, a most repectable procession of the inhabitants, chiefly with blue cockades, assembled in Park Place, to accompany the Mayor and Corporation to Church, attended by two troops of the 6th Dragoons, the non-commissioned Officers of the Local Militia, the Volunteer Cavalry, the Churchwardens and Constables, the Masonic Body, &c. The procession was preceded to the parish Church by a band of music playing "God save the King," by Standard Bearers carrying two blue flags, with suitable inscriptions, &c. The Rev. Miles Atkinson preached a most excellent and impressive sermon on the occasion, from the brief but **appropriate** text of "Praise ye the Lord." The collection for the **poor, afterwards,** amounted to upwards of £100. There was a procession of 600 men, women, and children, from the Linen Manufactory of Messrs. Benyon, Benyon, and Bage. It was a procession at once the most orderly and gratifying imaginable—The managers of the separate departments of the Mill were on horseback, with suitable **devices and** flags. The men, women, and children, were particularly clean and well-dressed. They proceeded to the house of Mr. Benyon, and afterwards to the **Mayor's,** where the band played, and the people sung "God save the **King**." Messrs. Clayton and Garsed's workpeople paraded in similar **order.** and were regaled by their employers. At the Flax Mill of Tennant, **Shaw** and Cobb, **200 men,** women, and children, were regaled with beef and strong beer.

MULGRAVE CASTLE.—The tenants, and labouring persons employed at the Alum Works of the Right Hon. Lord Mulgrave, upwards of 700 persons, were entertained in Mulgrave Castle, with the old English cheer of roast and boiled beef, strong beer, and punch. The entertainment concluded with a display of fire-works.

NEW MALTON.—The day was ushered in by the ringing of bells. Divine worship was performed both by the established church and dissenters. A subscription previously entered into for the poor of the place, enabled them also to participate in the festivities of this memorable day.

NORTHALLERTON.—Mr. R. Jackson gave a sumptuous dinner, and plenty of strong ale, to more than 100 persons employed in his linen manufactory. They walked in procession to church in the morning, and in the afternoon paraded round the crop with colours flying, and a full band of music, playing "God save the King," "Rule Britannia," &c., &c. The meat left at dinner was distributed to the lower class, by Mrs. Jackson.

NORTON—The whole parish was made to rejoice; towards which, Major Bower, of Welham, contributed with his accustomed munificence of spirit. This noble-spirited gentleman also sent two guineas and a brace of hares, to each of the 12 freehold innkeepers of Malton.

RICHMOND.—The morning was ushered in by the ringing of bells, &c., and at nine o'clock the 1st regiment of North York Local Militia, 1200 strong, now on permanent duty there, assembled on parade, and marched to church, when a most excellent discourse was delivered by the Rector, Mr. Goodwill. After service, the national and patriotic song of "God save the King," and a few appropriate verses to the old and popular tune of "Rule Britannia," were sung with striking solemnity by a number of men chosen from the regiment for that purpose, accompanied by the band. The remaining part of the day was spent in festive loyalty, unaccompanied by one instance of unbridled mirth. In the evening there was a ball, at which was present the most splendid assemblage of beauty and fashion from the town and neighbourhood, that ever was remembered—cheerfulness and happiness appeared in every face.

RIPON.—The morning was ushered in by a peal of bells, and other demonstrations of joy. At ten o'clock, the Mayor and Corporation met at the Town Hall, and voted a loyal address to his Majesty on the occasion: afterwards a procession to Church took place. After a very appropriate and excellent sermon, preached by the Rev. the Dean of Ripon, from Psalm 133, v. 1, the procession returned in the same order from the Church to the Market Place, where the 15th Regiment fired a *feu de joie*, amidst the acclamations of the surrounding inhabitants, who all seemed to vie with each other in demonstrations of joy and gratitude. Several select companies dined together at different houses in the town, and the evening concluded with an elegant and splendid ball at the New Rooms, where nearly 200 persons were present. A subscription having been previously opened for the benefit of the poor, a very handsome sum was distributed amongst them by a Committee appointed for that purpose. The Cross was brilliantly illuminated, and ale distributed to the populace. The kind aid, and liberal assistance and attention given on this occasion by Miss Lawrence, Lord Grantham, and the Hon. H. Robinson, one of the worthy Representatives in Parliament for Ripon, merit the highest praise.

SALTERGATE.—On the part of an estate belonging to Mr. Osbaldeston, in the neighbourhood of Saltergate, is a conical hill, seen from Whitby and Scarborough by all the country round to Malton and York. On the summit of this hill the standard of England was hoisted, on the morning of the 25th, and in the evening, a huge bonfire was made by his tenants, round which they emptied a barrel of ale, with repeated cheers to King George for ever.

SCARBOROUGH.—The Jubilee was observed at Scarborough with every mark of devout and grateful affection to the best of Kings. After a procession of the Corporation and principal inhabitants to Church, a large quantity of bread and soup were distributed to the poor, a liberal subscription having been made, not only to regale them on this happy occasion, but likewise for their further relief during the winter.

SELBY.—The 25th of October was ushered in at Selby by the ringing of bells and the firing of cannon. A fine ship was launched from the yard of John Foster, Esq., called the Jubilee, in honour of the day. Most of the inhabitants of the town were at some place of worship, and a crowded congregation, at Church, were much edified by a most excellent sermon from the Rev. John Turner, from part of the 11th v. 25th chap. of Leviticus, "A Jubilee shall that 50th year be unto you." At three o'clock, a sumptuous dinner was provided at the head Inn; most of the principal inhabitants of the town and neighbourhood attended, and had a most loyal meeting. In the evening, John Foster, Esq., gave a substantial supper to nearly 190 poor men; several of the poor families had provisions sent to their houses, so that from the highest to the lowest the **day** was spent with the greatest enthusiasm of loyalty and patriotism.

SHEFFIELD.—The Jubilee began at Sheffield by an act of mercy peculiarly suitable to the occasion: viz. by liberating on the preceding evening, all the prisoners of the Court of Requests; so that on the 25th not a single debtor remained in confinement either for the Manor of Sheffield or Ecclesall. Early in the morning, the bells rung a merry peal, which continued with little interruption, during the whole of the day. At ten o'clock, a grand procession proceeded from the Tontine Inn, to the parish Church. There were several appropriate Anthems sung. Collections were made at the Churches and Chapels to the amount of £145 17s. 6½d. for defraying the expense of great coats and hats, and a dinner for 71 poor men of the age of his Majesty, or upwards; and in aid of the General Infirmary, and the Schools for poor boys and girls. After divine service, all the Military marched to an elevated and commanding piece of ground, a quarter of a mile from the town, when the Artillery of the Local Militia fired 21 guns. The Dragoon Guards, after a general salute, fired a *feu de joie*, three rounds, in addition to three admirable volleys.—The Artillery then fired 50 rounds. The concourse of people was great, and three times three cheers, at the conclusion, echoed through the skies. The brigade then marched back to the front of the Tontine; and, after a general salute and three hearty cheers, they were dismissed to their various dinner engagements. The Master Cutler, the Town Regent, the capital Church Burgess, and a most respectable party of Gentlemen, dined together at the Angel Inn. The Officers of the Local Militia, the Officers from the Barracks, and others, besides a great number of respectable Gentlemen of the town, repaired to Messrs. Batty and Son's, the Tontine Inn, where a most elegant dinner was provided, with venison and other game in abundance: the wines were remarkably good. Dinners were given at almost every Inn in the town and neighbourhood. As 161 poor men of the age of his Majesty or upwards, were reported proper objects of charity, and the Committee being restricted only to provide great coats and hats for the number of 71, on the suggestion of a very respectable character, a subscription was entered into on Thursday, for the purpose of giving to the other 90 **old** men a crown each, in order that they all might be Kings on **the** day of his Majesty's entrance upon the 50th year of his government. The subscription was filled in a few hours, and it was accordingly distributed in the manner recommended. The High Court prisoners remaining in the gaol, were regaled with an excellent dinner, and good liquor to drink his Majesty's health, given to them by the Rev. Mr. Hedges, of Thriburgh, and for which they **were truly** thankful.

SKELTON GRANGE.—Sir James Graham, Bart., of Skelton

Grange, near Doncaster, distributed to the poor of that place beef, mutton, and bread, to the value of twenty guineas.

STAMFORD BRIDGE.—The township east and west, entertained all the poor families and others, who wished to partake of the same, with a good dinner of roast beef, plum-pudding, and good ale.

SUTTON HALL.—Sir Charles H. Harland, Bart., celebrated the joyous 25th of October, by dividing a fat ox and a plentiful quantity of ale, amongst the poorer class of inhabitants of the neighbouring villages of Sutton on the Forest and Huby.

WAKEFIELD.—The morning was ushered in with the ringing of bells; all the places of Public Worship were respectably attended by the members of their different congregations. The Royal Volunteers and the different parties of Military in the town, marched to St. John's Church, where an able and appropriate discourse was preached by the Rev. S. Sharpe, Chaplain to the Volunteers, from Psalm 21, v. 4—7. Every Club in the town commemorated the day with festivity; the noncommissioned Officers of the Wakefield Local Militia showed their attachment to their Sovereign, by a liberal entertainment at their Orderly Room, of which their wives partook. Many private parties passed the day with that hilarity which the occasion naturally inspired. Several individuals with laudable liberality caused their poor neighbours to rejoice. *Mr. J. Naylor gave a dinner of true English fare, roast beef and plum-pudding, to 25 of the oldest croppers in the town, the united ages of 20 of whom amounted to 1300 years. Twenty shirts and as many shifts were also distributed by him to 20 old men and women of the ages of 70 or upwards. At the Methodist Chapel, after an appropriate sermon by Mr. Taylor, from 1st Peter, 2. v. 7, the Sunday Scholars, upwards of 500 in number, were regaled with negus and plum-cake. No illumination took place; but a subscription was properly substituted, by a public meeting held on Monday, to furnish the poor with comfortable clothing and bedding during the winter.

WANSFORD.—John Boyes, Esq., gave 7 lbs. of mutton, 1 lb. of rice, and half a gallon of ale to nearly 70 families. The inhabitants proceeded to Nafferton Church, preceded by the Driffield Volunteer band. In the afternoon, a quantity of ale was distributed under a large elm, by the above Gentleman.

WETHERBY.—The inhabitants made a subscription, and had two fat heifers and one large sheep distributed in the Market Place, amongst the poor, together with a proportionate quantity of bread, also some loads of coals. After the principal inhabitants had attended divine service at the Chapel, and enabled the poor to enjoy themselves, they partook of a most excellent dinner at the Mason's Arms, where the day was spent in the utmost conviviality, each appearing to vie which could attest the greatest affection and loyalty to our beloved Sovereign.

WOMERSLEY.—Lord and Lady Hawke treated the whole of the inhabitants with an excellent dinner and supper on the occasion. Whole oxen were roasted, and barrels of ale, bowls of punch, &c., flowed in abundance. The evening concluded with a dance among the tenantry ; at which "God save the King," and several other loyal songs, were sung by Greenwood, the Trumpet-Major to the Regiment, of which his Lordship is Lieut.-Colonel. The utmost hilarity and good order prevailed.

———o———

NORTH AND SOUTH WALES.

BALA, *Merionethshire.*—At Bala the Jubilee day was celebrated by an attendance at the respective places of public worship, where collections were made in aid of general subscriptions in the town and neighbourhood, for supplying the poor with clothing and bedding. There was also a public dinner at the Bull Inn, R. W. Price, Esq., in the chair, when his Majesty's health was drank with the warmest effusions of loyalty, and the day closed with the utmost hilarity and good humour.

BANGOR, *Caernarvonshire.*—A very handsome subscription was entered into on the day previous, for furnishing the poor with coals and other necessaries during the ensuing winter. In the morning, the Members of the Friendly Society Club walked in procession to the Cathedral, preceded by the Dean, Archdeacon, and resident Clergy, and followed by a company of Volunteers, commanded by Captain Roberts. After divine service, the Volunteers were formed upon the mountain which overlooks the town, which, together with the fineness of the day, had a most pleasing effect ; several excellent volleys were fired, which were answered by the cannon from Port Penrhyn. In the afternoon, a large party assembled at the Penrhyn Arms to dinner, the Dean in the chair. After his Majesty's health had been drank, with three times three, the Dean in a most energetic and appropriate address, submitted to the company a proposal for establishing a Dispensary for this city and neighbourhood, an establishment which, he justly observed, " would hand down the commemoration of that day to the latest posterity." A liberal subscription was immediately entered into, both forming a present fund, and by annual subscription. In the evening the mountains in various directions presented a most pleasing spectacle, bonfires being displayed from their summits in every quarter.

BRECON, *Breconshire.*—In commemoration of the day, a school was instituted, for the instruction of poor children. A sermon was preached by the Archdeacon of Brecon, and a collection made in aid of the above benevolent undertaking. A handsome subscription was also made for the relief of the indigent, and the evening terminated by a ball at the Golden Lion.

CAERMARTHEN, *Caermarthenshire.*—A congratulatory address was voted—there was a full attendance at the different places of Worship, and a collection at the doors in aid of a general subscription for releasing persons confined for small debts in the gaol of the borough, and for relieving aged and indigent persons. There was also two public dinners.

CAERNARVON, *Caernarvonshire.*—The Corporation met at the Guildhall, at ten o'clock, and thence went to church in procession, the streets being lined by a troop of the 7th Dragoon Guards, and other military, when an excellent sermon was preached by the Rev. Mr. Jones, the Vicar of the parish; from church they returned in the same manner to the Guildhall, where an address was voted to his Majesty, expressive of loyalty and attachment to his person and government. A dinner was ordered for 50 poor men and 50 poor women of the town, and all the prisoners in the gaol. A liberal subscription was collected, and all the prisoners confined for debt (that were considered deserving) were discharged by the committee appointed to manage the subscription. Fifty volleys and a *feu de joie* were fired by the Dragoon Guards. The Corporation dined at the Sportsman Inn, where the evening was spent with great loyalty and harmony. The Jubilee subscriptions for charitable purposes amounted to upwards of £260.

CARDIFF, *Glamorganshire.*—The Vice-Lieutenant of the county, the High Sheriff, the Corporation, the Cardiff Troop of Cavalry, and the Military Stationed there, attended divine service; and the day was afterwards spent with the greatest loyalty, harmony, and hilarity, there being two public dinners—the High Sheriff presided at one of them, and Captain Wood at the other. The Local Militia, quartered at Cardiff, where liberally regaled with roast beef, plum-pudding, and Welsh ale, at the expense of their Officers.

CARDIGAN, *Cardiganshire.*—After divine service, a festive party, consisting of all the Gentlemen of the place and neighbourhood, sat down to an excellent dinner, and in the evening an Address was unanimously voted to his Majesty, and a sum of £60 subscribed for the poor.

CLIROW, *Radnorshire.*—A general rejoicing took place at the village of Clirow, both on Wednesday, the 25th, and on Sunday, the 29th, when the inhabitants were all regaled with beef and plum-pudding, and drank the King's health with affection and gratitude.

CONWAY, *Caernarvonshire.*—The day was celebrated with much loyalty. At one o'clock, the cannon were fired from the Quay, and in the evening, the fine ruins of the Castle were brilliantly illuminated, and was one of the grandest spectacle, it is possible to conceive. The opposite mountains blazed with innumerable bonfires, and frequent discharges of cannon announced the attachment of the ancient Britons to their King. Ale was distributed to the populace, and a subscription for the poor was cheerfully entered into, that they might also **rejoice,** and join their prayers and good wishes to those of their more opulent neighbours.

COWBRIDGE, *Glamorganshire.*—A splendid ball **and** supper was **attended** by a numerous and fashionable company, comprising nearly all **the respectable** personages **resident** within a circle of several miles. **Loyalty,** harmony, and happiness, prevailed **till** a late hour.

DENBIGH, *Denbighshire.*—**The Corporation** and inhabitants of Denbigh voted an Address to his Majesty. The Aldermen, Bailiffs, and Capital Burgesses, **met at eleven o'clock in** the morning at their Council Chamber, and **went** in procession, with the Rector and his Curate, attended by **the** Common Burgesses, the Inferior Officers **of** the Corporation, the **Local** Militia, and the Charity and other Schools, to Church, when **a very** impressive sermon **was** preached by Dr. Myddleton, **to a most** numerous **congregation.** After divine service, they returned to **the Town** Hall; **and the** Corporation, in their Council **Chamber, voted their** thanks **to Dr.** Myddleton, for **his** most excellent discourse. In the course **of the** day, 50 cannons were fired from the Castle, and several volleys with **a** *feu de joie* by the Local **Militia.** A most liberal subscription, at the head of which **was** R. M. **Biddulph, Esq.,** for thirty guineas; **the** Hon. **Mr. West,** twenty **guineas; and Miss** Myddleton, twenty guineas; **was made for** the **benefit of** the poor. Fifty Gentlemen dined together **at the** Crown **Inn, and** 151 of the other inhabitants, the Local Militia, and the regular soldiers **on the** recruiting service, with their recruits, were treated by the Corporation with a dinner at the Bull. The day was closed with a public ball, and, in short, spent by all the inhabitants **in a** manner which fully testified their **sincere** attachment to our beloved Sovereign.

DOLEMELYNLLYN, *Merionethshire.*—Mr. Bowes, of Dolemelynllyn, **called** together upwards of 120 peasants, with their wives and children, and feasted them **on** the grass-plot before his house, while he and his friends enjoyed **the** spectacle. The following letter, containing an account of the proceedings at Dolemelynllyn, to the editor of a provincial paper, may be interesting to many persons, as a picture of the gratification experienced **by** the lower orders **of** society upon this truly joyful occasion.

" SIR,—Being a farmer **of** the poorest kind, near Dolgelley, our market **town,** where I usually go once a week on business, and in the evening, over a **pint of** ale, hear your newspaper read, which last week contained abundance **of** news about the feastings and rejoicings at every place, and finding nothing about **our** feast at Dolemelynllyn, which strangers say is a beautiful place, where now lives (God be thanked for it!) Mr. Bowes, his wife, and two daughters, all strangers in this country, but who, ever since they have lived here, have done every thing in their power to make their poor neighbours happy. Please, Sir, to tell the world, that these gentlefolks did, on the Jubilee day, invite *me,* and above 120 more persons, who were poor and in low condition like myself, to **a** feast **on a** green before their house; we had beef, mutton pies, and puddings, such nice ones too, as few of the feasters ever tasted, or even saw before, and plenty, plenty of them. I thought my children, Evan and Lowry, never would have stopped eating. The gentleman and his friends stood behind our chairs, along with the common servants, without the least pride in the world; they would give us all clean knives and plates to eat our pudding. When the board was cleared, on came plenty of ale, and then the King's health, with *three hurras*. Next we were took to a large room, where the young folks danced until past midnight; in the mean time we had plenty of ale and cold meat. Never was such a happy day, never, never, God bless the founder! Now, Sir, I hope you will put this in among your news, for it is every word of it true, and a great deal more might justly be said about the feasting. I am sorry and ashamed that no better scholar than myself had not told you of this before.

Your dutiful servant, &c., &c."

DOLGELLEY, *Merionethshire*.—The morning was ushered in by an enlivening peal of bells, the incessant roaring of cannon, and reiterated acclamations of joy, until eleven o'clock, when the inhabitants repaired to Church, and to other places of public Worship, to return thanks to the Divine Disposer of all events, for his benignity exemplified in the preservation of our beloved Sovereign, and the blessings enjoyed in his favoured dominions. At one o'clock, every male and female pauper in the parish participated in the festivity, being regaled with Welch mutton, and as much Welch ale as was comfortable and proper: and there remained a surplus of a considerable sum of money reserved for the purchase of a quantity of flannel, the peculiar staple manufacture of the town, and each was supplied with a quantity to defend them from the piercing blasts of winter. At the same time, not a debtor, little or great, was left within the confines of the county gaol. At three o'clock, all the Gentlemen of the town and country sat down to an elegant dinner at the Golden Lion Inn, when appropriate toasts, songs and sentiments, were given. The evening was spent with the utmost conviviality, and in a manner highly expressive of their loyalty. Sir Robert Vaughan, though uniting in the general expense here, with that benevolent disposition by which he is so eminently distinguished and characterised, distributed a prodigious fine ox to the poor of his adjoining parish, in portions of 5 lbs. to each in a family; and on the summit of that stupendous mountain called Foef Offrum, the splendent side of which adorns the verdant Vale of Dolgelley, he had ordered a bonfire, which was of magnitude sufficient to throw lustre over the greatest part of that highly admired vale, the beauty of which was beyond every force of description. On that spot his five large cannon were in continual roar, the thunder of which, from their elevated situation, must have been distinctly heard over the major part of the adjoining counties. His munificence did not rest here, for on the following day, a most elegant and sumptuous dinner, with an exuberant quantity of the choicest wines, was provided at his hospitable Mansion, of which most of the respectable Gentlemen in the county round most heartily partook.

HAFOD, *Cardiganshire*,—The seat of Col. Johns, M.P. A very large concourse of honest Cambrians, after attending divine service, marched in procession to lay the foundation of an Arch, of very large rough stones, eighteen feet wide, by thirty-three feet high, across the turnpike road at Bwlch Boteol, in commemoration of the event; they then proceeded to the Hafod's Arms, Devil's Bridge, where upwards of 100 workmen and labourers were entertained with beef, plum-pudding and cwrw.

HANMER, *Flintshire*.—The morning was ushered in by the ringing of bells and the display of flags. After divine service, which was numerously attended, two large oxen, the one given by the Right Hon. Lord Kenyon, the other by Sir Thomas Hanmer, Bart., and a fine fat sheep, the gift of the Rev. John Hanmer, the worthy Vicar of the parish, were distributed, with a large portion of bread, cheese and ale, to the numerous objects of their liberality; and a double allowance of weekly pay was voted by a Vestry Meeting, to those who were dependents upon parochial relief. The two troops of Yeomanry Cavalry, commanded by Walden Hanmer, Esq., assembled and paraded the village, and were afterwards regaled by him at the Lion Inn; a large party likewise of the 1st regiment of Flintshire Local Militia, attended by their excellent band, fired repeated *feu de joie* in honour of the day, and afterwards partook of a dinner, at the Royal Oak Inn, given by their loyal Commander. The neighbouring farmers assembled at dinner in the village, and spent the day in temperate festivity and dancing.

HAY, *Breconshire*.—The day was observed with every manifestation of loyalty and attachment to our venerable Sovereign. At the parish Church, an excellent sermon was delivered by the Rev. E. Powell, and in the evening, a very numerous company attended a ball at the Swan Inn.

KIDWELLY, *Caermarthenshire*.—A congratulatory Address was voted to his Majesty; there was likewise a general attendance at divine service, and festive rejoicings concluded the day.

LLANDAFF, *Glamorganshire*.—All the debtors in the county gaol and prison in the county of Glamorgan, after being regaled with beef and plum-pudding, were liberated on the happy day, as was also the only prisoner confined for debt in Swansea gaol, by the very handsome subscription entered into by the Gentlemen, &c., of the county; and there is still a considerable surplus, which will be applied to such charitable purposes as may be determined on by the Gentlemen present.

LLANDEGAI, *Caernarvonshire*.—Lady Penrhyn, with her usual goodness, distributed two fat oxen to the poor of the parishes of Llandegai and Llanllechid, and provided a sumptuous dinner at Penrhyn Hall for the most respectable inhabitants. The evening concluded with a dance.

LLANDENIOLEN, *Caernarvonshire.*—The tenants of Asheton Smith, Esq., were regaled with plenty of cwrw da, at the village of Llandeniolen, as were also the persons employed in the Cilgwyn Slate Quarries.

LLANDILO, *Caermarthenshire.*—A meeting of the Nobility, Gentry, Clergy and Freeholders, of the county of Caermarthen was held, at which it was resolved to present a congratulatory Address to his Majesty. The Rev. D. Prothero preached a very excellent sermon to a crowded congregation, which he was requested by the Meeting to print. After service, nearly 70 Noblemen and Gentlemen sat down to one of the most splendid entertainments that the principality ever witnessed; Lord Dynevor presided. Nothing that the most ardent loyalty could suggest was omitted, and after the festive glass had freely circulated, the company retired to partake of the amusements of an elegant ball in the evening, which was honoured with the presence of a very large assemblage of Nobility and persons of distinction, who protracted the general happiness which prevailed until the following morning's dawn.

LLANELLY, *Caermarthenshire.*—The Church was fully attended, and the ships displayed their colours and discharged several rounds of cannon; there was a public dinner at the Falcon, and a ball in the evening at Sir John Stepney's Mansion; there was likewise a very handsome subscription for the relief of the poor.

LLANFYLLIN, *Montgomeryshire.*—The Corporation of this ancient Borough and the other inhabitants of the place attended divine service, where an excellent discourse was delivered by the Rev. Mr. Hassal, the Curate of the parish.—They afterwards dined together; and in the course of the day, fifteen sheep were apportioned amongst the poor of the parish, and in the evening, a sheep was roasted and divided amongst the populace.

LLANVIGHANGLE, *Radnorshire.*—At Llanvighangle, Nantmellan, Percival Lewis, Esq., distributed a sum of money to the poor, sufficient to find each a comfortable dinner of roast beef and pudding, and a quantity of bread was also given by the gentlemen of the parish.

LLANYMYNECH, *Montgomeryshire.*—The inhabitants of this village and its vicinity, having made a very handsome subscription, met at the Cross Keys Inn, where they partook of an elegant dinner, and drank the health of our good old King, with three times three, which was, by signal, immediately followed by firing 21 rounds from the Rock, and the blaze of a bonfire on the point of the Hill. Some excellent songs, trios, &c., were given, the Llanymynech band playing at intervals "God save the King," "Rule Britannia," &c. Much praise is due to the President, the Rev. Mr. Howell (who gave a most impressive discourse in the morning), for his mode of conducting the entertainment. At the close of the day a grand display of fireworks took place, conducted by the Vice-Presidents, Mr. T. Yates, and Mr. Williams, Surgeon, who sent up two balloons in good style, to the great amazement of many of the spectators, to whom the sight was novel. A ball for the Ladies, concluded the celebration of the day. In these scenes of mirth and festivity, the poor were not forgotten; a large quantity of bread was distributed in the Church, to the relief of many needy families, out of the subscription money.

MERTHYR, *Caermarthenshire.*—His Majesty's numerous and loyal subjects in this populous place observed the day with the utmost attention and solemnity. After divine service (which was fully attended at all the places of public Worship), five shillings were distributed at the Church, to every aged and infirm house-keeper in the parish, by order of S. Homfray, Esq., of Pennydarran Place, to enable them to celebrate the day.

MILFORD, *Pembrokeshire.*—Among the general rejoicings in South Wales, few places have shown more eagerness to welcome that auspicious day, on which our beloved Sovereign entered the 50th year of his Reign, than the new and flourishing town of Milford, united with the adjoining parishes of Stainton and Hubberstone. After divine service in St. Catherine's Chapel, the Battery on Hakin Point, manned by the Volunteer Artillery Company of Milford, fired a royal salute, which was answered from the Haven by his Majesty's Revenue Cutters on this station, viz., the Speedwell, Capt. Hopkins, the Diligence, Capt. Dobbin (decked on this occasion with the colours of various nations), the Fox, Capt. Cuff, the Pursuit, Capt. Williams, and the Endeavour, Capt. Peregrine; while a *feu de joie* by the detachment of the Royal Brecon and Monmouth regiment of Militia, under Capt. Lewis, added to the general display. The inhabitants of Milford and its neighbourhood, avoiding feasting and illuminations, marked their respect to this day by a liberal subscription to the poor of Milford, and the adjoining parishes of Stainton and Hubberstone: nor were the sailors, the soldiers, the artificers of the Dock Yard, and the farming labourers around forgot, and these drank "Long life and happiness to their most valued King," with joyful acclamations. The brightness of the day cheered the willing homage of the spectators of this joyful scene, and which the beauty of Milford Haven, adorned by numerous colours from the ships, rendered peculiarly interesting, and gratified their loyal endeavours.

MONTGOMERY *Montgomeryshire.*—A subscription was entered into for the relief of the poor during the winter, which was immediately filled up to the very considerable amount. A noble ox was roasted, and distributed to the poor after divine service, with plenty of bread and ale, when "Long life to the best of Kings," was drank amidst peals of the bells and the shouts of the multitude. Soon after, a large party of the inhabitants and neighbours dined together at Read's, and the patriotic festivities of the day concluded with a ball in the Town Hall, which was illuminated, and attended by all the beauty of the town and neighbourhood. A dutiful Address was resolved unanimously to be presented to his Majesty on his entrance into the 50 year of his Reign.

NANTCOS, *Cardiganshire.*—Mr. Powell made many loyal hearts happy, by the distribution of fifty guineas to the poor of his neighbourhood.

NEATH, *Glamorganshire.*—A public dinner was given at the Ship and Castle. In the evening the Rev. Mr. Davies gave a ball to the young gentlemen of his Seminary, and a select number of young ladies, in celebration of the day.

PENGLUISE, *Cardiganshire*—Mr. Richards displayed his liberality and in the vale of Airon, beef and cwrw da were distributed by Col. Lewis, to a numerous assemblage of the peasantry. In the evening, Aberystwith was illuminated.

POLE, *Montgomeryshire.*—The Rev. Mr. Lloyd entertained 50 of his poor neighbours, whose united ages amounted to 3,751 years, with a good substantial dinner of beef and pudding. It is worthy of remark, that this cheerful assemblage of old age lived within a mile of Mr. Lloyd's Mansion, 14 of whom were considerably above 80, and 20 above 70 years of age.

TAN Y BWLCH, *Merionethshire.*—After divine service 50 pieces of cannon were discharged, and a very numerous and respectable company partook of an excellent dinner, prepared by Mr. Thomas Redding, at Tan y Bwlch Inn. The poor in the neighbourhood were regaled with a good dinner and plenty of ale, at the expense of the company. The charitable benefaction of William Oakley, Esq., of Tan y Bwlch, procured a good suit of clothes for each of the poorest and oldest inhabitants of the parishes of Festinog and Maentwrog; he also distributed two barrels of ale. In short, every heart was filled with joy. A large bonfire lighted the whole vale at night, and a very extensive exhibition of fire-works took place.

TENBY, *Pembrokeshire.*—The morning was ushered in by the ringing of bells, and the guns on the Fort were fired repeatedly in the course of the day. A large ox was given to the poor by the Corporation, which was distributed under the inspection of the worthy Mayor, Mr. Griffith, in portions according to the size of their families, with a proportionable quantity of potatoes, and thus every heart was impressed with a joyful remembrance of the blessings which Britons have so long enjoyed under the best of Sovereigns.

TRE-MADOC, *Caernarvonshire.*—In the evening the inhabitants of Tre-Madoc and its vicinity, assembled to commemorate the 50th Anniversary of our beloved Sovereign's Accession to the Throne. The evening commenced with a general illumination of the whole town :—at the same time an immense column of light appeared at the top of the very high mountain over the town (Moel y Gest) which commands **the whole of** the Cardigan Bay and the promontory of Llyn, and had a very fine effect. The Town Hall Assembly Rooms were brilliantly illuminated. "God save the King" was sung in **grand** chorus, accompanied by the **harp,** which was immediately suc**ceeded by a** discharge of 50 volleys **of** musketry. The whole con**cluded with a** ball and supper.

ST. ASAPH, *Flintshire.*—That **the** poor might partake of the general festivity on the 25th, Fleetwood Williams, Esq., brother to Sir J. Williams, Bart., of Bodlewyddan, sent twenty guineas, for a barrel of ale, to drink **the** King's health, and the rest of the money to be distributed among **the** poor families there, it being his native place. Mr. Williams **was** amongst the most active in celebrating the day in Liverpool, **his** name standing foremost in all the public subscriptions there, **which have** been noticed before.

SWANSEA, *Glamorganshire.*—The celebration of the happy event began, **on the clock** striking **twelve** on Tuesday night, by the bells ringing **a** joyous peal; an elegant and numerous company which had assembled **at the** ball at the Mackworth Arms, in honour of the event, drank his Majesty's health with enthusiasm, and cordially joined in the favourite national strain "God save the King." The attendance at divine **service** was universal. The Rev. Mr. Basset, **over** whose head **77 winters** have **passed,** delivered a **very** appropriate discourse from Proverbs 23, 21; he expatiated on the inestimable blessings which have resulted to us from our present happy establishment in Church and State, and recommended a strict adherence to religion, conformity **to** the laws, and affection for the King, as the certain means of securing to ourselves a continuance **of** these inestimable blessings. An **anthem** was introduced in the **course of the** service. After divine **service,** the armed ships **fired a** royal salute, the Staff of the West Glamorgan Local Militia also fired three excellent volleys, and the Swansea Cavalry a *feu de joie.* The boys and girls in the Lancastrian Charity School, about 300 in number, were regaled with a plentiful dinner of beef, bread, and beer, by the munificence of John Llewlyn, Esq., and other respectable subscribers. The petty Officers and men employed in the impress service, partook of a good dinner provided at the expense of the recruiting Officer, Capt. New.—The poor persons in the Castle were likewise regaled with a dinner. At four o'clock, a large party of Naval, Military, and other Gentlemen, sat down to a sumptuous dinner at the Bush Inn; Capt. New, R.N., was unanimously called to the chair;—on the cloth being withdrawn, the chairman rose, and, in a neat and pertinent address, pronounced **a just** panegyric on the happiness we enjoy under the mild and **beneficent** sway of our gracious Sovereign, contrasting our internal situation with the miseries endured by the unhappy countries which had been subjected **to the** control of France. He noticed, in warm and complimentary terms, the release of the prisoners confined for debt **in** the gaols of this county, which he considered an act that must ever reflect the highest lustre on the Welsh character; and concluded by proposing "**The** King, **and** long life to him." This toast was drank with every expression of the most ardent attachment, and the thrice three cheers, which succeeded, made the "the welkin ring." "God save **the** King," was **sung in** high style by a Gentleman present, **the** whole company joining **in** chorus, and the united **voices** of so many loyal **subjects** produced **a** grand effect.—"The Queen, **and** Royal Family,"—"Prince and Principality," and many other **loyal** toasts, **were** drank with great spirit; the interval being filled up by **some excellent songs,** and a number of patriotic airs performed by the **band of the West Glamorgan** Local Militia, occasionally relieved by **the martial strains of** the drums **and fifes of the** same regiment; **and the company** retired, much gratified **with the festivity** of the day.

WELSHPOOL, *Montgomeryshire.*—The morning was **ushered in with** the ringing **of** bells; and the whole of the time before **Church service, was** taken up with cheering the hearts of nearly 300 families, **by** the supply **of a** sum to each, to enable them to participate **in the** general joy of our venerable Sovereign having attained the 50th year of his Reign. The Bailiffs, Aldermen, and inhabitants, went in procession **to** Church, accompanied by **a** band of music. Dinners were provided at the principal inns, where **numerous and** respectable companies attended, and expressed the **fulness of their** hearts in loyal toasts and songs. At night a numerous assemblage of persons resorted to **a ball at** the **Oak Inn.**

WENVOE, *Glamorganshire.*—Robert **Jenner,** Esq., **gave** twenty **guineas** to the **poor of** that parish, and the same sum to **each** of three **neighbouring parishes,** together with **a plentiful** dinner, ale, &c., to **all his tenants.**

WREXHAM, *Denbighshire.*—The day was ushered **by early peals** of ringing, **which** continued, at intervals, until a late hour. **The** Wrexham **Cavalry** marched in procession to Church, where a **most excellent discourse was** delivered by the Rev. Mr. Jones.—They afterwards fired **three** volleys, **and** partook of a sumptuous dinners **at the** Lion Inn (Major Lloyd, of Pen-y-lan, **in** the chair). His Majesty's health was drank with that enthusiasm which may be **more** readily conceived than expressed. Several appropriate toasts **were** drank, and the evening was spent with conviviality and good **order.** Much **to** the credit of **this** long and well established corps, they liberally contributed £50 **to the** fund, already **subscribed** by the inhabitants **of the** town and neighbourhood, **to relieve the** wants of the necessitous poor during the ensuing winter; they likewise purchased a **quantity of fire-works** which were displayed **on** the evening of **that day,** and had a pleasing and splendid effect. **The** paupers **in** the parish Workhouse were bountifully **regaled with** roast beef, &c., **and a** quantity of their native ale; **and those** receiving parochial **relief received double pay** for the **week.** Richard Lloyd, Esq., **Banker, in a very handsome manner came forward upon** the **present** occasion, by subscribing liberally to the fund, and undertaking to serve the poor with five hundred measures of corn at a shilling per measure below the Market price; and likewise to furnish the Committee with any loan of money they may want, without interest. Most of the Gentlemen in this county killed an ox, and gave dinners to their tenants, the poor, &c.

---o---

ISLE OF ANGLESEA.

BEAUMARIS.—A party of the Royal Anglesea Militia, and the Officers' Staff of the Local Militia of the county, paraded at Beaumaris, and marched to the Church, where an excellent and appropriate sermon was preached by the Rev. Mr. Williams, Chaplain of the regiment. A *feu de joie* was then fired by the Military, and the guns on the Batteries were discharged. The Staff and Band of the regiment, and the inferior Officers of the Corporation, were treated by Lord Bulkeley to a dinner at the Bull's Head Inn, and the populace to copious libations of cwrw, to drink his Majesty's health. At night, there was a great display of bonfires in the town and neighbourhood. The Corporation of Beaumaris, and the Officers were entertained with a splendid supper at Baron Hill, by their Colonel, Lord Viscount Bulkeley, where several loyal toasts were given, and the evening passed with great hilarity.

HENBLAS.—The Jubilee was celebrated with the utmost loyalty and hilarity, at the hospitable mansion of Hugh Evans, Esq. A sumptuous dinner was given to numerous circle of his friends; after which, appropriate toasts were drank, each breathing the purest attachment to their beloved Sovereign and country. As the same time, his neighbouring tenantry, labourers, and their families, to the number of about 150 were regaled with beef, plum-pudding, and unlimited libations of cwrw da. The whole was conducted with the utmost good humour, highly creditable to the worthy donor, who is always forward to evince his unshaken adherence to the best of Kings.

PLASNEWYDD.—The Jubilee was celebrated at Plasnewydd, the seat of the Earl and Countess of Uxbridge, by a distribution of beef, cheese, oatmeal, and strong beer, to the poor families, consisting of upwards of 700 individuals, of the parishes of Llandaniel, Llanfair, and Llandisilio. A plentiful dinner was likewise given at the mansion, to his Lordship's workmen, labourers, and their families. In the evening, there was a magnificent display of fire-works; and it may be added that the well known loyalty and attachment of the noble owners of the place to his Majesty, was most gratefully seconded on this happy occasion by their numerous dependants.

---o---

THE JUBILEE AT EDINBURGH.

THE day was ushered in by the ringing of bells. An immense crowd of people filled the road to Leith, and increased by the procession of many Lodges, who met in Edinburgh, and marched down in Masonic order. The Magistrates, Grand Lodge, Nobility and Gentry, &c., met in the Leith Assembly Rooms at nine, where a public breakfast was given. It was near eleven o'clock, before the procession began to move. The streets and road, from the Leith Assembly Rooms to the site of the intended military work, were lined by the Prince of Wales's Loyal Edinburgh Volunteers, and a detachment from the Aberdeenshire Regiment of Militia. The procession moved in the following order :—1. Society of High Constables of Edinburgh, and Constables of Leith. 2. A detachment of the crew of the Egeria, in clean jackets and trowsers, headed by two Officers. 3. The Lord Provost, supported by the Sheriff of the county, the Earl of Morton, and Sir Patrick Murray, the Magistrates of Edinburgh, in their robes, preceded by a band of music, and followed by the Merchant Company of Edinburgh, attended by many Gentlemen, the Admiral, and resident Bailiffs of Leith, &c. 4. The Grand Lodge of Scotland, the Earl of Moira officiating as Grand Master, in their appropriate insignia, followed by the Lodges of Edinburgh and neighbourhood, in the order of seniority, and accompanied by a band of music. The Masonic decoration were extremely rich, and the whole had a fine effect. The ships in the harbour and wet dock, had all their flags displayed; and were, particularly those in the wet dock, crowded with an immense assemblage of people. On many of them scaffolding was erected, on which were numerous parties of Ladies—and shrouds and yards were completely covered with boys. On arriving at the ground, the crew of the Egeria, who had joined in the procession, filed off to man the guns, which were to fire the grand salute. These were ranged on the west side of the bason. The usual ceremonies of Masonry passed at laying the Foundation Stone, and appropriate speeches were made by the Lord Provost, and the Grand Master.

Inscription deposited under the Foundation Stone :—

On the 25th day of October, in the year of our Lord 1809, and of Masonry 5809, the Right Hon. the **Earl** of Moira, past acting Grand Master of the Grand Lodge of Scotland, in the absence of the Hon. William Maule, of Panmure, M. P. acting Grand Master, laid the FIRST STONE of this BASTION, for the security of the extended Commerce of the PORT of LEITH; the day on which his Majesty King GEORGE the THIRD entered into the 50th year of his Reign, being chosen for the foundation of a Structure which is to bear his Royal name; that a work of public utility, founded amidst the universal thanksgivings of a happy and grateful land, might commemorate, as the most suitable memorial, the Accession of a Prince, to whom, at all times, the most acceptable homage is that which marks the increasing prosperity of his people.

Inscription on the Plate :—

Regi optimo, Patri Patriæ, pio, clementi, benefico, virtutes ob insignes, tam privatas quam publicas, populo suo semper carissimo, imperii Britannici in rebus secundis decori, in arduis præsidio, GEORGIO TERTIO. Regni, quod, annuente Deo, sit longissimum, quinquagesimum annum jam ingresso, cives Edinburgensi, urbis præfecto iterum Gulielmo Coulter, armigero, hoc monumentum posuerunt ovantes, VIII. Calendes Novembris, A.D. MDCCCIX.

Translation.

To the best of Kings, the father of his country, pious, mild, beneficent, by his great private, as well as public virtues, always endeared to his people, in prosperity the ornament, in dangers and difficulties the safeguard of the British Empire, to GEORGE THE THIRD, just entering the 50th year of his Reign, which God prolong, the Citizens of Edinburgh, in the 2nd year of the Provostship of William Coulter, Esq., rejoicing with thanksgiving, erected this Monument, 25th Oct. **1809.**

When the business **was** over, **the** guns planted on **the** west side of bason, fired a grand **salute** of 50 rounds, which **was answered** by the ships in the Roads, **and** the acclamations of 20,000 people. The procession moved back in nearly the same order, the junior Lodges only marching off first, **to a** certain distance, and then forming a line inside the soldiery, through which the procession passed in returning to the Assembly Rooms. On passing one of the King's ships, then in the wet dock, **the** crew mounted the shrouds, and saluted the Magistrates with **three cheers.** The music which preceded **the** Magistrates, in going and returning, played the King's Anthem. **At** 12 o'clock, the **guns** were fired from the Castle, followed by a *feu de joie* from **the** regi**ment** of Militia, drawn up **on** the Castle Hill. At 1 o'clock, the 2 regi**ments** of Edinburgh Volunteers, with the Mid-Lothian and Trinity House Artillery, formed a line in Princes'-street, and fired a royal salute, &c. At 12 o'clock, divine **service was** held in the different Churches and Chapels. The collections, **which were** liberal, are to be applied to benevolent purposes. **At** five o'clock, a numerous body of Noblemen and Gentlemen **dined** together in the Assembly Rooms, George-street. The company consisted of about 500; and a variety of toasts, appropriate to the occasion, were given. At seven in the evening, the illu **mination of** the public buildings, and fire-works began. Sievwright's **Rooms—his** Majesty's Printing House—Post Office—Register Office—**Excise** and Custom Houses, were most superbly illuminated with variegated lamps, emblematical devices, transparencies, &c. The Register Office far exceeded any thing ever exhibited in Edinburgh; on the right was **an** emblematical transparency of Commerce, with appropriate ornaments—left, a Sailor reclining on his arm—the centre transparency, **very large,** exhibited his Majesty seated, crowned by an angel, **the enemies of his** country falling before him; behind the throne, **on his** Majesty's **left,** was pictured a Highland Chieftain; the **drapery executed** by lamps suspended from chains: the crown, etc., **had a splendid** effect. These paintings were executed by Mr. Lizars; **the decorations** of lamps, &c., by Mr. Smith. Excise Office, under **initials and** crown, had *"Pater Patriæ"* in lamps; the Custom House, *"Anno Regni* 50," beautifully executed. The inscription on the King's **Printing Office,** in gigantic letters, formed of lamps, was, "*Long Live the* **King."** Mr. Trotter, Princes'-street, exhibited two very beautiful transparencies. Messrs. Nimmo and Co., of the Adelphi Soda Water Warehouse one—and Mr. Urquhart, George Street.—The Theatre Royal (late Corri's rooms) had a crown, and G. R. in variegated lamps. The weather was most favourable ; a more delightful day and night have seldom occurred. The streets were crowded by persons of all ranks and descriptions: and it may with pleasure be added that they dispersed at an early hour, without the smallest confusion or disorder.

JUBILEE FOR JUBILEE;

OR, FIFTY YEARS SHEPHERD FOR FIFTY A KING.

The following simple and beautiful Verses, addressed to his Majesty on entering the 50th year of his Reign, are the production of an old inhabitant of the Grampian Mountains, who lives in the Cottage in which Norval (in the Tragedy of Douglas) was bred.

FRAE the Grampian hills will the Royal ear hear it,
　An' listen to Norman the Shepherd's plain tale,
The north win' is blawing, and gently will bear it,
　Unvarnish'd and honest, o'er hill and o'er dale,
When London it reaches, at Court, Sire, receive it,
　Like a tale you may read it, or like a sang sing,
Poor Norman is easy—but you may believe it,
　I'm *fifty years* Shepherd—you're *fifty* a King.

Your *Jubilee*, then, wi' *my ain* I will mingle ;
　For *you an mysel'* twa fat lambkins I'll slay,
Fresh turf I will lay in a heap on my ingle,
　An' wi' my auld neebours I'll raut out the day.
My pipes that I play'd on langsyne, I will blaw them,
　My chanter I'll teach to lilt over the spring ;
My drones, to the tune, I will roun' and roun' thraw them,
　" O' Fifty years Shepherd, an' Fifty a King !

The flock o' Great Britain ye've lang weel attended,
　The flock o' Great Britain demanded your care ;
Frae the *tod* and the *wolf* they've been snugly defended,
　An' led to fresh pastures, fresh water, an' air.
My flocks I hae led day by day o'er the heather,
　At night they aroun' me hae danc'd in a ring ;
I've been their protector thro' foul and fair weather,
　I'm Fifty years Shepherd—*you're* Fifty a King.

Their fleeces I've shorn, frae the cauld to protect me,
　Their fleeces they gave, when a burden they grew ;
When escaped frae the shears, their looks did respect me,
　Sae the flock o' Great Britain still looks upon you.
They grudge not their monarch a mite o' their riches
　Their active industry is ay on the wing ;
Then you an' me, Sire, I think are twa matches—
　I'm Fifty years Shepherd— you're Fifty a King !

Me wi' my *sheep*, Sire, and *you* wi' your *subjects*,
   On that festive day will baith gladly rejoice ;
Our twa hoary heads will be fu' o' new projects,
   To please our leal vassals that made us their choice.
Wi' sweet rips o' hay I will **treat** a' my wethers,
   The juice o' the vine to your lords you will bring,
The respect they hae for us is better than brithers,
   I'm Fifty years Shepherd—you're Fifty a King.

I live in the cottage **where Norval was bred** * in,
   You live in the **palace your** ancestors rear'd ;
Nae guest uninvited dare come to our weddin',
   Or ruthless *invader* pluck us by the beard.
Then thanks **to** the island we live, whar shipping
   Swim round **us abreast,** or like geese in a string,
For safe, **I can** say, **as** my brose I am sipping,
   I'm Fifty **years** Shepherd—you're Fifty a King !

But ah ! Royal George, and ah ! humble Norman,
   Life to **us** baith draws near to a close ;
The year's far awa that has *our* natal hour, man,
   The time's at our elbow that brings us repose !
Then e'en let it come, Sire, if conscience acquits **us,**
   A sigh frae our bosoms death never shall wring ;
An' may the niest *Jub'lee* amang angels meet us,
   To hail the auld Shepherd, and worthy auld King.

NORMAN NICHOLSON.

Grampian Hills, Oct. 1809.

* Vide Douglas, a Tragedy.

THE JUBILEE AT DUBLIN.

DUBLIN.—The Jubilee was celebrated in this city with a spirit of loyalty and patriotism in the highest degree honourable to the feelings of the inhabitants. The dinner at the Rotunda was magnificent. His Grace the Lord Lieutenant was pleased to honour the company with his presence, and remained in the rooms until a very late hour. Upwards of 500 persons were assembled, together with all the nobility in town, several of the Judges, the Attorney and Solicitor General, the Commander of the Forces, and a number of General and Staff Officers, the Right Hon. W. W. Pole, Sir E. B. Littlehales, Sir Charles Saxton, **the** Commissioners of the Revenue, **the** Lord Mayor and Sheriffs, and several of the board of Aldermen, &c. Soon after seven o'clock, dinner was served, which was laid out in the circular room, at one end of which was exhibited a magnificent transperency, representing his Majesty and the Royal Family, with various emblematic figures, the composition of Mr. Williams, which deserved and received the highest approbation. At the different tables, the Lord Mayor and several Magistrates presided—every table was full, and never were guests served with a more exquisite banquet. The wines were circulated in profusion, and when the health of our great and good King was announced, it was received with an enthusiasm never exceeded on any former occasion. Immediately after this toast was drank, a full band placed in the orchestra, performed an ode composed for the occasion, and set to music by Mr. Logier. After the ode, the following toasts were given:—Prince of Wales, Queen and Royal Family, Lord Lieutenant of Ireland, the Archbishop of Dublin, and the Church of Ireland, &c. About half past three o'clock, his Grace the Lord Lieutenant, who appeared highly delighted with the happiness manifested in every countenance, gave as a toast, " The Lord Mayor's health," which was drank with three times three. His Lordship then gave his Grace's health, which was received with rapturous expressions of pleasure, and drank in the same manner. His Grace was pleased to notice this attention in the kindest manner, and having in a short speech thanked his Lordship and the assembled company, departed to his carriage. There never was known an entertainment better or more splendidly conducted; and it is difficult to say, whether the Lord Lieutenant appeared more delighted by this proof of loyalty, or the guests more gratified by the affability and condescension of his Grace. The poor debtors in the several prisons also had their Jubilee dinner; Mr. Sheriff Stanley, with an activity in the cause of benevolence worthy of the highest approbation, undertook the management of this part of the festivity, and by the application of comparatively a small sum from the general fund, made many a poor person happy for the day. Trinity College also distinguished itself on this joyous occasion. The Students recited Latin compositions in prose and verse, in honour of the day, which received the warmest approbation. The Castle was splendidly illuminated, as was the Royal Exchange, the Head Police Office, Nelson's Pillar, the Post Office, the University; and indeed, every part of the city demonstrated a zealous desire to testify the highest affection for our venerable Monarch. The admirable sermon preached at Christ Church, by the Lord Bishop of Cork, excited universal attention; his Lordship very happily selected for his text, 2 Kings, c. 23, v. 25:—" And like unto him was there no King before him, that turned to the Lord with all his heart, and with all his soul, and with all his might, according to all the law." Independent of the numerous company that dined at the Rotunda, to celebrate the Jubilee, almost every public room in town was occupied by parties, who assembled together in clubs and convivial meetings in honour of the day. Thursday being the second day of the Jubilee, a grand illumination took place in the evening, and a brilliant display of fire-works at St. Stephen's Green. On Friday, the third day, the Jubilee was concluded by a grand ball and supper at the Rotunda, at which their Graces the Lord Lieutenant, the Duchess of Richmond, Lady Mary Lenox, and their suite were present. Her Grace appeared in Windsor uniform, with a profusion of diamonds. The rooms were most elegantly decorated with emblematical paintings and devices suitable to the occasion; and being well lighted, the whole had a most brilliant effect. To describe the whole company would be impossible; it consisted of all the rank and fashion in town, with most of the respectable citizens. —Crowds of beautiful women were seen promenading the different rooms—the ball was opened by Lady Mary Lenox and Mr. Pole, and **the** dancing continued until a late hour. The Windsor uniform was much worn by the Gentlemen. The **supper was announced at** one **o'clock, at** which upwards of **1,000 persons were** accommodated. **Several** delightful catches and **glees were** sung, and at intervals a **band of** music contributed to the general festivity of the evening. **Their** Graces did not leave **the** room until past three o'clock, and the whole company did not separate till a much **later hour.**

The celebration of **the Jubilee was not** merely confined to the Capitals of the Sister Kingdoms, but spread to the remotest corners of each. This, in every point of view, is a pleasing consideration, and constitutes an unequivocal proof **of** that union and harmony of sentiment, which now prevails over, and in particular is so essentially necessary **to the** welfare of this once distracted land.

The Islands of Guernsey, Jersey, **St.** Vincent, Antigua, &c., celebrated **the** day with equal demonstrations of enthusiastic ardour; in **short,** those who had the happiness of witnessing the gratifying scene **in** any place, or whoever peruses these pages must, it is presumed, **be** satisfied, that the beloved Monarch of these Realms reigns indeed in the hearts of an affectionate and grateful people.

CELEBRATION OF THE JUBILEE BY THE GOVERNMENT OF BOMBAY.

Bombay, June 9th, 1810.

On Monday last, being the 4th of June, the hon. the governor gave a splendid ball and supper at Parell to the ladies and gentlemen of this settlement, surpassing even the many former elegant entertainments which we have had the pleasure of witnessing at the same mansion. The arrangemements for this fete were conducted with a degree of liberality and magnificence, worthy of the occasion for which the party was assembled: to celebrate not only the Birth-day of our Beloved Sovereign, but the Fiftieth Year of his arduous and eventful Reign.

The avenue leading to Parell was illuminated a considerable distance from the house, which appeared a solid blaze of light. The area before the entrance, was brilliantly ornamented with lights, suspended in the most fanciful and elegant manner among the branches of the trees, and on arches and festoons, erected for the purpose. Over the principal entrance was a transparency representing a medallion encircled by a wreath of laurel, and surmounted by a crown with the rays of the Sun reflected from the black ground. On the centre was the following inscription:

GEORGIUS TERTIUS

REX

ANNO 50. REGNI.

And underneath was the following beautiful and highly appropriate motto from the Scriptures:

"The hoary head is a crown of glory when found in the path of righteousness."

The large hall on the ground floor was also decorated with transparencies, the floor, together with the grand staircase, being painted so as to resemble marble.

Over the door at the western end, was a transparency of his Majesty's arms, with the following memorable words, from the first speech which he addressed to his Parliament after ascending the throne:

"BORN AND BRED A BRITON, I GLORY IN THE NAME.

On the right was seen the plume of feathers of his Royal Highness the Prince of Wales, with the letters G. P., while the Royal Arms were supported on the left by the transparency representing MAGNA CHARTA resting on the lion and the unicorn in a recumbent posture, with the Rose and the Thistle, and the Shamrock in the foreground; whilst the national flags with the masts of a ship, and the other emblems, completed the rear.

At the opposite extremity of the Hall, over the great door leading to the gardens, was another transparency, on a very extensive scale, presenting a view of the constitution of Great Britain, on several medallions.

On the upper part immediately over the medallion, on which was engraven ENGLAND, sat BRITANNIA; the rays of the Sun were connected on the right with the PARLIAMENT over which stood LEGISLATURE resting upon a rock; the Parliament was again subdivided into the LORDS and COMMONS, with their appropriate emblems. The JUDICIAL with the JUDGES and JURIES were connected by the same means with the left, with a figure of JUSTICE supporting with her right hand the sword, and the balance with her left. In the centre between these two divisions, was seen a Star, representing the executive part of the constitution, with the KING engraven in large letters of gold, and encircled by the garter with the motto, "*Honi soit qui mal y pense*"—below this was the CHURCH surmounted by the cross and the commandments, and again subdivided into the SPIRITUAL LORDS and the CLERGY, with the mitre over the former, and the Book of Common Prayer and the chalice over the latter. On the lower part of this beautiful representation, was seen St. George on horse-back contending with the dragon, while above Britannia were engraved the following lines:—

THE LAWS, THE RIGHTS,
The generous plan of power, delivered down,
From age to age by your renowned forefathers
So dearly bought, the price of so much blood,
O let it never perish in your hands;
But piously transmit it to your children.
Do thou, great LIBERTY, inspire our souls,
And make our lives in thy possession happy,
Or our deaths glorious in thy just defence.

The upper Hall was likewise decorated in a novel and elegant manner with transparencies in the several windows, having inscribed on them some of the most important events of the present reign. At the eastern extremity was a portrait of his Majesty, with a full-length painting of Britannia, recording, under the directions of Fame, the Naval Heroes of the Nile; over which we observed on a rich drapery the beautiful designation bestowed on her by our immortal poet,

"The green-haired Heroine of the west."

with the following motto in allusion to the taunts of our enemies.

Dives opûm, Studiisque asperrima belli.

On the window on the right hand of Britannia appeared

ELLIOTT,
GIBRALTAR,

with the following line selected not so much for its beauty, as from the circumstance of its having been placed on the Medal presented by the celebrated Frederick the Great to General Elliott, on the termination of the memorable defence of that fortress.

Celebris in flammis, celebris Gibraltar in undis.

The following inscriptions appeared in the several other windows.

RODNEY.   HOWE.
12th April, 1782.   1st June, 1794.
Muturate fugam, regique hæc dicite vestro;
Non illi imperium pelagi, sævumque tridentem,
Sed mihi sorte datum.

DUNCAN, ST. VINCENT,
11th Oct., 1797. 14th Feb., 1798.
    Britannia needs no bulwarks,
    No towers along the steep,
    Her march is on the mountain waves,
    Her home is on the deep.

NELSON,
1st Aug., 1798 ; 2nd April, 1801 ; 21st Oct., 1805.
    Blood of the Brave, thou art not lost
    Amid the waste of waters blue ;
    The waves that roll to Albion's Coast
    Shall proudly boast their sanguine hue ;
    Thy blood shall be the vernal dew
    To foster Valour's daring seed,
    The generous plant shall still its' stock renew,
    And hosts of Heroes rise when one shall bleed.

UNION OF GREAT BRITAIN AND IRELAND, 1st January, 1800.
    Paribus se legibus ambæ
    Invictæ gentes æterna in fœdera mittant.

WILBERFORCE,
Abolition of the African Slave Trade, 1st January, 1808.
The blessing of those who were ready to perish came upon him.

ABERCROMBIE : ALEXANDRIA.
    The Father of the fight
    Who snatched on Alexandria's sand
    The Conqueror's wreath with dying hand.

SIR SIDNEY SMITH : ACRE.
    Or of the redcross hero teach,
    Dauntless in dungeon as on breach ;
    Alike to him, the sea, the shore.
    The brand, the bridle, or the oar.

MOORE : CORUNNA.
    Fallen to save an injured land,
    Imperial Honour's awful hand
    Shall point his lonely bed ;
    The warlike dead of every age,
    Who fill the fair recording page,
    Shall leave their sainted rest,
    And half reclining on his spear
    Each wondering chief by turns appear,
    To hail the Hero guest.
    Old Edward's sons unknown to yield,
    Shall crowd from Cressy's laurelled field,
    And gazed with fixed delight,
    Again for Britain's wrongs they feel,
    Again they snatch the gleamy steel,
    And wish the avenging fight.

HARDINGE, 8th March, 1808.
    'Tis not th' embattled host,
    Nor fleets that line a coast,
    That claim alone the mead,
    Of Valour's sacred deed,
    Nor whether Admiral or Captain bleed ;
    No 'tis the Hero's soul
    Which gives the high controul ;

> This saves a falling state,
> This signs a Tyrant's fate,
> This flamed in Hardinge's eye
> At Battle's cheerful cry,
> And bade him like the mighty Nelson die!
>
> WELLESLEY: VIMEIRA—TALAVERA.
>
> Victor ab aurorœ populis.
> Duo rapta manu diverso ex hoste trophæa,
> Bisque triumphatas utroque ab littore gentes.
>
> STUART: MAIDA.
>
> On you, noblest English,
> Whose blood is fetched from **Fathers of** war-proof.

The above inscriptions are derived from sources too generally known to require specification, unless we except those which relate to the two naval heroes, Nelson and Hardinge, who fell alike in the hour of victory. The beautiful lines on the former, are by Dr. Leyden of Calcutta, and the no less beautiful verses on the latter, are from a Poem written at Parell House, in March, 1808, by a lady who has recently left this settlement for Europe, who long filled the first rank in this community, but who was much more distinguished by her genius and virtues, than by the highest rank which any community could bestow. It is only for strangers that it is necessary to add, the name of *Lady Mackintosh.*

The ball was opened about 10 o'clock by the Hon. the Governor and Mrs. Lechmere, and the dancing continued with great spirit, considering the extreme heat of the weather, until about 1 o'clock, when the party retired to an elegant supper, after which the following toasts were given.

THE KING, and may he continue to wear the Crown for many years.
THE QUEEN AND ROYAL FAMILY.
THE HONOURABLE UNITED EAST INDIA COMPANY, &c., &c.

The party afterwards proceeded to the extensive gardens which were illuminated in a very grand and magnificent manner, having a triumphal arch between the fountains, and the great terrace which runs parallel with the water.

From the terrace, the company were gratified with a splendid display of fireworks, which illuminated the whole of that beautiful picturesque scenery, which extends from the gardens by successive ranges of hills, interspersed with wood and water until it terminates with the high land on which the flag staff is erected.

On this occasion the flag staff was decorated with the colours of various nations, which produced a magnificent effect, when appearing through the extreme darkness of the night, by the assistance of a strong light which suddenly rose behind the hill.

The company afterwards returned to the ball-room, when the dancing recommenced and continued till a late hour in the morning.

We must not omit to mention that many of the ladies, unwilling to show any want of loyalty on so memorable an occasion, wore Bandeaus with the following motto:

G. R.
50.
God prolong His Majesty's Reign.

LIST OF HIS MAJESTY'S MINISTRY, AS IT STOOD

In July, 1809.   In Dec., 1809.

CABINET MINISTERS.

In July, 1809	Office	In Dec., 1809
Earl Camden	President of the Council	Earl Camden.
Lord Eldon	Lord High Chancellor	Lord Eldon.
Earl of Westmoreland	Lord Privy Seal	Earl of Westmoreland.
Duke of Portland	First Lord of the Treasury (Prime Minister)	
Rt. Hon. Spencer Perceval	Chanc. and Under Treasurer of the Exchey. and also Chanc. of the Duchy of Lancaster...	Rt. Hon. Spencer Perceval.
Lord Mulgrave	First Lord of the Admiralty	Lord Mulgrave.
Earl of Chatham	Master Gen. of the Ordnance	Earl of Chatham.
Earl Bathurst	Pres. of the Board of Trade	Earl Bathurst.
Lord Hawkesbury	Sec. of State for Home Department	Hon. Richard Ryder.
Rt. Hon. George Canning	Sec. of State for Foreign Affairs	Marquis Wellesley.
Lord Castlereagh	Sec. of State for the Department of War and the Colonies	Earl of Liverpool.

NOT OF THE CABINET.

In July, 1809	Office	In Dec., 1809
Rt. Hon. R. Saunders Dundas	Pres. of the Board of Controul for the Affairs of India	Rt. Hon. R. Saunders Dundas.
Rt. Hon. George Rose	Vice-Pres. of the board of Trade, and Treasurer of the Navy	Rt. Hon. George Rose.
Sir James Pulteney, Bt.	Secretary of War	Vicount Palmerston.
Lord Charles Somerset, Rt. Hon. Charles Long	Joint Paymaster-Generals	Lord Charles Somerset, Rt. Hon. Charles Long.
Earl of Chichester, Earl of Sandwich	Joint Postmaster Generals	Earl of Chichester, Earl of Sandwich.
William Huskisson, Esq., Hon. Henry Wellesley	Secretaries of the Treasury	Richard Wharton, Esq., Charles Arbuthnot, Esq.
Sir William Grant	Master of the Rolls	Sir William Grant.
Sir Vicary Gibbs	Attorney-General	Sir Vicary Gibbs.
Sir Thomas Plomer	Solicitor-General	Sir Thomas Plomer.

PERSONS IN THE MINISTRY OF IRELAND.

In July, 1809	Office	In Dec., 1809
Duke of Richmond	Lord Lieutenant	Duke of Richmond.
Lord Manners	Lord High Chancellor	Lord Manners.
Sir Arthur Wellesley	Chief Secretary	W. Wellesley Pole.
Rt. Hon. J. Foster	Chancellor of the Exchequer	Rt. Hon. J. Foster.

ODE FOR HIS MAJESTY'S BIRTH-DAY—June 4th.

By Henry James Pye, Esq., Poet Laureate.

WHILE Europe with dejected **eye**
Beholds around her rural reign
Whilom of Peace the fair domain
The scene of desolation lie;
  Or if with trembling hope she cast
  Her looks on hours of glory past:
  And burn again with virtuous fame
  Her ancient honours to reclaim,
    And brace the corslet on her breast,
    And grasp the spear and wave the crest;
Yet lies her course through war's ensanguin'd **flood**;
Yet must she win **her** way through carnage **and thro'** blood.

  Ah! happier **Britain,** o'er thy plain
  Still smiling Peace and Freedom reign.
  And while thy sons with pitying eye
Behold the fields of ruin round them lie;
The storms that shake each neighbour-realm with fear,
Like distant thunder die upon the ear;
  They bless the halcyon hours that gave,
  To rule a people free and **brave,**
  A patriot Monarch all their own,
Their swords his bulwark, and their hearts his throne,
  And while to this auspicious day
  The Muse devotes her tributary lay,
  A nation's vows in choral Pæan join,
And consecrate to Fame a 'verse as mean as mine.'

  Yet not to selfish thoughts confin'd,
  Are the warm feelings of a virtuous mind:
  The Royal Patriot, while he views,
  Peace o'er his realms her bliss diffuse,
  Mourns for the sorrows that afflict mankind.
  Go forth, my sons, he cries; my Britons, go,
  And rescue Europe from her ruthless foe.
  Behold, in arms, Austria's Imperial Lord;
  Behold Iberia draw the avenging sword;—
  O **let,** with their's, your mingling ensigns fly,
  In the great cause of injur'd Liberty!
Go forth, my sons, and to the world declare,
When suffering Freedom calls, Britannia's arms are there!

JUBILEE:

Or, Lines on the 25th of October, 1809, being the Day on which our beloved MONARCH *entered on the 50th Year of his Reign.*

BY SAMUEL ELSDALE,

Author of "Short Pieces in Verse."

Fair Orb of day, with heav'nly splendour bright,
Chase from yon crystal arch the shades of Night;
Let brazen trumpets pour a shrill-ton'd voice,
To hail the day that bids our hearts rejoice.

Let thund'ring cannons roar with loud acclaim
Till ev'ry shore re-echo GEORGE's name;
At that lov'd name innum'rous shouts arise,
And loud huzzas ring through the vaulted skies.

Twice five-and-twenty years their course have run,
Since o'er our hearts his gracious reign begun;
Beneath his sacred sway and mild command,
Freedom and Plenty crown Britannia's land.

Her hardy offspring till her peaceful shore,
While round her coast the hostile thunders roar;
No fairer virgins through the world are found,
Than the sweet Nymphs who grace our native ground.

Our Merchants are like princes, ev'ry sea
Wafts the rich freight of British industry;
No hearts so gen'rous other lands can show,
To melt with Charity, with Valour glow.

On all alike Freedom her gifts bestows,
No slave can breathe the air which o'er her Island blows;
Soon as he springs on England's sacred shore,
His chains are broken, Slav'ry galls no more.

Shrouded in storms the Fiend of Discord low'rs,
And deluges the world with bloody show'rs;
From land to land she drives her iron car,
Her fell attendants, Pestilence and War.

The murd'rous Corsican, with furious mind,
To death or bondage dooms all human kind;
Where'er his sanguinary hordes advance,
By force or fraud subdued, all bow to France.

Britons alone, triumphant in the field,
On land and ocean make the Tyrant yield ;
A proud superiority they claim,
And join a Moore's to Nelson's honoured name,
Alike in death, alike in deathless fame.

May our lov'd Isle, for god-like deeds **renown'd**,
The pride and glory of the World be crown'd ;
May foreign wars, domestic quarrels cease,
And ev'ry clime be hush'd in smiling Peace !

Long may **our** gracious Sov'reign's rule extend,
The King **of** Freemen, and his people's friend ;
To Britain's cry, may bounteous Heav'n give ear,
And GEORGE's Life, so lov'd, so honour'd, spare !

God save the King, and grant him long to reign,
Britannia's guardian, monarch of the main!
And when that hour shall come, which comes to all,
When Heaven shall give the signal of recall,
Still may his soul in endless Glory live,
And for an earthly crown a heav'nly Crown **receive** !

ODE FOR THE ROYAL JUBILEE.
OCTOBER 25, 1809.
BY WILLIAM-THOMAS FITZ-GERALD, ESQ.

Olympic games by Greece were **given,**
   And Circus sports by Rome,
But Britons raise their voice to Heaven,
   For virtues thron'd at home !
And from the Peasant to the Peer,
They hail this **day, to** millions dear !

The fiftieth sun's autumnal **ray,**
   Beholds the mildest Sov'reign **sway,**
     A People happy, **great,** and **free** ;
That People, with one common voice,
From Thame's to Ganges' shores rejoice,
   In universal Jubilee !

May Heaven the cherish'd life extend
Of Albion's Monarch, Father, Friend,
   For many a future year !
Long be postpon'd that hour of fate,
When He, the Just, the Good, the Great !
   Shall cause the general tear !

To Henry's reign, and Edward's sway*,
    A few more years were given ;
But Hist'ry never mark'd that day
    As bless'd by Earth and Heaven,
While ages yet unborn shall own
Our Monarch's virtues grac'd his Throne?

The upright Judges of the land,
    From worldly influence free,
Were made by his benign command ;
    The surest pledge of Liberty†!
This act alone endears his name,
Beyond the pride of Cressy's fame !
By this our rights are made secure,
And the deep spring of justice pure !

While bounty opes the dungeon's door,
To liberate the suff'ring poor,
    And set the wretched free ;
Each heart shall feel—(and grateful beat)
That George's Throne is Mercy's Seat,
    And bless the happy Jubilee !

Age shall his weight of years beguile,
And Poverty reliev'd, shall smile ;
Care's wrinkled brow shall disappear,
And Sorrow intermit her tear !
For rich and poor one voice shall raise
To England's glory—George's praise !

If there's a traitor in the land
Who will not raise for George his hand,
Whose heart malignant grieves to see
All England rise in Jubilee ;
Let the detested monster find
Some cavern blacker than his mind !
There let him waste his life away,
Nor with his presence blast THIS DAY.

While half the world in shackles groan,
Beneath a cruel Tyrant's throne ;
    Drench'd in an hundred people's blood !
Britons, with glowing bosoms, sing,
May GOD preserve our PATRIOT KING !
    The moral, pious, mild, and good !

* Henry III. reigned 56 years, and Edward III. 50 years and some months.

† The first act of his present Majesty's reign, was to render the Judges independent of the Crown.

Where **is the** virtue which he has not shewn,
To honour man, and dignify a Throne?
Be this his praise—all other praise above,
A Prince enthron'd upon his People's love!
His subjects' rights are foster'd in his mind,
The lov'd, and honour'd Titus of mankind!
O'er whom may Heaven its awful Ægis throw,
To blast the traitor, and confound the foe!
Then let the Nations **who** confess his **sway,**
For ever celebrate this happy day,
And ev'ry loyal subject sing,
May GOD preserve our PATRIOT KING!

INDEX OF PLACES.

Abingdon, 23
Adderley Hall (Salop), 138
Albrighton (Salop), 138
Aldborough (Suff.), 153
Aldermaston, 24
Alfreton, 45
Allensmoor (Heref.), 79
Allesley (War.), 169
Almeley (Heref.), 80
Alnwick, 129
Alresford, 72
Amersham, 27
Andover, 72
Ardwick (Manchester), 96
Armeley, 180
Armitage (Staff.), 147
Ashborne, 45
Ashburton, 49
Ashby-De-La-Zouch, 105
Ashford, 85
Ash—Henley Park (Surrey), 157
Ashton-Under-Lyne, 95
Aston Clinton, 27
Astrop Wells, 121
Axminster, 49
Baddesley (War.), 169
Badminton, 65
Bakewell, 45
Bala, 192
Banbury, 133
Bangor, 192
Banstead (Surrey), 157
Basingstoke, 72
Bath, 141
Bawtry, 181
Beach Hill (Berks.), 24
Beaford, 49
Beaulieu, 72
Beaumaris, 202
Bebington, 31
Beccles, 154
BEDFORDSHIRE, 21
Bedford, 21
Belton (Lin.), 107
Berkeley, 65
Berkhamstead, 82
BERKSHIRE, 22
Berkswich (Staff.), 147
Bernard Castle (Dorset), 58
Berwick-upon-Tweed, 129
Beverley, 181
Bewdley, 178
Biggleswade, 21
Binfield (Grove House), 24
Birmingham, 169
Bishop's Castle, 133
Bishop Wearmouth, 60
Bitton (Glo'ster), 65

Blenheim, 133
Blithfield (Staff.), 147
Bletchington (Oxon.), 133
Bletchington (Sussex), 164
Bluntisham, 29
Bockhampton, 175
Bodmin, 35
Bognor, 162
Bolton (Lanc.), 96
Bolton (Lan.), Wallsuches Bleach Works, 103
Boughton (Northamp.), 121
Bracon, 118
Bradden, 121
Bradfield (Essex), 62
Bradford (Wilts.), 175
Brampton (Westmor.), 174
Brandon, 154
Brayfield, 121
Brecon, 192
Brentford, 108
Bridgenorth, 138
Bridlington, 181
Brighthelmston (Brighton), 161
Brightling, 163
Bristol, 66
Broadstairs, 85
Broad Windsor, 54
Brockhall, 121
Brockhampton (Heref.), 80
Brockton Hall (Staff.), 147
Bromsgrove, 178
Broseley, 139
Brough (Westmor.), 174
Browsholme (Lanc.), 96
Bruton, 142
BUCKINGHAMSHIRE, 27
Buckingham, 27
Burghclere (Hants), 72
Burley-on-the-Hill (Rut.), 136
Bures (Essex), 62
Burslem, 147
Bury (Lanc.), 96
Bury St. Edmunds, 153
Caermarthen, 193
Caernarvon, 193
Camborne, 35
CAMBRIDGESHIRE, 28
Cambridge, 28
Camelford, 35
Cannock, 148
Canterbury, 86
Cardiff, 193
Cardigan, 193
Carlisle, 42
Carythanick, 35
Castle Bromwich, 170
Castle Donington, 105

Index of Places.

Castle Hill (Devon), 50
Castle Howard (Yorks.), 181
Catterick, 181
Charlton Kings, 68
Cheadle (Staff.), 148
Chelmsford, 62
Chelsea, 109
Chelsea Farm.—Lord Cremorne's Seat, 109
Cheltenham, 68
Chepstow, 115
CHESHIRE, 30
Cheshunt, 83
Chester, 30
Chesterfield, 45
Chester-Le-Street, 58
Cheveley Park, 29
Chichester, 161
Chil-Grove (nr. Chichester), 164
Chorley (Lanc.), 96
Chorlton-cum-Hardy (M'chester), 97
Cirencester, 68
Clifton (Glo'ster), 68
Clirow, 193
Coalbrooke Dale, 139
Colchester, 62
Coleby, 107
Combank (Kent), 87
Combe (Sussex), 164
Combhay (Som.), 142
Compton (War.), 171
Conisborough, 181
Conway, 193
CORNWALL, 34
Cosby. 105
Cote House (Glo'ster), 68
Court House (Som.), 142
Coventry, 171
Cowbridge, 194
Coxwold, 181
Craven, 182
Crowcombe Court (Som.) 143
Crowsley Park (Oxon.), 133
Cuby (Corn.), 36
Cuckfield Place (Sussex) 164
Culham Court (Oxon.), 133
Culworth, 121
CUMBERLAND, 42
Darlington, 58
Dartmouth, 50
Daventry, 122
Dawlish, 50
Deal, 88
Denbigh, 194
DERBYSHIRE, 44
Derby, 44
Devizes (Wilts.), 175
DEVONSHIRE, 48
Dodington, 69
Dolemelynllyn, 194
Dolgelley, 195

Donhead Lodge (Wilts.) 175
Donington (Salop), 139
Dorchester, 54
Dorking, 157
DORSETSHIRE, 54
Dover, 88
Dronfield, 46
DUBLIN, 206
Dudley, 178
Dukinfield (Lanc.), 97
Dunchurch, &c., 172
Dunstable, 21
Dunster Castle (Som.), 143
Durdens (Epsom), 158
DURHAM, 57
Easingwold, 182
Eastbourne, 164
Eastham, 31
East Hampsted (Berks.), 24
East Hoathley (Sussex), 165
Eccles (M'chester), 97
Eccleshall (Staff.), 148
Eckington, 46
EDINBURGH, 203
Edmonton, 110
Ellesmere, 139
Eltham, 88
Ely, 29
Emsworth, 73
Endon (Staff.), 148
ESSEX, 62
Evesham, 178
Exeter, 48
Fairfield (M'chester), The Moravians, 104
Fakenham, 118
Falmouth, 36
Fareham, 73
Faringdon, 24
Farley Hill, 24
Farnham (Bucks.), 27
Farnham (Surrey), 158
Farnley, 182
Faversham, 88
Fawley (Hants), 73
Fenton Potteries, 149
Fladbury (Worc.), 179
Fletching (Sussex), 165
Fordwich, 89
Forton (Staff.), 149
Fownhope (Heref.), 80
Frampton, 69
Frimley House (Surrey), 158
Frocester, 69
Frogmore, 19
Frome, 143
Frowlesworth, 105
Garnons (Heref.), 80
GLOUCESTERSHIRE, 65
Gloucester, 65
Gorton (M'chester), 97

Index of Places. 221

Gosport, 73
Grampound, 37
Great Dunmow, 63
Great Ness (Salop), 140
Greenford, 111
Greenwich, 89
Greenwich Hospital, 89
Grimsby, 107
Grove House, Binfield, 24
Guernsey, 208
Hadley, 111
Hafod, 196
Hales Owen (Salop), 140
Halifax, 182
Halliwell (Lanc.), 98
Hambledon (Hants), 73
Hambledon (Oxon.), 134
HAMPSHIRE, 71
Hampton, 112
Hanbury (Staff.), 149
Hanmer, 196
Hannington, 122
Hardingstone, 122
Harefield, 112
Harewood (nr. Leeds), 183
Hartlepool, 58
Hartwell, 27
Harwich, 62
Hassop (Derby), 46
Hastings, 166
Haughton, 58
Havant, 73
Hay, 196
Hedon (nr. Hull), 183
Heighington (Lin.), 108
Helmingham, 154
Helmington Hall (Durham), 59
Helston, 37
Henblas, 202
Henley (Oxon.), 134
Henley (War.), 172
HEREFORDSHIRE, 79
Hereford, 79
HERTFORDSHIRE, 82
Hertford, 82
Heslington (nr. York), 184
Hexham, 130
Higham Ferrers, 122
Highgate, 113
Hinckley, 105
Hindleap (Worc.), 179
Hinton (Berks.), 25
Hinton St. George (Dorset), 55
Hinton St. George (Heref.), 80
Hirthington, 134
Honingham, 119
Horsham, 167
Horsington, 143
Huddersfield, 184

Hull, 184
Hungerford, 25
Hunmanby (Yorks.), 186
HUNTINGDONSHIRE, 84
Hursley Lodge (Hants), 74
Hurstbourne Park (Hants), 74
Husbands Bosworth, 105
Hythe, 90
Ibbetson, 54
Ilfracombe, 50
Illogan, 37
Ipswich, 154
ISLE OF ANGLESEY, 202
ISLE OF WIGHT, 77
Itchen Abbas, 74
Jersey, 208
Kelham, 131
Kendal, 174
KENT, 85
Kettering, 122
Ketteringham, 119
Kew, 158
Keynsham, 143
Kidwelly, 196
Killerton (Devon), 50
Kingston-upon-Thames, 159
Kington (Heref.), 80
Kington (War.), 172
Kirton (Lin.), 108
Knaresborough, 187
Knowle (War.), 172
Knutsford, 31
LANCASHIRE, 94
Lancaster, 94
Lanrothal, 81
Lansallos, 37
Lapworth, 172
Lathom House (Lanc.), 98
Launceston, 34
Lavenham (Suff.), 155
Lawford Place (Essex), 63
Ledbury, 81
Leeds, 187
Leek (Staff.), 149
Leek Wootton, 172
LEICESTERSHIRE, 104
Leicester, 104
Leigh (Kent), 90
Leigh (Lanc.), 98
Leighton Buzzard, 21
Leominster, 81
Letton (Heref.), 81
Lewes, 167
Lichfield, 149
Lillingstone Dayrell, 27
LINCOLNSHIRE, 107
Lincoln, 107
Linley (Salop), 140
Liskeard, 37

Littlebourne, 90
Liverpool, 99
Llandaff, 196
Llandegai, 196
Llandeniolen, 197
Llandilo, 197
Llanelly, 197
Llanfyllin, 197
Llanvighangle, 197
Llanymynech, 197
Lyme, 55
LONDON, 1
Longdon (Staff.), 150
Long Ashton, 144
Longleat (Wilts.), 176
Lostwithiel, 38
Ludlow, 140
Lulworth Castle (Dorset), **55**
Lydney, 69
Macclesfield, 32
Maddern, 38
Maidenhead, **25**
Maidstone, 85
Manchester, 100
Manningtree, 63
Mapledurham House (Hants), 74
Margate, 91
Market Harborough, 106
Market Overton, 136
Marlborough, 176
Marlow, 27
Marshfield, 69
Medmenham, 28
Melbury House (Dorset), 55
Melton (Suff.), 155
Mereworth, 91
Merthyr, 198
MIDDLESEX, **108**
Milford, 198
Milton (Dorset), 55
Miserdine Castle (Glo'ster), 70
Mistley (Essex), 64
MONMOUTHSHIRE, 114
Monmouth, 114
Montgomery, 193
Morpeth, 130
Mount-Edgcumbe, 51
Mulgrave Castle (Yorks.), **188**
Much Marcle, 81
Muncaster Castle (Cumb.), 43
Mylor, 38
Nantcos, **199**
Neath, 199
Nedging (Suff.), 156
Netherbury, 55
Nettlecombe (Som.), 144
Newbury, 25
Newcastle-on-Tyne, 127
Newcastle (Staff.), 150

Newchurch in Rossendale (M'chester) 100
Newhaven, 167
Newent, 70
New Lodge (Staff.), **150**
Newlyn, 38
New Malton, **188**
Newmarket, 30
Newport (Corn.), 39
Newport (I. W.), 77
Newport (Mon.), 115
Newport (Salop), 141
Newton (Lanc.), 101
Newton Park (Glo'ster), 70
Newton Park (Som.) 144
Nore (The), His Majesty's **Ships at**
 the Nore, 91
NORFOLK, 115
Northallerton, 188
NORTHAMPTONSHIRE, 120
Northampton, 120
Norton Canon, 82
North Shields, 131
Northstoke, 25
NORTHUMBERLAND, 127
North Petherton, 144
Norton (Yorks.), 188
Norwich, 115
NOTTINGHAMSHIRE, 131
Nottingham, 131
Nuneaton, 172
Oakes, The (Derby.), 46
Oakham, 136
Oakhampton, 51
Oldham (Lanc.), 101
Olney (Bucks.), 28
Olveston, 70
Orchardleigh (Som.), 144
Ormesby (Norfolk), 119
Osmastone (Derby.), 47
Oswestry, 141
Otterton, 51
Ottery St. Mary, **51**
Oundle, 123
Overstone, 123
OXFORDSHIRE, 132
Oxford, 132
Packington, **172**
Paddington, **113**
Padstow, 39
Palgrave, 156
Pattingham (Staff.), 150
Painswick, 70
Pencombe, 70
Pengluise, 199
Penkridge (Staff.), 151
Penrith, 44
Penryn, 39
Penzance, 39

Index of Places.

Peterborough, 123
Petersham (Surrey), 150
Plasnewydd, 202
Plymouth, 51
Plymouth Dock, 52
Pole, 199
Poole, 55
Portchester, 74
Portsmouth, 74
Poynton, 33
Preston (Lanc.), 101
Preston Candover, 75
Prestwich (M'chester), 101
Probus, 39
Radborne, 47
Ramsbottom (M'chester), 102
Ramsgate, 91
Ratcliff, 113
Ravensworth (Durham), 59
Reading, 22
Redruth, 39
Rendlesham, 156
Renholt (Beds.), 22
Ribby House (Lanc.), 102
Richmond, (Yorks.) 188
Rickmansworth, 83
Ripon, 189
River (nr. Dover), 92
Rochdale, 102
Rochetts (Essex), 64
Routon (Staff.), 151
Ross, 82
Rothley, 106
Rudge Hall (Staff.), 151
Rugby, 173
Rugeley, 151
RUTLANDSHIRE, 136
St. Albans, 83
St. Asaph, 200
St. Austell, 40
St. Columb, 40
St. Germans, 40
St. Giles (Wilts.), 176
St. Ives (Corn.), 40
St. Ives (Hunts), 84
St. Mary Bourne, 76
St. Oswyth, 64
St. Peters (Kent), 93
Salisbury, 175
Saltergate (Yorks.), 189
Saltram (Devon.), 52
Sandbach, 33
Sandhill Park (Som.), 145
Saxmundham, 156
Scarborough, 189
Seal (Kent), 92
Sedgley, 151
Selby, 182
Sevenoaks, 92

Severton Hall (Notts.), 132
Shadwell, 113
Shadwell Market, 113
Shaftesbury, 56
Sheffield, 190
Sherborne, 56
Sherborne St. John, 76
Sherborne Castle (Oxon.), 134
Shifnal, 141
Shipston-upon-Stour, 179
Shirehampton, 70
Shotton (Durham), 59
Shrewsbury, 136
SHROPSHIRE, 136
Sittingbourne, 92
Skelton Grange (nr Doncaster), 190
Solihull (nr. B'ham), 173
SOMERSETSHIRE, 141
Southampton, 75
Southgate, 113
Southill House (Beds.), 22
South Mimms, 114
Southport, 102
South Shields, 59
Southwark—see London
Southwick, 76
Sowe (nr. Coventry), 173
Spilsby, 108
STAFFORDSHIRE, 146
Stafford, 146
Stamford, 108
Stamford Bridge (Yorks.), 191
Stanmer (Sussex), 168
Stanton Prior, 176
Staplehurst, (Kent), 92
Stapleton (Glo'ster), 70
Stepehill (I. W.), 79
Stivichall, etc., 173
Stock House (Dorset), 56
Stoke-upon-Trent, 151
Stoke (Suff.), 156
Stoke D'Alborne (Cobham), 160
Stoke House (Notts.), 132
Stoke Lacy (Heref.), 82
Stockport, 34
Stockton, 59
Stonehouse (Devon.), 53
Stoneleigh, 173
Stonyhurst (Lanc.), 102
Stony Stratford, 28
Stratford-on-Avon, 173
Stroud (Glo'ster), 70
Sudbury (Suff.), 156
Sudbury (Derby.), 47
SUFFOLK, 153
Sunderland, 60
SURREY, 157
SUSSEX, 161
Sutton Coldfield, 174

Index of Places.

Sutton Hall (Yorks.), 191
Swallowfield, 26
Swansea, 200
Syrencot (Wilts.), **177**
Tan y Bwlch, 199
Taunton Dean (Som.), 145
Tellisford (Som.), 145
Temple Guiting, 70
Temple Sowerby, 174
Tenby, 199
Tewkesbury, **70**
Tew Lodge **(Oxon.), 135**
Thame, 135
Thatcham (Wilts.), 177
Thornham (Suff.), 156
Thorpe (Suff.), 156
Thrapston, 123
Ticknall, 47
Tideswell, 47
Titchfield, 77
Titfield, 124
Tortworth, **71**
Tottenham **Park** (Wilts.), 177
Towcester, 124
Tregony, 41
Tregothnan, 41
Trellissick, 41
Tre-Madoc, 199
Trevennen, 41
Trewarthenick, 41
Truro, 41
Tunbridge **Wells, 93**
Twerton-on-Avon, **145**
Tynemouth, **131**
Unton-cum-Chalvey (Bucks.), **28**
Uppingham, 136
Urmston (M'chester), 103
Uttoxeter, 153
Uxbridge, 114
Wakefield, 191
WALES, North and South, 192
Walgrave, 126
Wallingford, 26
Wallsuches Bleach Works (near Bolton, Lanc.), 103
Walsingham Abbey, 119
Wansford (Yorks.), 191
Warminster, 177
Warrington, 103
WARWICKSHEIR, **168**

Warwick, 168
Washingboro' (Lin.), 108
Wellingborough, 126
Wellington (Som.), 145
Wells (Norfolk), 119
Welshpool, 201
Wenvoe, 201
Weobly, 82
Westerham, 93
West Haddon, 127
WESTMORELAND, 174
Weston (Staff.), 152
Weston Park (Sussex), 168
Wetherby, 191
Weymouth, 56
Whitchurch (Salop), 141
Whitehaven, 44
Willesley, 106
Wiln (Derby.), 47
WILTSHIRE, 175
Wimpole, 30
Winchester, 71
Windsor, 17
Wirksworth, **48**
Wisbech, 30
Witham (Essex), 64
Witham (Oxon.), 135
Wokingham, 26
Wolverhampton, 152
Woodbridge, 156
Woodbury, 53
Woodchester, **71**
Woodley, **26**
Woodstock, 135
Woolley (Wilts.), 177
Woolwich, **93**
Wooton-under-Edge, 71
WORCESTERSHIRE, 177
Worcester, 177
Workington, 44
Wornersh (Guildford), 160
Worthing, 168
Wrexham, 201
Wynyard (Durham), **61**
Yalding, 94
Yarmouth, 119
Yately, 26
Yeovil (Som.), 146
YORKSHIRE, 179
York, 179

APPENDIX.

Bombay, 209
H. M. Ministry, 213
Ode for His Majesty's Birthday by the Poet Laureate, 214
Jubilee Verses by S. Elsdale, 215
Jubilee Ode by William-Thomas Fitz-Gerald, Esq., 216
Index of Places, 219

S. & J. BRAWN, Printers, 13, Gate Street, Holborn, **London,** W.C.

www.ingramcontent.com/pod-product-compliance
Lightning Source LLC
Chambersburg PA
CBHW020812230426
43666CB00007B/982